HOMŒOPATHY

FAIRLY REPRESENTED.

A REPLY TO PROFESSOR SIMPSON'S

"HOMŒOPATHY" MISREPRESENTED.

BY

WILLIAM HENDERSON, M.D.,
PROFESSOR OF GENERAL PATHOLOGY IN THE UNIVERSITY OF EDINBURGH.

FIRST AMERICAN, FROM THE LAST EDINBURGH EDITION.

PHILADELPHIA:
LINDSAY & BLAKISTON.
1854.

PROF. SIMPSON'S HOMŒOPATHY.

LINDSAY & BLAKISTON

HAVE JUST PUBLISHED,

HOMŒOPATHY:

ITS TENETS AND TENDENCIES,

THEORETICAL, THEOLOGICAL AND THERAPEUTICAL.

BY

JAMES Y. SIMPSON, M. D.,

PROFESSOR OF MIDWIFERY IN THE UNIVERSITY OF EDINBURGH, ETC., ETC.

IN ONE VOLUME, OCTAVO.

Price $1,25.

WM. S. YOUNG, PRINTER.

CONTENTS.

CHAPTER III.

CHAPTER IV.

CHAPTER V.

PREFACE TO THE SECOND EDITION.

So short a time (scarcely three weeks) has elapsed between the publication of the first edition of this work, and the demand for a second, that, besides the correction of such oversights of composition as were scarcely avoidable in a treatise written somewhat hurriedly and amidst many interruptions, there is little or no difference between this new edition and its predecessor.

I have observed nothing in the public journals, which have noticed the work, that calls for any reply; nothing indeed but the personal abuse, and the party mis-statements, which my experience of the habits of some of our professional opponents, and of the blamable partiality of some newspaper editors, who are of course unacquainted with the subject in dispute, had led me to anticipate, and accustomed me to disregard. That the more important part of this work, the statistics of acute inflammations, can be successfully attacked by the allopathic party, I have taken too much pains with the facts and calculations to have the smallest misgiving. That they will attempt it is to be expected—they cannot help themselves, they must put on the appearance of disputing the results to which I have been led, but I defy them to unsettle a single conclusion which is recorded in that part of the work.

The only event which has happened since the publication of the first edition, that calls for particular notice, is the appearance of a paper, to which the following observations refer:—

In a late number of an allopathic journal,* a passage occurs that would have demanded some notice from me, (acquainted as I am with the particulars of the case to which it refers,) even though I had no personal concern with it. And it is not in the very least degree because I am the "homœopathist" referred to in that passage, it is not even on account of the manner in which the reference is made to myself and the practice I prefer, that I think it both expedient and proper to comment upon it in this place. Personal responsibility for the way in which I discharge my professional duties, I am of course prepared to incur; and with the support of my deliberate convictions of what is true in medical science, and right in professional conduct, it is a very insignificant matter to me by whom that truth is condemned, or that conduct aspersed. It is by no personal motive regarding either myself or the author of the article to which I have referred, that I am actuated in my present purpose. The narrative I am about to quote suggests far more important reflections than are merely personal to either of us, and it is to these that I wish to direct the attention of the reader.

In considering the deaths from dysentery and diarrhœa, the author of the "Investigation," after stating that eleven such deaths had occurred in the quinquennial period, from 1845 to 1850, to which his labours were confined, observes,—

"A scrutiny of the certificates shows that five of the eleven

* An investigation of the Deaths in the Standard Assurance Company. By Robert Christison, M. D., V. P. R. S. E., Professor of Materia Medica in the University of Edinburgh, and Ordinary Physician to the Queen in Scotland. Monthly Journal of Medical Science, August 1853.

might be justly considered first-class lives at the time of assurance. To these may be added a sixth, as to whom the certificates supply no information, but who was familiarly known to the directors as a healthy citizen and of a long-lived family. This gentleman fell a victim to the delusions of Homœopathy, now happily on the wane in this city. He was seized with acute dysentery, for which his attendant, notwithstanding its swift and steady advances, administered with fearful pertinacity only infinitesimal nothings. On the fourth day his family gathered courage to put an end to this mockery; the Homœopathist withdrew, and I was consulted, but only to see the patient in a state of hopeless collapse, afflicted with incessant, fluid, bloody, involuntary discharges, a fluttering pulse, a husky voice, and cold extremities; under which symptoms he expired early on the fifth day. This was the swiftest case of dysentery I have ever seen. But I never before saw a case of acute dysentery left to nature. This party very nearly attained his expectations of life." (P. 131.)

I shall not take the trouble now to describe the surprise with which I perused these sentences, but shall restrict myself to a calm narrative of facts, and to such dispassionate observations as they appear plainly to suggest. And, first, it is worthy of being noticed that, for the special and avowed purposes of the "Investigation," all that it was necessary for the author to do, in connexion with the case adverted to, was to specify the death by dysentery at a certain age, and after a certain period of insurance, or, if anything additional was to be expected, that the allopathic investigator should express, as he had every right to do, his honest opinion, however ill-founded, regarding the "delusions of Homœopathy," in connexion with the result of the case. So much the "Investigation" might demand: more than this, and especially a professed account of the early progress of the malady, of which he knew nothing, the courage of the family, the withdrawing homœopathist, &c., &c., was quite uncalled for,—a voluntary intrusion of irrelevant and unedifying particulars into a disquisition on life assurance. I draw attention to this matter in order to remark that, in referring to this case, the author of the Investigation obviously did not feel himself hampered by want of space, and compelled by an imperative necessity of being brief, and of excluding whatever did not bear upon the immediate and primary objects of his paper, to omit mentioning any important particulars bearing upon the issue of the case, but considered himself at liberty to say all he had a mind to say.

Secondly, The reason for the case in question being added to the list of first-class lives is very extraordinary. It is solely on the ground that a board of "directors," composed of non-professional persons, regarded the gentleman as a "healthy citizen." "The certificates supply no information:" nothing is ascertained regarding the illnesses he may have had, or the care in regard to diet, &c., he may have needed in order to preserve his healthy appearance, and no medical evidence exists as to any one point in his actual condition at the time of his being insured, or as to anything in his previous history. I am bound, however, to say, that this is the only instance throughout the investigation in which the usual evidences regarding the quality of a life are entirely dispensed with. In all the other cases the strictness necessary to entitle the Investigation to the confidence of the reader appears to be maintained with scrupulous propriety.

But, under this second head, there is much more to perplex and surprise than the particulars I have just noticed. The question occurs, What "directors" are referred to as the parties whose decision regarding the health of the gentleman is held to be so conclusive? That it cannot be the board who presided over the institution when the gentleman in question was admitted to the benefits of insurance is obvious, for of the fifteen gentlemen who composed that body in 1828, when the insurance in question was effected, I understand that thirteen at least have been long dead, and the author of the Investigation, whose connexion with the company is of a comparatively recent date, can therefore have had no opportunity of learning their opinions on the subject. Not one of these gentlemen belonged to the board of directors in 1849, the year in which the individual whose case is the theme of this disquisition died. Nor can any of the more permanent office-bearers of the company have given information regarding the opinion of these directors,—for the manager of 1828 has been for many years in another part of the world, and the secretary has been long out of the world altogether. The only other directors who can be supposed to be the parties to whose opinion the reference is made in the Investigation, are those who were members of the board during the period embraced by the Investigation, which includes, of course, the year 1849, when the death in question took place. But it cannot have been intended by the author of the Investigation to appeal to the directors of 1849 as cognizant of the existing and habitual state of health of a citizen twenty-one years before, which they had no opportunity of personally knowing, even were they competent to judge, and of which they had avowedly no documentary evidence to enable them to form an opinion. Their testimony, therefore, can only have been reasonably appealed to in regard to the apparent health of their fellow-citizen, (who was also, by the by, their fellow director,) at the time he became affected with the acute disease which made him "a victim to the delusions of Homœopathy."

Now, what are the facts? There cannot have been a single director of 1849 who was not aware that their fellow-citizen, during the winter and part of the spring preceding his death, and down to the time at which he was seized with the acute disease of which he died, had been "breaking up," his health undermined by chronic cough and chronic disease of the stomach, and, for aught I know, by allopathic drugging, until, long before his last and acute illness, he had become sallow, haggard, and greatly reduced in strength and flesh! All this happening to a man in his sixty-eighth year, constituted a state of general decay which no medical man of experience, be he of what party he may, can deny to have been one of the most unfavourable conditions in which it was possible for a severe attack of acute dysentery to have occurred. His age itself was an unfavourable circumstance, but it was as nothing compared to the inroads which chronic disease had made on his whole constitution. Nearly about the same time, I witnessed quite as sudden and acute an attack of dysentery in a gentleman of seventy-six, but he was not worn with previous disease as well as old age, and he recovered in a few days.

I was first consulted by the gentleman whose case is adverted to in the Investigation on the 31st of March, 1849. The notes of his chronic illness, which I committed to writing at the time, were as follows:—

In the beginning of December last he became affected with cough and expectoration, and continues to be so to a considerable degree, though now better than formerly. No physical signs of disease of the chest.

Tongue clean in front, loaded and pasty behind. Appetite much diminished, and he soon tires of anything. His habitual sensation is that he is already full, and needs no food. After eating he experiences an uneasy turning sensation in the stomach, and nausea, producing a desire to vomit, or a wish that he had eaten nothing. Sometimes he does vomit, and experiences relief. After eating, too, he is liable to feel as if a hard lump existed in the stomach. He has always much flatulence after food, and is liable to be affected with nausea, and filling of the mouth with water, at any time. Bowels pretty regular. In the evenings after dinner he is inclined to sit cowering over the fire, is taciturn and chilly. All these symptoms date also from the beginning of winter. He had some homœopathic remedies prescribed.

5th April.—Cough and expectoration much less. No flatulence till last night, after an indigestible meal; appetite much improved. No "burden" about the stomach till yesterday, after the indigestible food referred to. No sickness, Altogether better, and feels a new activity and pleasure in business. Much less chilliness. More medicine.

16*th.*—Has been really very well. Knows a great difference in his strength. Continue medicine.

It was while thus improving in health, but before time enough had been afforded to enable the improvement to repair the ravages made by the previous months of disease, that he was seized, on the evening of the 22d of April, with dysentery, in consequence of prolonged exposure to cold; and on the following day, the first of my attendance for the acute disease, it had acquired a character of significant severity: the pulse was 100 in the minute, skin hot and dry, thirst, and the evacuations already sanguineous and slimy.

Had the history of this case prior to the last illness been even hinted at, however inadequately, in the Investigation, I should not have considered myself called upon to make any comments on the opinion of the allopathic author regarding the unsuitableness of the homœopathic treatment. It was not to be expected that, with his views and practical unacquaintance with Homœopathy, he should have entertained any other opinion, or have hesitated to express it. Those who practise homœopathically have no right to demand that their cases shall not be commented on by physicians who dissent from their principles. Homœopathists may, indeed, even when their cases are represented by their opponents fully and fairly, very reasonably observe that they do not pretend to cure every case of acute inflammation that may occur in their practice, and they may, with undeniable justice, retort on their too stringent critics, that Allopathy, in every city and hamlet in Christendom, in the best as well as in the worst hands, loses many a case of acute inflammation, dysentery among the rest, at every age and in every phase of general health, good and bad, that human creatures can possess. These remarks remind me of an anecdote which I have heard in connexion with the case I have been describing. At a dinner party in this city, soon after the decease of this gentlemen, two allopathic physicians commented with much emphasis on the unhappy event: "It was very melancholy,—really dreadful,—a sad, sad business," &c., &c.; and many the shake of the head, and half-sorrowful, half-indignant phrase, betokened or appeared to betoken their wounded feelings. A non-medical friend who had reason to think more favourably of the offending practice, began to shake his head too, and to groan in concert, while now and then he muttered to the gratified ears of the two, "Sad, very sad,—the most melancholy case I have known for years." "Yes," said the two; "dreadful,—you may well say so." "I was thinking," said the other, "of poor J. H.; a man in the prime of life; little above 50; a rising man; really a great loss; and so likely to have lived long." "But, but," said one of the Allopaths, "he wasn't treated homœopathically!" "True, true; but still a very melancholy case,—very melancholy, —and of dysentery too!"

Though we have no right, as I have said, to demand that our cases shall not be commented on by our opponents, we *have* a right to expect and to require that they shall not be misrepresented, or, what comes to the same thing, represented in such a way as to leave abundant room for misconstruction. In the present instance I am far from saying or insinuating that the misrepresentation or room for misconstruction was deliberate and intentional. But I do say, that care was not taken by the author of the Investigation so to represent the case as to allow his readers to judge for themselves whether it was really such as would have made recovery a probable occurrence in any circumstances or under any treatment. And, in addition to the previous history of the patient, he should have mentioned that, on examination of the body, the mucous membrane of the stomach was found to bear traces of the chronic disease which had for so long a time made healthy and healthful digestion impossible. My informant as to this point was merely a non-medical member of the family, to whom the fact had been communicated, so that I am not prepared to say to what extent the anatomical change had gone.

In other particulars, of minor importance, the Investigation is so incorrect as to furnish the clearest proofs that the author wrote without reflection, and without notes to assist his memory. What does he know of the "swift and steady advances" of the disease? Nothing. On the second day of my attendance, I had hopes that the disease would yield, for the pulse had fallen in frequency from 100 to 78 in the minute, during the previous twenty-four hours. And though the amendment did not advance, the pulse on the last day of my attendance had not risen above 86, while it continued of good size and strength. Besides, though they always maintained the peculiar character they exhibited at my first visit, the other symptoms did not increase so swiftly and steadily as the author of the report very uninformedly asserts. At my last visit, about 5 P.M. on the fourth day of the disease, I found the pulse 86, full and soft, the *skin warm*, the evacuations scanty, though about once an hour.

The allopathic physician visited the gentleman *three* hours afterwards, "but only," he says, "to see the patient in a state of hopeless collapse, afflicted with incessant, fluid, bloody, involuntary discharges, a fluttering pulse, a husky voice, and cold extremities;" were all this correct, this great change in three hours' time, then it would be also correct that "he expired early in the course of the fifth day," or that immediately following the day (the fourth) on which this physician had made his first visit. But, and this is a remarkable instance of the strange peculiarity that characterizes the whole narrative, the patient did not die till the *day after*, or the *sixth* day! I don't know whether it will still be held as the "swiftest case of dysentery" the reporter ever saw. I have heard that the other case referred to in my anecdote was a swift one, but I do not assert that it was, for I do not know. At all events, the question comes now to be, why was *this* case so very swift? Had a day and a half of Allopathy nothing to do with the swiftness? I don't mean to say that the patient would have recovered but for Allopathy, for I am not at all sure that he would, but I incline to think that he would have lived longer. The author of the Investigation hints that it was the swiftest case he ever saw, because he had never before seen a case of dysentery "left to nature," which he facetiously suggests to be equivalent to being left to Homœopathy. I am obliged to contradict him again, and to assert that he *has* seen cases left *as long* to nature seriously, as he affirms of this case facetiously. In his notice of the dysentery of 1826,* he says certain effects followed his treatment "if the patient was seen within three or four days," and he mentions of a particular case which died in his hands, that he "entered the hospital on the *eighth* day of his illness." Now we have no express affirmation that these cases had had *no* treatment, prior to

* Edinburgh Medical and Surgical Journal, 1829.

their being "seen" by the writer of the report, or before admission into his hospital wards; but the whole tenor of his remarks justifies the conclusion that there had been no treatment previous to his own,—for he is giving an account of the alleged effects of a certain medicine on the peculiar symptoms of dysentery, and, in order to be a fair and unequivocal account, it must refer to dysentery untampered with, and not sophisticated by drugs previously administered. Besides, every hospital physician in Europe *must* have seen cases of severe and acute dysentery that had undergone no medical treatment whatever for four, five, six days, and even more, previous to their being admitted as hospital patients. The poor everywhere are well known to put off the services of the doctor as long as they can. The author of the Investigation, in addition to what he knows on this subject from his own hospital experience, will find instances in point recorded in Mr. Brown's account of the dysentery of Glasgow,* where cases are mentioned that were seven and fourteen days without medical treatment, though the disease was so severe as to prove ultimately fatal. After all this, it certainly must appear very strange that the author of the Investigation should endeavour to appal his readers by the allegation that as he had never seen a case of acute dysentery "left to nature" for four days, the rapidity of the example he comments upon must have been due to that unprecedented circumstance. Not only has he seen cases left as long to nature, as I have shown, but he knew, or ought to have known, that even when not "left to nature,"—that when enjoying or enduring the inflictions of allopathy, cases of acute dysentery have been fatal in six days, and that, therefore, the case he animadverts upon was not by any means a unique one. In Mr. Wilson's notice of the dysentery of Glasgow, in 1827,

* Glasgow Medical Journal, vol. i.

it is remarked, "death sometimes took place so early as the sixth day," which was the date of the death selected for special remark in the Investigation. To be sure it is there made to occur on the *fifth* day, but that allegation, as has been seen, is incorrect, and in consequence of its being so renders the exultation of the author over the imaginary swiftness of the case rather awkward.

Before concluding these remarks on dysentery, I may be allowed to ask, if one of the eleven cases referred to in the Investigation "fell a victim to the delusions of Homœopathy," what delusion proved fatal to the other ten? Allopathy does not appear to be always a very successful opponent of acute dysentery, for the author of the Investigation admits that, in 1826, the allopathic mortality was "dreadful,"—twenty deaths out of eighty cases, or one in four! No doubt the disease was epidemic, and epidemic dysentery often presents a considerable proportion of severe cases; but I ask any physician of candour and experience to say, if, among eighty old gentlemen, broken down by chronic disease, so many as three out of four, or even one out of four, would have escaped under the best allopathic treatment? And yet the investigation more than insinuates, pretty broadly intimates, that the case it so partially represents died for want of Allopathy!

Lastly, Homœopathy is said to be "happily on the wane in this city." The correctness of the Investigation in other particulars, will not dispose the readers of this account of it to put much faith in this crowning allegation. No doubt the wish was father to the thought, in the absence of a more legitimate parent. On this point, so momentous to Allopathists of every grade, I must content myself with referring to page 205 of this work.

PREFACE TO THE FIRST EDITION.

AFTER many announcements, from time to time, of the approaching event, the Professor of Midwifery brought his tedious gestation of twelve months to a happy issue in the middle of March last. Anticipation was high among the professional kindred, the allopathic side of the family, during the interesting period; and we of the other party, who are but the step-sons of "our ancient mother," could gather from the significant looks of our half-brothers that we were expected to gird up our loins for a speedy retreat on the appearance of the young stranger. He was to be, for modern times, quite an unprecedented production; without a parallel, in fact, since the famous progeny of the cock's egg, whose breath, and even very look, was fatal. We would take no hint, notwithstanding, however kindly intended, thinking it would be time enough to pack up our chattels, if we must do so, after we had looked the awful creature in the face; for, great as our credulity is said to be, we had no faith in prodigies, and a strong suspicion that the powers of the new cockatrice, introduced with so much noise, would prove as imaginary as those of its fabulous predecessor. And now that the thing is fairly before us, "combed, wattled, and spurred like the dunghill cock with a serpent's tail," as the heralds have it, we hope to be pardoned for laughing at the ridiculous astonishment of our friends on the other side, at the absurd object presented to them by the parturient professor. We don't mean it offensively, and hope they will take it in good part; for we can honestly assure them that we never felt so kindly towards them in our lives, or so disinclined to injure their feelings. We are quite aware that this was looked upon as their last hope, and we are not the people to triumph over chop-fallen opponents with an ill-timed merriment—when it can possibly be restrained. But really the present is altogether an exceptional case; and if we do look a degree or two merrier than in the strictness of friendly sympathy we ought, it is in a great measure because we hope that this last and sore disappointment will disenchant them, ere we part, of their delusion, both as to their own position and ours, and be the means of a better understanding among us for the future, if not of a speedy and entire coincidence of opinion regarding the matters at present in dispute.

Dr. Simpson's tactics strongly remind me of the ingenious conduct of the Dutch in Charles the Second's time, who kindled bonfires and set their bells a-ringing whenever they had been thrashed at sea, in order to evade the acknowledgment or appearance of disaster. For, I believe, it was generally admitted, and even by not a few of his own party, that in the last engagement he was very handsomely beaten; his personal authority as to facts and doctrines shown to be quite infinitesimal; his information to be singularly defective, not only in homœopathic matters, but in the truths that are common to all medical science; his logic to have its point turned destructively towards himself and his friends; and his theological zeal to be entirely out of place. Yet, with the *face* of an old Dutchman, here he is again with as much of the former tattered material as he can get to hang together, and as much new canvass of the same originally bad quality as his crippled spars will carry, trying to look as if he was unconscious of defeat. But the device won't do: the former discomfiture can be forgotten only in the new calamity of a still greater. This I may venture to promise, and without laying myself open to the charge of vain confidence; for such is the mode of attack Dr. Simpson has selected, that almost any one might beat him who chose to take the trouble. Nay, the work is, for the most part, done to his hand; for the author's mind has been so confused with the undigested mass of raw material he had swallowed in his twelvemonth of hard reading, that he frequently contradicts and refutes in one page what he had affirmed on the preceding, and loads his paper with commonplace dissertations on human credulity and knavery, which tell with double effect when turned the other way.

In his preface, Dr. Simpson, alluding to me, takes occasion to observe in the Dutch style,—"It is said that in a hopeless and hollow law-suit, an English barrister had his brief on the day of trial handed to him with this note: 'No case; but take a chance of decision in our favour by personal abuse of the opposite counsel.' The homœopathic author of the principal reply to my previous pamphlet seems to have taken up the same tactics as the best or only line of defence for his system. And I have no wish to disturb him in it; more particularly as, like an unhappy lawyer pleading a bad cause, he has himself, in my opinion, evidently no faith whatever in his own irrelevant arguments and diversified mis-statements." On the first of these charges, which always falls so easily into the imagination of persons in Dr. Simpson's situation, I would observe, that I am of course aware that my former reply was at least as severe (for plain outspoken truth is sometimes very severe) as there was any occasion for, and that others, besides the individual who naturally felt it the most, are of opinion that the lash was laid on with more than necessary good will. I would, however, remind the objectors that, as Lord Jeffrey says, there are occasions "when severity becomes a duty"—a duty to the public, to the erring brother, and to one's self; and I would remind them, moreover, of the circumstances in which that reply was written. To the persecuted party, the occasion appeared one of life or death to their principles and themselves, a time for courage, energy, and plain speaking. The aggressors seemed powerful, merciless, and bent on mischief to the uttermost, so that we had but one choice—to crouch and be crushed like cowards, or to face the odds that were against us, as devoted men who neither gave nor looked for quarter. There was Dr. Simpson, President of the Royal College of Physicians, with all the weight of a "European reputation" in his arm, and all the strength of Colleges and Societies, and hordes of "free companions," at his back, intent on destroying us root and branch, and careless of the weapons he employed, if they seemed but fitted for his purpose. The emergency appeared critical and dangerous in no ordinary degree, and to call for prompt and decisive measures. It is all very well, after the champion—on the credit of whose supposed personal authority and character so much of the issue was made to depend—was disarmed, prostrated, and "disembowelled," as one of his own party expressed it, for mere spectators to say, that there was an unnecessary violence in the treatment he received. Skilful and experienced artillerymen can so estimate the strength of their powder as to make it do its work economically, but I had no scientific data, and no practice, to guide me as to the precise force that was needed gently to upset a President, loaded with the "European" thing and what not, and buttressed behind by so many backers. As to the more important of the latter, the Colleges, they had so long ruled the profession, and lorded it over the "sea of troubles" which afflict the public, that it is no wonder their power and importance, as props to the bellicose Professor of Midwifery, appeared greater than we now know them to be. We mistook them for something like the bluff and bearded Venitian Doge of the thirteenth century, who could say, and effectually too, with his war-ships at his elbow, to Pope and Pagan who would fish forsooth in the Adriatic, "Be off—that sea is ours!" It is all very well to laugh at their peremptory words, now that they are discovered rather to resemble a certain sapient bird, of which Goldsmith relates the following anecdote:—"Once upon a time, a goose fed its young by a pond side; and a goose in such circumstances is always extremely proud, and excessively punctilious. If any other animal, without the least design to offend, happened to pass that way, the goose was immediately at it. The pond, she said, was hers, and she would maintain her right to it, and support her honour, while she had a bill to hiss or a wing to flutter;" and then he goes on to say, how a mastiff, which I take to have been a type of ourselves, the strong-jawed Homœopathists, chanced to pass by, and thought it no harm if he should lap a little of the water, as he was thirsty; and how he had a mind twenty times to snap off her head,—but finally contented himself with the remark, "A pox take thee for a fool; surely those who have neither strength nor weapons to fight, at least should be civil." For my part, I wish them no such miserable punishment; but certainly think that the "Physicians," in commemoration of Dr. Simpson's presidentship, should inaugurate an effigy of the unreasonable fowl beside the philosophers of their porch, Charon, Pandora, and the other.

After the experience we have now had in controversy, there would be no excuse for me, or any one of my way of thinking, employing such deadly weapons as the seeming dangers of an earlier stage of the struggle demanded. We are now comparatively at ease and in safety, and have no other desire than to cultivate the arts of peace; in which I, at least, hope to excel so much, that, as it was wittily said of Cæsar, when some one sneered at his baldness, "He has covered that defect with laurels," so the courtesy and forbearance of all future productions of my pen shall gracefully conceal the roughness of their predecessors. At the same time, I cannot cancel in this work all the just severities of the former; for Dr. Simpson—while he groans under inflictions applied to himself, suppresses in his new production several of the personalities which brought down on him much of the exposure he formerly underwent, and professes an anxiety to avoid "unnecessarily mixing up any personal disputations" with the matter of his new lucubrations,—has done little else from beginning to end of the strange medley he has produced, than labour to load his opponents with charges of quackery, deception, avarice, falsehood, blasphemy, witchcraft, and almost every other conceivable wickedness and folly. He has violated the sanctity of the grave, and insulted the dead, who cannot defend themselves, as well as the living who can; though in the latter respect, in order to plead for exemption from personal retaliation, he has been more careful than formerly to avoid specifying the individual objects of his aspersions, as if he could escape from the guilt of misrepresenting any in particular by misrepresenting all without distinction.* Therefore it is that in defending myself and my friends from

* To the best of my recollection, the dead Hahnemann is the only person pointedly and by name vilified by the brave Professor of midwifery. He, alas! is not here to reply. Death is a sad obstacle to fair play, giving all the safety to one side. Truly, as the proverb says, "Better a living dog than a dead lion." Another fact of an equally valiant nature, observable in the "Tenets," is the putting of the insulting and abusive charges with which it abounds, in the form of quotations from other allopathic works against Homœopathy.

such reckless imputations, I find it still necessary to expose the author of them to the merited censure of the reader, as it is impossible to bring to the light of public observation a tissue of extraordinary misrepresentation and abuse, without exhibiting the artificer along with his inventions. Besides, *Cumque opere in proprio soleat se pingere pictor*, "As every painter paints himself in his own works," and most authors, too,—Dr. Simpson has drawn such a likeness of himself in his various publications on Homœopathy, as makes him in a great measure harmless to the cause he so ardently aspires to injure; and, therefore, I feel bound, in fairness to that cause, to bring the lineaments a little more prominently before the reader than the mere attractions of the portrait would justify. Had he managed the execution of his purpose with more skill, —assumed a tone of dignity that could not stoop, or but with seeming reluctance, to make use of the assertions of the low and worthless writers who had preceded him,—had put on an air of candour and charity which could "scarcely believe so, and so," "hoped that things were not quite so bad as they appeared," and "feared that our friends the Homœopaths had made some mistake here," in short, "would not for the world impute bad motives without proofs clear as they are painful," and finally, had he, with real caution, but the show of forbearance, declined entering into details on various scientific questions, hinting merely that a great deal might be said if he had chosen, or had time, and so forth; by thus concealing his dispositions, purposes, and quantum of information, he might have proved, because not so easily caught and exposed, a more formidable opponent than we find him to be. But, like too keen a swordsman, he forgets half his art, which ought to consist not less in covering himself than in striving to vanquish his adversary. By abandoning himself to the passion of the hour, he has exposed himself on every page, and painted a likeness equally absurd and surprising. I can fancy how happy his antagonist, Dr. Mure, will be to appropriate such an object from the head of the allopathic party.* Dr. Simpson's readers will remember that he mentions an outlandish personage of that name, from somewhere in the neighbourhood of Patagonia, as a dealer in a very unmentionable kind of insect, which he recommends as a homœopathic remedy when duly comminuted. He will now have a suitable remedy for moral as well as bodily taints, for Milton tells us, in the preface to his Sampson Agonistes, that Aristotle held the exhibition of certain passions to purge the mind of the beholder of whatever he entertains that is of the like kind. "Nor is Nature," continues the poet, "wanting in her efforts to make good his assertion: for so, in physic, things of melancholic hue and quality are used against melancholy, sour against sour, salt to remove salt humours." With such high authority, then, for a homœopathic way to "minister to the mind diseased," Dr. Mure is doubly armed, and holding the mirror up to Nature, in the shape of Dr. Simpson, in the one hand, and carrying his brayed insect in the other, he may well regard himself as a match for any corporeal or spiritual *psora*.

The passage which I have quoted from Dr. Simpson's preface, besides the erroneous allegation that I had made my defence of Homœopathy to consist of a mere personal attack upon himself, contains the charge, that I indulged in "diversified mis-statements." This affirmation, of course, is intended to signify that the personalities were unfounded. As it is not my intention, in this work, to reproduce in detail several of the most serious of the charges which I formerly

*In a newspaper article,—written by whom?—Dr. Simpson was lately said to be at the "top of his profession." In a review of my first edition in the *Caledonian Mercury*, August, 1843, written by a person who has an equal contempt for truth and good taste, he is said to be a great discoverer, and to enjoy the confidence of his Sovereign—as if he were, on these accounts, even supposing them true, entitled to insult and misrepresent with impunity.

proved against him,—and for the simple reason that, by suppressing, in his new work, the statements which had called for the exposure of which he complains, the reproduction of them in an extended form has become unnecessary.—I refer to them briefly in this place, merely for the purpose of observing, first, that they are not withheld on the ground of having been unjust or improper; and, second, that the establishing of them was of material consequence in dealing with some of the accusations Dr. Simpson and others had made against the adherents of Homœopathy. In the postscript of my Letter to the President of the Medico-Chirurgical Society, the following passage occurs, which I quote in order to illustrate the second of these observations. "Those who believe Homœopathy to be a great and invaluable system of practical medicine have been, with unsparing acrimony and in the most offensive terms, stigmatized as unworthy of credit: all the courtesies that are usual among gentlemen have been denied us, and now that an occasion apart from all the perplexities that pertain to the operation of medicine, has presented itself, of testing the candour and uprightness of the contending parties, those who have been heretofore maligned have a right to appeal to the public,—in a question which the public is qualified to comprehend,—to decide between them and their opponents, as to which shall henceforth be esteemed the most entitled to confidence. This controversy, therefore, ceases to be a merely personal one: it is rather to be regarded as a combat in which those who are engaged do battle for the honour of their respective hosts." In these sentences reference is made to a question which had arisen between Mr. Syme and Dr. Simpson on the one hand, and myself on the other, as to the truth of contradictory affirmations regarding certain matters of fact, with which we were all in circumstances to be equally and fully acquainted. No matter how trifling these matters were in themselves—(and probably no *casus belli* at Donnybrook was ever more paltry)—the two champions of the allopathic party attached great importance to them, and, doing so, thought proper to make public affirmations respecting them which were diametrically opposed to previous statements of mine. Here, then, was a fair opportunity of testing the credibility of persons who occupied prominent places on opposite sides, and of coming to some just conclusion regarding the alleged difference between the contending sections of the profession, in respect to accuracy of statement—to use the mildest expression; for I have no desire to make this necessarily a question of veracity, in the moral sense of the term. It may or may not be so: I give no opinion; but speak only to what appeared on the surface. By referring to the testimony of third parties, the allegations of the allopathic belligerents were proved, to the conviction, if not to the satisfaction of both sides, to be totally at variance with fact. It would be a miserable use of this result, and of every other imperfection that could be brought home to individual Allopaths, to make them the grounds of grave and sweeping accusations against the whole or the majority of the allopathic body. I am not so foolish as to believe, and not so wicked as to pretend to believe, that many of them would deliberately state what they know to be false, any more than they would pay their debts like Professor Webster of America, or discharge a confidential trust like Sir Everard Home, or fabricate their cases, like M. Lisfranc, or revenge themselves like Dr. Fickel.* But Dr. Simpson, when he

* Sir Everard, it will be remembered, published the MSS. of Hunter, or the researches they contained, as his own. Dr. Fickel, I formerly apprized the public, was convicted of gross deceit during his professed attachment to Homœopathy, and to revenge himself on his homœopathic castigators, he published a book, "Die Nichtigkeit der Homœopathie,"—the Nothingness of Homœopathy,—professing to be a proof, from cases, of the inutility of the practice. He was not long afterwards in jail for *swindling*. Dr. Simpson

finds, or supposes he finds any departure from moral rectitude in one who has the misfortune to differ from him as to the proper dose of a drug, and the proper rule for prescribing it, hesitates not to hold all who entertain the same offensive opinions as liable to the same moral accusations. A great proportion of his industry during the existence of this controversy has been employed in striving to detect something reprehensible in the conduct of individuals opposed to him, and in affixing the stigma of their real or fancied blemishes on their party in general. He must not, therefore, be surprised if some of the calumniated body put the worst construction on his own conduct in the instances I have referred to, and argue from what they believe to be proved against him, that, since the very leader of their opponents, whose reputation in the profession has acquired so considerable an eminence, has stooped to such behaviour, his colleagues of a lower grade must be capable of conduct at least as bad. If he is conscious, as he may be, that he was not guilty of intentional untruth in the instances in question, he ought to feel that others may be equally unfortunate in appearing to be guilty, while really innocent; and he ought to be specially careful how he advances the loathsome accusation of deceit. Happily, the very excess of his criminality in this particular has defeated his discreditable purpose, as is proved by the following quotation from a judicious and candid review of his work, in a common organ of public opinion:—"It is, in truth, most repellent to every honest mind to read the open charges of fraud so constantly flung against Hahnemann and his disciples; as if every homœopathic doctor in Europe were an arrant knave whose only object is an unblushing system of deception, in order to enrich himself at the expense of

knew all this; yet refers to him as an authority against us. He is, doubtless, as good an authority as most of the others.

the lives and pockets of the community. Human nature instinctively revolts at the thought,—and human nature is right."*

As to the accuracy of my statements in the other particulars contained in my reply to Dr. Simpson's former publications, I shall bring the sincerity of his general accusation to the test, by pledging myself to submit to any penalty even the College of Physicians may impose, if he will point out a single misstatement made by me; and all I ask in return, without, however, making it a stipulation, is, that he will make an honest confession for but one in every ten that I can prove to exist in his various attacks on Homœopathy. And here I am tempted to notice a little episode in the majestic march of these medical wars, which I think will prove to the satisfaction of the most incredulous, that the author of the "Tenets" has refrained from specifying any one misstatement as chargeable against me, for the very good reason that he could discover none. A work was published some short time ago, in which the demise of a gentleman was erroneously referred to as having been due to a chronic organic disease. As the individual in question had been attended by me, it appeared probable to Dr. Simpson, that I was the author of the statement as to the cause of death, and that if he could ascertain that point to his satisfaction, he would have a great triumph over a troublesome opponent, and indisputable

* Edinburgh Advertiser, April 19, 1853. As an additional warning to Dr. Simpson to refrain hereafter from reckless imputations of falsehood against his brethren, I may recall to his notice a complaint of his own of somewhat similar conduct towards himself of his friend Mr. Syme, in the course of one of their quarrels:—"He adds, indeed, that if his object were to convict me of the most gross and explicable inaccuracy he could easily multiply examples of it, but that as he merely desires to prevent the patrons from being misled by my statements, he trusts that enough has been said to attain this object." —Memorial, &c., &c., by J. Y. Simpson, M. D.—1841.

evidence of the dishonesty of the whole homœopathic body. Well, he, being President of the Royal College of Physicians, &c., &c., condescended to call privately in person on the author of the work, to learn if Dr. Henderson was his authority for that statement, "because it was not true." But no, alas! Dr. Henderson was too knowing a man, to say the least of him, to affirm an untruth, for he had somehow learnt, what many are slow to believe, that honesty in all things is the best policy; and so had no more to do with the erroneous statement than Dr. Simpson himself. Now, do not suppose, gentle reader, that I have given this anecdote merely in order to get you to join me in a laugh at the expense of the curious Professor of Midwifery. Far from it; my chief object in entering into these pitiful matters at all, is to show that where Dr. Simpson and I are at variance regarding a matter of fact, the yea or nay as to which depends on our personal authority, *I* am entitled to be esteemed by far the more likely to be in the right. Now we are at direct issue concerning the trumpery story which Dr. Simpson has related about a box of homœopathic medicines, which had once been "his own former homœopathic box," and while it was so had the contents of its many phials mixed together, as he says, by some juvenile member of his family; but which, notwithstanding, had been the means in my hands of so convincing me of the truth of Homœopathy, that some time afterwards, I assured him, as he avers, that I "had seen some wonderful effects and cures from using the drugs contained in it;" or, as he said to himself, (in a conversation we had on several memorial topics before he published this altered version of the words put into my mouth,) were my actual expressions, "your box has converted me." To both versions I give now, as formerly, an unqualified denial, and for the simple and sufficient reason, that for me to have uttered either the one or the other would have been an untruth. In the words of my former refutation of the whole fable—"My first experiments on Homœopathy were made by medicines from *five* different sources, in addition to Dr. Simpson's box. The respected Secretary of the Medico-Chirurgical Society favoured me with a box, in connexion with which there was, as became his character, no trick, but all that was fair and honest. Dr. Russell supplied me with many other medicines; Headland of London did so too; the Chemist in this city, at a later period, did the same; and some I prepared with my own hands, The results were published, and drew from Dr. Forbes of London the admission, that had the cases been treated according to the rules of the ordinary school, he would have regarded the results as 'very satisfactory.' Among them were some 'wonderful effects and cures,' which I have always regarded as evidence of the power of homœopathic remedies; but that they were due to Dr. Simpson's 'own former homœopathic box,' in which the trick was, I do not believe that I could ever have averred, because I was not in the habit of noting in each case from what source the medicines I employed were taken, for I suspected no trick. Since Dr. Simpson made his trick public, I have suspected, reasonably enough, that some of the failures which I could not formerly account for but on the ground of my own want of skill, must have been due to the dishonest box."* In his new work, Dr. Simpson incautiously enters so much into a pretended history of the box and its contents, while it belonged to him, as to furnish the means of a satisfactory refutation of another and very material part of the business, which is no less than this, that the whole account of the medicines being mixed is imaginary. The box containing sixty-six phials, each labeled *on the glass and on the cork,* with the name, in Latin, of the included drug. Every phial was full,

*Letter to the President of the Medico-Chirurgical Society.

and every cork in its right place, when the box came, unexpectedly by Dr. Simpson, into my possession. Now, are we asked to believe that a child, some three years old, in the habit, as is alleged, of uncorking the bottles of his "occasional plaything," emptying their contents into a heap, and then refilling them from the general mass, was so precocious a scion that he could replace each cork of the sixty-six in its proper place, according to its inscription? And if not, as is perfectly certain, what learned Theban was at the trouble to rejust the disordered elements of so despised a machine?

These are disagreeable topics, and such as I would never have stooped to discuss here or anywhere, if they had been brought forward by Dr. Simpson merely to injure me. I believe I could afford to let them pass unnoticed. But, through me, they are designed to bring the only rational system of practical medicine into contempt; and since I know how to dispose of them, I feel bound to waive my own feelings for what I believe to be required by the general good. And now the reader may rest assured, that I am almost done with the *personnel* of Dr. Simpson, whom, indeed, I hope scarcely to bring on the boards again, but with his company of *sauteurs* to tumble a little for our diversion. Not that I can allow his whole band to make their bow to the public on these pages, for many of them are such dull and vulgar rogues as to be unfit to give entertainment to any one, and they must therefore go their way to the tune of their own particular march, a sentence which proceeds from no anger or ill-will towards them, for Homœopathy can well afford to imitate the good-nature of my Lord Derby's "tall navvy," and, smiling on the whole generation of such small men, give them full liberty to practise their vocation, with the benevolent and senatorial reflection, "It amuses them, and don't hurt me. A selection, then, of the best performers being necessary, I shall introduce first a foreigner of some note in his own line.

It seems that a transatlantic gentleman, who rejoices in the classical denomination of *Mr. Horace Green*, related an instance to Dr. Simpson, in which a nervous lady had been recovered from a tedious state of fancied inability to walk, by what she supposed homœopathic globules, but which were in reality percussion pellets of fulminating silver that had been brought to her by mistake. The patronymic of our respectable contemporary is suggestive of much that is incompatible with the *curiosa felicitas* and knowledge of men that distinguished the celebrated heathen from whom he derives his baptismal appellative, and I scarcely know in what capacity to take him. Considering him simply as Mr. Green, we have one explanation of the anecdote; but regarding him as Horace, we have another totally different. Verdure is inseparably associated with ideas of simplicity and play, and allusions to the connexion abound in our finest pastorals; while so intimate is the association in the popular mind, that the moment a Mr. Green appears, he is instinctively appropriated to amusement. Viewing him, therefore, patronymically, I would incline to the opinion that, as *green*, (and, no doubt, as young too, for I find it as impossible to conceive of an old American, as De Quincy does of a young Chinese,) our innocent friend has been played upon by the knowing husband, who did not choose to own his conversion to Homœopathy by the miraculous recovery of his wife, and sought to justify his incredulity in the amazing circumstances by such cock-and-bull story as might obstruct the tender vision of his professional friend. Regarding him, again, in his more Pagan aspect, and decking him in fancy with the attributes of his harmonious name-father, who somewhere sings,—

> "Sine amore et jocis
> Nil ést jucundum,"

one may be disposed to conclude, that the playful Horace, discerning something greenish in the eye of his obstetric acquaintance, as they sipped their Falernian together, and mistaking its import, (for alas! there is a wide difference in the characters expressed by that optical tint,) conceived on the moment to relieve the monotony of their professional talk about moonstone and windpipes, (a weak point with our exotic brother,) the pleasantry about homœopathic globules and fulminating pellets. And it is, no doubt, though manufactured and issued under the poetical license, an apt instance of the power of imagination on the nervous hypochondriac, and as such deserves to be recorded among the thousands of a similar nature which in every age have made fame and fees the fruits of *allopathic* delusions.

The fertile Horace can, of course, diversify his narratives to meet every imaginable aspect of the great question, and, accordingly, he next assumes the tragic vein, and concentrating his fierceness on some allopathic rival, he enjoys in prophetic vision the delight of pouring a phial of homœopathic globules over his throat, medicated for the occasion with enough of imaginary strychnia to despatch him to his place. The whole story will remind the reader of Newman Noggs' pugilistic enjoyments on the image of Mr. Ralph Nickleby. Of course, no mortal was ever slain by such means as Mr. Horace pretends; but I shall stretch courtesy and imagination so far as to assume, that it actually happened that "a gentleman swallowing in sport a number of homœopathic globules" that did not belong to him, suffered on the spot the extreme penalty of the law due to such freedoms with property and poisons; and I shall slump this well-authenticated case with two others equally entitled to credit. One of them is the melancholy demise of the Duke di Cannizzaro, some twelve years ago, in Sicily, asserted by Mr. Edwin Lee (apparently a bookseller's traveller) to have been due to an over dose of nux vomica; the second is the alleged instance, in which Dr. Taylor of London detected in a powder, also professing itself to contain only a "homœopathic dose," one-third of a grain of morphia, quite an allopathic quantity. Now, these examples, supposing them true, may be regarded in one or other of two lights. First, they may be said to prove that three medical men, out of the many hundreds, if not thousands in the world, who now *avow* themselves homœopathists, were guilty of deceiving their patients, and were actually treating them with *allopathic* quantities, (as doses are termed when they reach or approach the poisoning potency,) while they professed to be giving only the *homœopathic*, (as doses are termed without the risk of killing.) No doubt such deception was extremely wrong—highly dishonourable and immoral; but it tells nothing against the multitude of homœopathic practitioners who do not practise any such deception. If we apply to the allopathic body in general, the discredit of similar deceptions (*mutatis mutandis*) practised by some among them, Dr. Simpson will perhaps see that the principle he attempts to apply so injuriously to us tells with a hundred-fold greater severity against himself and his friends. For it is an undoubted fact that a proportion of professedly allopathic practitioners employ, for particular diseases, the remedies which were discovered and announced by Hahnemann, as due to his homœopathic law for the selection of remedies; while with extraordinary meanness they ignore the discoverer, and treat his more honest followers with an affected disdain. Far different was the conduct of the late Mr. Liston, of whom Edinburgh has reason to be proud, as the greatest surgeon she has produced. He had the manliness, the *honesty*, to avow in public, that he derived his knowledge of the remarkable powers of aconite in subduing inflammatory fever, and of belladonna in curing erysipelas, from homœopathy, and to declare besides, that he had given the medicines "in much smaller doses than have hitherto been prescribed."* Others of the allopathic body go still farther in their secret use of homœopathic remedies, for I have been informed by a homœopathic chemist in London, that his shop is chiefly supported by practitioners who procure from him homœopathic remedies which they distribute to their patients *disguised as allopathic mixtures.*

So much for the first aspect in which these tales may be viewed. According to the second light in which they may be regarded, it may be maintained, as was no doubt intended by Dr. Simpson, if he had any distinct idea on the subject, that the detection of such large doses of strychnia and morphia in the hands of three homœopathic practitioners proves, or makes it likely, that the whole body of Homœopathists use doses of the like magnitude, while they profess to employ only the "infinitesimal" quantities. Now, granting the reasonableness of this generous allegation, it may be replied, first, that Homœopathists must be very verdant gentlemen indeed, if they attempt to impose on the public, by falsely professing rules, as to doses, which make Homœopathy absurd in the ignorant eyes of the very persons intended to be entrapped; for it is undeniable that the only obstacle to the progress of Homœopathy in the world is the incredulity which meets it on the ground of the unprecedented minuteness of its doses. The truth is, so little relish have many Homœopathists for the ridicule bestowed on the doctrine of minute doses, that there is a far greater risk of some of them being guilty, like so many of their professedly allopathic brethren, of pretending to give large doses, while they actually give the small. Small doses they know from experience to be the safest and best, and they are, with an exception or two, determined at all hazards to adhere to them; but it may

* See Lancet, 1836; where the reader will find, *in extenso*, the Clinical Lectures by Mr. Liston, containing a distinct recommendation of homœopathy to his pupils.

sometimes be difficult for them to do so, and keep their foolish patient at the same time, who may have a preference, even in physic, for things he can taste and smell, like the majority of silly mankind. Again, if Homœopathists are really believed by Dr. Simpson and his friends only to *pretend* that they give small doses, while they are *known*, as is alleged, to give doses as large as do the gentlemen of the other school, what is the use of calling in the aid of mighty mathematicians to prove that there can be nothing in the pretended homœopathic attenuations? The whole of this charge against them assumes that such attenuations are never actually made, or never employed, and if the accusers really believed this, as they profess to do, the calculations might be left, for any necessity they are of to the success of the charge, to the wisdom of Toby the learned quadruped. But the bare fact that such calculations have been regarded as of immense importance to the opponents of Homœopathy, proves that they have themselves no confidence in the statement that Homœopathists do in reality practise the deceit of which they are so shamefully accused. If they felt secure in the evidence and credibility of that statement, where was the necessity of bothering respectable elderly gentlemen, who happen to have a calculating faculty, with sentimental journeys to the sun, moon, and stars, in search of an argument which Mr. Horace Green had found without going a yard from his own door? And, lastly, if Homœopathists are believed by their opponents to use no other doses than are used by ordinary physicians, to what end are the elaborate endeavours to prove that the success of Homœopathists in treating diseases is inferior to that of their rivals, while the whole object of the assertion now under review is to prove that the practice of the two bodies is the same? This is surely a robbing of Peter to pay Paul, and a very stupid and foolish consummation of the whole argument.

There is yet another aspect in which these asserted instances of homœopathic deception can be viewed, and a far more rational one it is than either of the others, namely, that let Mr. Horace Green, Mr. Lee, Dr. Taylor, and Dr. Simpson, assert what they may, the deceptions that are alleged were and are *impossible*. The charge is, not simply that large doses were used in the cases referred to—that would be a minor matter, as a man is at liberty to employ what dose he prefers—but that the said doses were pretended to be *minute*. Now, reader, I hope you will be in a humour to apply the knout to the inventors of foul charges against their honester brethren, when I tell you, that such a dose of strychnia, nux vomica, or morphia, as these persons specify, could not possibly be taken by any man, in possession of his senses, without being detected by the *intense bitterness of their taste!* Had the accusers remembered this difficulty in the way of their instances being credible, they would not have ventured to prefer the charges they have made, in connexion with such substances at least; for they must have bethought them that, as "homœopathic doses" are well known to have no taste, no Homœopathist could dream of deceiving his patients by drugs so furiously bitter as these. To give the unmedical reader some idea of the obstacle to the alleged deception, presented by the bitterness of strychnia, I may observe that, according to Sir Robert Kane, one part "requires 7000 parts of cold water for solution, and yet, if *one* part of this be diluted with 100 parts more of water, this liquor tastes strongly bitter."* Or, what is the same thing, one grain of strychnia, dissolved in seven hundred thousand grains of water, or above eleven gallons, may still be detected by its strongly bitter taste. If, then, the 700,000th part of a grain of strychnia is strongly bitter, what must be the bit-

* Elements of Chemistry. 842.

terness of the 16th of a grain, the ordinary dose, diffused in a spoonful of water, which Homœopathists are accused of giving to their patients as "infinitesimal," and therefore tasteless! The bitterness of morphia is well known, but I may mention that Pereira says of it that, "notwithstanding that it is *insoluble*, or nearly so, in cold water," the water, which can hardly be said, therefore, to dissolve an appreciable quantity of it, "has a distinctly bitter taste." Yet Dr. Simpson wishes us to believe that a Homœopathist expected to elude the senses of his patient by so large a dose as a third, or half of a grain! Now I hope these gentlemen have tumbled to some purpose, and that the spectators will express their sense of the performance with their usual judgment.

Dr. Simpson's work abounds in charges as demonstrably untrue as those I have just disposed of, but, as I have no ambition to write a work so tiresome and unreadable as almost every body declares his to be, I shall pick out for notice in this place only the one remaining example which has an appearance of resting on respectable authority, and which may possibly be believed by very credulous and unreflecting people. Dr. Glover of Newcastle asserts that the *agent* of a London wholesale firm for the manufacture of homœopathic drugs, which prepares "60 lbs. weight of them every fortnight," (*i. e.* 1560 lbs. weight per annum,) stated to a company of *allopathic* druggists in Newcastle, that his firm, aware that the homœopathic method of preparing drugs was a "farce," gave up the troublesome proceeding, and put *nothing* into the powders and pilules which they sold as *medicated.* I do not know that Dr. Glover makes the assertion on his own authority; if he does not, of course he will not be implicated in the unavoidable inference suggested by the following considerations. The story is *incredible*, first, because it would be at variance with the known principles which regulate human intercourse, that the agent of a mercantile firm should reveal, (supposing the fraud to be actually practised,) to the most implacable enemies of his house, what must destroy his trade if generally believed; it is incredible, secondly, because it is infinitely more likely that the allopathic druggists would *invent* a story that would be to their own advantage, than that the other would disclose a fraud, the public knowledge of which must be to his own ruin; it is incredible, thirdly, because no London homœopathic wholesale druggist exists who prepares 60 lbs. weight of drugs, or pretended drugs, in a fortnight, for most of the homœopathic chemists in London, and throughout the country, prepare all, or nearly all, their own drugs, and there is no market for such a wholesale business; it is incredible, fourthly, because Dr. Glover, having been repeatedly called upon to give the name of the fraudulent firm, has declined to do so, which it is plain he never would if he were certain of his ground, and did not fear that compliance with the demand would explode the whole story. But, even supposing that some swindling company of homœopathic druggists actually do dispense unmedicated powders, and pilules, and tinctures, how does that tell against Homœopathy? Those who are unfortunate enough to deal with the swindlers will be unsuccessful in their practice, and be instrumental in making a few skeptics as to the power of homœopathic drugs. This is the whole result, and is quite on a par, and no more, with the following allopathic anecdote, which has the advantage of being credible:

"Making and Taking Pills.—We remember (says the *Englishman*) an occurrence which took place in the practice of a country apothecary in England. He had only one apprentice upon whom the entire duty of pill-making fell. A patient of rather inquisitive and nervous temperament called one morning with a pill-box in his hand, to show the apothecary that by cutting the pills in halves he had discovered something extraordinary in the manufacture. The apprentice was sent for, who confessed, that being naturally of a gay disposition, he preferred spending his evening with friends to wasting his time in weighing, and adjusting, and rolling into pills, the various drugs which his master had prescribed in the course of the day. After much consideration, he had found no method so quick as that of wetting a quantity of juniper berries in gum water, and next shaking them up in powdered chalk, and then most impartially filling all the boxes. He stated that he had continued this practice for a year and a half without a single complaint, except from the gentleman who had just called; and he insisted that the cases under treatment had all done exceedingly well."

I shall conclude these prefatory samples of the credibility of the representations Dr. Simpson has made, partly from the fruits of his own inventive genius, partly from the equally reliable stores of his friends, of the practice of homœopathic physicians, by two very characteristic specimens of his scrupulous honesty as a controversial writer. To one of them I drew the notice of the public in my former reply, but, as he repeats the same offence in his new work, after he had been told that it had led to false conclusions in the minds of some of his readers, and had been apprized, if he did not know the fact right well before, that his authority was notoriously fictitious, I am induced to advert to it again. A single sentence will dispose of the deception, and I presume of the last remaining fragment of confidence which the most partial of his readers may have retained in his candour. He quotes in a note a passage from the "Confessions of a Homœopathist," in which the author pretends to confess that homœopathic physicians employ "powerful doses" of "morphia, strychnia, arsenic, corrosive sublimate, and such like," in the form of "globules," and without allowing the patient to know that he is getting any thing but some hundred-thousandth part of a grain, Dr. Simpson quotes this pretended confession as authentic evidence against us, without informing his readers that the work from which he quotes is a *work of fiction*, as he well knew it to be when he selected his extract!

The other specimen is still worse, if worse can be. He begins by asserting that there are homœopathic physicians "who doctored people according as people themselves wished, either with drachms of drugs, or billions of a grain of the same;" a charge which he sustains by the authority of the veriest zany in the profession, and then proceeds to quote the following passage, as if it was a passage which confirmed his accusation, from his "colleague, Professor Henderson," who observes in one of his publications, "I rejoice to say that I know many physicians, who, while they adhere to the homœopathic law as the great regulator of their practice, consider themselves entitled, in the free exercise of their profession as independent men, to prescribe any quantity of medicine they think necessary for their patients, and where the homœopathic principle cannot be of service to them, whether from its present or necessary limitations, or their insufficient acquaintance with it, consider themselves not only entitled, but bound in duty, to employ any other expedients for the benefit of their employers that may be within their knowledge." And then, still further to persuade his readers that his colleague is an advocate for treating people "according as people themselves wished," he subjoins a quotation from my excellent friend, Dr. Black, as affording a view of "the due estimation of such a combination of principles and practices" entertained by homœopathists themselves; the quotation being as follows: "There is a class of practitioners who merit the indignation of every right-minded man,—a class who, viewing medicine only as a trade, a mere barter for pounds, shillings, and pence, act obsequiously *as the patient wishes; at his desire* their practice is either homœopathic or allopathic." Now, Dr. Simpson's work has been termed *clever* by one or two of his admirers, and I grant the justice of their assertion if it be clever to misrepresent, to suppress the truth, to give that as a true version of an opponent's doctrine which is the very reverse of it; and I add, may I and my friends be patterns of stupidity in all time coming, if this is to be *clever!* Why, immediately before the sentence he has extracted in order to show that I approve of physicians "doctoring people according as people themselves wished," I had actually said as follows—"That Dr. Simpson knows of any such persons I do not believe. I know a great deal more of those whom he delights to calumniate than he does, and I solemnly aver, that I neither know, nor ever have known, a single instance of the conduct he has ventured to lay to their charge." My information on the subject of such practices might be defective, and even incorrect, but my disapproval of the practice of allowing patients to choose how they were to be treated, and my refutation of it personally, are abundantly manifest in the two sentences I have just given, and yet Dr. Simpson makes me appear an advocate for the very practice which I plainly condemn! A concern for the "laurels" I hinted at on a previous page, restrains me from uttering a single word in the way of commentary.*

Having touched on the question of the need there may be for Homœopathists sometimes employing an allopathic expedient, I shall finish the subject in this place; and the more willingly that it admits of a very summary treatment. The amount of allopathic medicine which I would retain for occasional, though unfrequent employment in CURABLE diseases, is an aperient, chiefly a *teaspoonful of castor oil.* For *incu-*

* The truth is, that instead of Homœopaths being chargeable with treating their patients *either way,* it is *allopaths* to whom the remarks of Dr. Black apply, who, finding Homœopathy "go down" with some of their patients, give their services on the homœopathic principle when required.

rable diseases that have nearly reached their final stage, and are the occasions of sleepless nights and weary days, of pain and misery to decaying nature, I would give whatever promises to smooth the way a little to the not distant grave. For this end, there may be some two or three drugs, each suitable to his own class of cases;—too often, alas! there are none. As to ancient appliances that are not properly medicinal,—do not consist of medicines in the proper sense, I would reserve my right to employ heat and cold as I think best, and, speaking for myself personally, I would also regard myself at liberty, and without forfeiting my title to the honour of being a homœopathic physician, to facilitate the action of my homœopathic remedies by local abstraction of blood in some acute diseases,—a practice which I have followed some ten times in about as many years. These are the true "Confessions of a homœopathist;" and they are complete. Give me the little I have mentioned, and the rest of your physic to the dogs. In these views and conclusions all the homœopathic physicians of my acquaintance, with the exception, I think, of two, substantially agree. Among the exceptional dissentients is my respected friend, Dr. Scott of Glasgow. He is of opinion, that, when an allopathic expedient is required, an allopathic physician should be called upon to administer the same. I am not sure that our friends of the opposite party would altogether relish this proposal: it would make occasional demands on their exertions not quite up to the mark of professional dignity. But I have no objection to the proposal; provided always, that the gentlemen of the other side will bind themselves scrupulously and honestly to use *none of our remedies*, and to leave to us all the diseases that we can treat more successfully than they. It seems to me that a much better contract would be this: that both we and they should employ the very few allopathic drugs that are of any service as palliatives, and that they should honourably acknowledge the many instances in which they make use of homœopathic remedies. We claim no exclusive right to the latter; we merely expect and ask that they shall not be used without acknowledgment.

Dr. Simpson, at least, cannot object to the small modicum of Allopathy I would retain; for he not only, like his brethren universally, employs many drugs whose operation is homœopathic, as we shall by and by see, when they are accidentally of any benefit to his patients, but, notwithstanding his pretended unbelief in the homœopathic law of Therapeutics, has actually, in his place as a Professor in the University, commended a remedy in circumstances where its action is confessedly homœopathic, after having employed it himself, moreover, by the advice of a homœopathic friend of his own. Behold the evidence: "Ipecacuanha causes vomiting; and the celebrated Dr. Simpson of Edinburgh, as he stated in my hearing, failed to cure a case of chronic vomiting from pregnancy, until he took the advice of Dr. Arnt, a Homœopathist, and gave half a grain of ipecacuanha, and so cured his patient." (Homœopathy: by George Wyld, M. D. Page 25.*)

*Dr. Stewart, in his controversy with Dr. Christison, gives substantially the same version of this passage in the Lectures of Dr. Simpson. Both he and Dr. Wyld were pupils of Dr. Simpson at the time it was delivered. The lecturer, however, denies one part of their statement, and says that the ipecacuan did no good, but the reverse; and he refers to the alleged testimony of a person whose patient the lady in question is said to have been, in corroboration of his assertion. This, however, must relate to another case, and seems to show that Dr. Simpson employed ipecacuan for vomiting more than once—successfully when the proper occasion for it was pointed out by a Homœopath, unsuccessfully when he used his own discretion. Both of his former pupils aver that he gave credit to the ipecacuan in the instance they heard him speak of; and two witnesses are better than one, especially when that one has a personal interest in representing the subject of dispute in his own way. Internal evidence, too, is strongly against Dr. Simpson in this

In this instance we have the admission by the Coryphæus of Allopathy, that he did employ a homœopathic remedy, and with success, too, when all his other remedies (?) had failed. Will he have the goodness to reconsider the following sentences he has composed against the Homœopath who would dare to use an allopathic palliative, and tell us, in his next publication on medical ethics, if he continues to regard the opinions expressed in them as candid and honourable: "Some men pretended they could honestly and honourably mix up the two practices. Most physicians naturally doubted whether any man could in honour and honesty combine such incompatible incongruities. Neither any true Homœopath, nor any true Allopath, would give this spurious set credit for their integrity of purpose and principle." P. 21.

There are many more of this "hybrid and equivocal class of practitioners," as he terms them, in the ranks of Allopathy, besides Dr. Simpson. Belladonna, as a preservative against scarlet fever, and as a remedy for the disease in some of its aspects and stages, was first proposed by Hahnemann; and it has been employed, in the former character especially, very generally throughout the civilized world by allopathic physicians, from Dr. Locock down to the obscurest Sangrado of the sect. Dr. Simpson cannot deny this fact, although he attempts to show that belladonna has not the protective power ascribed to it. The latter question will be discussed in its

matter. For what end did he allude to the ipecacuan in his class, in the presence of the friend who recommended it, if not for the purpose, partly, of paying a compliment to the latter, a stranger from a far country, who honoured the lecture by his presence? Surely not to point at him by name, in so public a place, as having advised a remedy which did harm instead of good! This is incredible. Dr. Simpson is surely too hospitable a man to be rude to a foreigner, and he a friend too. Dr. Simpson tries to get out of this scrape by another plea. He didn't know, forsooth, that Dr. Arnt was homœopathic! Well, what of that? He knew that *ipecacuan* was so to vomiting, and no one accuses him of having prescribed Dr. Arnt.

proper place, and the medical knowledge of the objector put "through its paces." Meanwhile, the adoption of the homœopathic preventive — (whether truly so or no)—by allopathic practitioners, stands condemned by Dr. Simpson as at variance with "honour and honesty;" and thus is included in the same category of crimes with his own employment of ipecacuan in the instance mentioned above.

I had almost forgotten the Magnetoscope! This is an instrument invented by Mr. Rutter, Manager of the Gas-Works at Brighton; and was supposed by the inventor to be so sensitive a machine that its pendulum would make certain motions under the influence of impressions not discoverable by ordinary means. My able friend, Dr. Henry Madden, was the first medical man who saw the instrument, and probably, for that reason, was the first physician who was deceived by it. Had it come first in the way of the Allopaths, they would have had the priority in being duped; but as the thing happened, the deception fell to one of us in the first instance, and, *of course*, Homœopathists must bear the undivided reproach of gullibility. I wonder, now, if a Homœopathist, with the best intentions in the world, were to get his neck broken, whether we should not all be accused of being "shaky" in the cervical region, or if he should chance to swallow a plum-stone, whether he would not be charged with doing it "o' purpose," and because we all had gizzards. Well, Dr. Madden was the first to be taken in by the magnetoscope, but he is entitled to the credit of having been the first also who discovered and exposed its worthlessness; and, to conclude this eventful history, while the two or three homœopathists, who of all the body were imposed upon by the deceitful machine, have long seen their mistake, it remains the appropriate *protégé* of a knot of their allopathic brethren, who certainly need something more than human to discover the curative value of their drugs, when administered on their distinctive principle.

Having now gone over a long list of most contemptible "arguments" against homœopathy, the reader may be inclined to ask how it is to be explained, that Dr. Simpson, commonly reputed to be among the advocates of progress in scientific matters, should be found so bitter and unscrupulous an opponent of the new practice. It cannot be from an intelligent conviction of its unsoundness, for he is practically but little acquainted with it, and the little he knows is, as we have seen, rather in favour of its claims than otherwise. But Dr. Simpson's medical glory, such as it is, is pinned to the old standard, and his medical existence is all but ignored by the followers of the new. The discerning student of such affairs will have no difficulty, then, in finding a parallel to, and an explanation of, the conduct of the Professor of Midwifery in the instructive history of Haman, the once prosperous son of Hammedatha the Agagite.

HOMŒOPATHY FAIRLY REPRESENTED.

CHAPTER I.

Comparative View of Homœopathy and Allopathy, as adapted to acute diseases: in which the latter is proved to be a fatal delusion—Homœopathic Statistics proved to be accurate—Alleged success of Laennec and army surgeons in inflammation of the lungs shown to be incredible—Allopathic cases, when *selected*, proved to present a much greater mortality than the Homœopathic unselected—Allopathic treatment of pneumonia destroys human life—Acute inflammation of the lungs better left to nature than to Allopathy—Dietl's experiments—Allopathic fatality in pleurisy, peritonitis, &c.—Pretended Allopathic cures of consumption more extravagant than those of the most ignorant Homœopaths.

A CONSIDERABLE portion of Dr. Simpson's work is occupied with the usual diatribe on human credulity, and the usual illustrations of human folly, from Mesmerism, amulets, charms, Mormonism, &c. The reader who peruses this chapter to the end will probably be of opinion that the author ought to have added Allopathy to the list, which, like its twin sister Calamity, is "of so long life," merely because of the fears which lead men rather to "keep those ills they have, than fly to others that they know not of," though the latter, as in the case of Homœopathy, may be only imaginary. At all events, the parallel between these delusions and Homœopathy foolishly takes for granted the very point at issue, and assumes that Homœopathy is a delusion. Every previous great step in scientific discovery has had to undergo a similar novitiate of obloquy from the prejudiced and the ignorant; and if Homœopathy did not, it might be fairly regarded as but little, if at all, better than the system it purposes to supplant, and therefore not worth quarreling about. It is absurdly supposed by those who have no acquaintance with "scientific" men, and know not the mettle of which they are made, that they are always gratified by the addition of new facts and principles to their respective sciences. Nothing can be generally more untrue than such a conclusion; nay, I suspect the instances are comparatively few in which the disposition of men, already matured in their own field, towards all that is new, may not be illustrated by an anecdote of a late eminent professor of chemistry, who, on receiving from a colleague an answer in the negative to his inquiry, if there was anything new in the fresh Number of a scientific Journal, replied, "I am very glad to hear it;" or by another, of a professor of the same science in a northern university, who, compelled at last to advert to the discoveries of Sir Humphrey Davy, regarding the composition of certain alkalis, dismissed them with the shortest possible notice, and dubbed their author, "a verra troublesome person." Of course there are exceptions in every pursuit, but fewer, it may be justly said, in medicine proportionally than in any other. Medical men, in general, are more concerned to ply their arduous vocation with the instructions they may have received in early life, and such small and easy additions to their stock as they have leisure to pick up from the journals of the day, than to sound the depths of science, and seek the treasures of knowledge that lie hid in her bosom, by the light of the midnight oil, when a "good soft pillow" for their tired heads, whether white or black, is what the proprieties of the time demand. And of the exceptional instances—the busy-minded men who roll in their carriages by day, and are fresh enough for study by night—it may be justly said, that their welcome, when they have any to spare for the researches of others, is offered very rarely to doctrines opposed to the labours of their own lives, but is reserved for such as are in harmony with their previous opinions, and with the views to which all their success and importance in the medical world is inseparably linked.

It is nothing, that second or third rate men, whose field of vision is naturally and unavoidably of small extent, should be incapable of perceiving new and great truths just in proportion as they *are* new and great, and therefore far aloof from their own habitual trains of thought, or petty additions to the common currency. We look for blemishes of this kind in ordinary mortals, and are in no degree moved by their occurrence. But when first-class men, standing so high above their fellows as to command the whole field of intellectual enterprise, fix their eyes with a fond partiality on the fruits of their own genius, and what may be closely akin to them, to the neglect of other objects good in their way and important in their own place, we remember with regret that man in his best estate is but vanity, and that to expect among terrestrial beings freedom from weakness is but to look for

"A faultless monster, which the world ne'er saw."

We cease, then, to wonder that even Hahnemann, with all his genius and learning, and keen-eyed scientific instinct, overlooked a few things in medical science, which he might have studied with advantage to his reputation, and to the credit of his system. In the brightness of his own discoveries, these inferior objects "hid their diminished heads," and the eye that dwelt so long and so intently on the light that appeared amidst the general gloom, from its first faint glimmering in his path, as he meditated mournfully on the surrounding chaos where "darkness brooded," on through its gradual kindling into the dawn of a better day to patient humanity, may well be pardoned its insensibility to the ineffectual glow-worm lights that could do little else in his day than make the darkness visible. This plea is specially applicable to his contempt for morbid anatomy, and to his ignoring of ordinary palliatives that are capable of producing temporary ease in incurable organic diseases. With him the office of the physician was to *cure;* on that grand consummation his heart was set, and he had no eyes for any end short of the best that could be wished for. Morbid anatomy presupposes death; and whatever light the scalpel shed on disease, to Hahnemann it showed only the discomfiture, the imperfection, sometimes even the deadly error of the art that should have healed. He sought only for the means of *curing* diseases, and believed that means existed which, known and rightly used, were equal, by the goodness of the Almighty, ("compared to which," he says, "the tenderest mother's love is as thick clouds beside the glory of the noonday sun,") to the cure of almost all maladies: so that morbid anatomy was in his opinion merely the proof, if not the result of error. Hence it was that he threw on Allopathy and its disciples so much blame for the anatomical disorders which death enabled them to study. And true it is, beyond all question, that as the proper science of the physician becomes more understood and effective, there will be less for the anatomist to contemplate, though it may well be doubted whether, even were remedies fully ascertained for every ill that flesh is heir to, men would generally submit to them at the right stage of their disorder, continue them for the proper time, or give them a fair field for the full and free exercise of their virtues. *That*, however, is the business of the sufferer: the chief duty of the physician is to know how to cure him if he will but give the opportunity. But even in order to acquire this coveted knowledge, Hahnemann should have remembered, that to every honest man on the right road "his failures are the preparation of his victories," and that the morbid anatomy of the dead was capable of teaching much that might be of service to the still living, even on his own therapeutic principle; for medicines taken to a poisonous excess, or given to the lower animals in experiment, have, of course, *their* morbid anatomy too, the effects of their action on the living organs, and therefore *similar* to those producible by disease.

To leave these examples of human imperfection, even in the wisest of physicians, I would devote some space now to a subject of the gravest interest—to an exhibition of homœopathy in the capacity of the curer of maladies esteemed destructive of a large amount of human life in the hands of the ordinary practitioner. It is in the treatment of acute inflammatory diseases that Homœopathy appears in its most striking aspect to common observers. Such maladies are naturally regarded with the greatest apprehension, on account of the suddenness of their invasion, the intensity of their symptoms, the rapidity and brevity of their course, which is so liable to terminate fatally under the ordinary treatment, in a very large proportion of cases, within a few days from the date of its commencement. Hahnemann, however, never esteemed the curative powers of Homœopathy in acute diseases, remarkable as he knew them to be, to afford the greatest triumphs of his art. He looked upon the cure of chronic maladies as far more difficult, and therefore far more honourable to the physician and to the method which were capable of accomplishing it. Chronic ailments, unimposing at their outset, insidious and seemingly inconsiderable through a great part of their course, and tardy in their issue, are not the less fatal or the less productive of suffering, when unsuccessfully opposed by the physician, but either directly or indirectly are much more fertile sources of misery and devastation among mankind, than all the acute inflammations in the world taken by themselves. Hence it is that Hahnemann refers to the latter with an indifference bordering on contempt, as the assumed tests of medical prowess. Many of them he speaks of as ceasing spontaneously, and in spite of the many ingenious appliances of his contemporaries, that had a tendency to thwart the curative powers of nature. But of chronic diseases his estimate was very different. Of them he entertained the opinion that they were not capable of spontaneous recovery, and arose from or rather were the signs of constitutional taints that could not be eradicated without the greatest skill on the part of the physician, and much perseverance and circumspection on the part of the patient. To this question I shall claim the attention of the reader when I come to the consideration of the "psoric" hypothesis, when I hope to prove that there is far less of gratuitous speculation, and much more of accurate observation and sound pathological doctrine in it, than superficial observers and shallow thinkers appear to suppose.

The statistics which have been published of the results of the homœopathic treatment of acute inflammatory diseases by the hospital physicians of Germany, have, as might be expected, been attacked with peculiar virulence by the writers of the allopathic party. The small proportion of deaths which they exhibit is so astounding a contrast to the mortality of the same diseases when treated by even the best allopathic physicians, that it is no wonder it should be regarded with astonishment by those who have no practical knowledge of Homœopathy, and be treated with every injustice by those who are resolved at all risks to disparage that practice. Without any acquaintance with the character of the homœopathic physicians who report these results, the allopathic writers have not scrupled to attack their integrity and their professional discrimination. They sometimes accuse them of falsehood, sometimes of inaccurate diagnosis. By one or both of these defects their alleged success must be explained, for that their statistics are correct the opposing party are determined not to allow.

I shall not contend for the invariable accuracy of the homœopathic statistics, because I know that physicians of the greatest name and largest experience are liable to occasional mistakes. But I have not the smallest doubt that the number of mistakes is exceptional on both sides among hospital physicians of considerable experience, and that an equal allowance should be made for such imperfections in all statistics of the kind issued by either party. In the more common acute inflammations, diagnosis is acknowledged to be simple and easy in all but a small proportion of cases, and if it were even to be granted that wherever it was *difficult* it was *incorrect*, I do not think that a very material element of inaccuracy would exist, after all, to vitiate *comparative* statistical results. That mistakes in diagnosis would be all on the homœopathic side must be incredible to every one who reflects on the indubitable truths, that profound diagnosticians, who greatly excel such of their brethren as have fair abilities and practice, in the art of discriminating one disease from another, are exceedingly rare, and that public professional duty is discharged by men of both parties, who are endowed with but an average amount of talent and insight. Dr. Simpson, following the example of Dr. Routh and others, adduces from the medical statistics of the army examples of an apparently remarkable success in the treatment of inflammation of the lungs, and it is with these more particularly that they attempt to prove the superiority of allopathic practice. Now, I have no disrespect for the medical service of the army; on the contrary, I have no doubt that there are many able and efficient men in that department, but at the same time I take the reasonable liberty of questioning very much whether every young dandy or ancient beau (for such there are) who carries a sword and a lancet, is nearly so perfect in the art of undoing a difficulty in diagnosis, as in the correlative cunning of tying a knot on his cravat. Some, again, of the allopathic writers, adduce the statements of Laennec in favour of the allopathic treatment of pneumonia. He says that he lost only one case out of twenty-eight, which is about the same mortality as is mentioned in some of the army statistics. Louis, however, one of the best diagnostic physicians of the allopathic school, expresses his belief that Laennec had committed errors of diagnosis among his alleged cases, having mistaken the "crepitation" due to other diseases in the lungs for the "crepitation" of pneumonia; for Laennec tells us, with a confidence pardonable in the discoverer of auscultation, that his only evidence that pneumonia existed at all in some of his cases, was the presence of some crepitation; "therefore," says Louis, "he must have confounded acute pulmonary catarrh, which attacks the last bronchial twigs, and is accompanied by a subcrepitant rattle, with pneumonia; and thence doubtless the immense apparent difference between the results of his practice and mine."—(*Rech. de la Saignée*, p. 66.) Are the ordinary allopathic hospital physicians, here or elsewhere, in civil or military service, better diagnosticians than Laennec? By the by, Dr. Simpson adverts to the remarkable *success* of Laennec, but carefully shuts his eyes to M. Louis' explanation. It is a pity he can't shut ours.*

* There is no need, however, of charging the allopathic authorities with any peculiar deficiencies; and in adducing a few among the many instances of errors in diagnosis committed by eminent allopathic physicians that have come to my knowledge, I have no desire to ask the reader to conclude that bad diagnosis are peculiar to gentlemen of the other side, but simply to apprize him, that if they are chargeable against us, they are likewise chargeable against them, and, considering the parties who were at fault, that it is

As to the other question, the integrity of the homœopathic physicians, I shall say very little, because the details I have to lay before the reader must settle that point triumphantly, and on clear allopathic authority too.* It is no small pleasure to be able to take the accusers by the ears, and pointing their unwilling eyes to the proofs that their injured

likely they are at least as common on the one side as on the other. I have, then, *known* an accomplished consulting physician, and an eminent general practitioner, overlook our mistake in double pneumonia, of great extent, and discover it only on dissection; I have *known* a great advocate for cod-liver oil consumption mistake chronic pleurisy for the other disease; I have *known* an eminent stethoscopist, for mere irritation of the throat, which he treated with caustic as usual, mistake pulmonary consumption which was fatal within the week by the bursting of a tubercular abscess into the pleura; I have *known* an instance in which a notable hospital physician, not finding on dissection the pulmonary disease he had mapped out and described to his pupils, adroitly remarked, "Gentlemen, you perceive the appearance on dissection don't correspond with the stethoscopic signs heard during life," (the lung was sound;) and, not to be tedious when *samples* alone are required, I believe Dr. Simpson knows of a case of *diabetes mellitus*, which a whole bevy of "foremost" physicians mistook for some chronic inflammation within the cranium, and treated accordingly. Let us hear no more of errors of diagnosis, else the list may be greatly enlarged. *Humanum est errare.*

* It may be worth noting, notwithstanding the conclusive evidence about to be adduced of the accuracy of the homœopathic statistics, that Dr. Forbes, a distinguished allopathic physician, bears the following testimony to the character of Dr. Fleischmann, the physician of the principal homœopathic hospital in Vienna:—"Dr. Fleischmann is a regular, well educated physician, as capable of forming a true diagnosis as other practitioners, and he is considered by those who know him as a man of honour and respectability, and incapable of attesting a falsehood."—*British and Foreign Medical Review.* Dr. Simpson, however, is made so desperate by the statistics of Dr. Fleischmann, as to catch at the merest straws to help his halting argument. Thus, he adduces the authority of a youth, fresh from his elementary studies, and known to no human being as competent to distinguish any one chest disease from another, as superior to Dr. Fleischmann's in regard to the fact of a certain case having been pneumonia or not; Fleischmann's having stated two deaths from that disease to have occurred during a particular period, and the modest youth asserting that there were three.

brethren were guiltless, to ask them, with closed teeth, and an excusable twisting of the imprisoned appendages, how they dared to put so foul an affront on innocent men. As the unprofessional reader may have some difficulty in apprehending by what magic we have thus been enabled to clap the "twitch" as farriers have it, on our ferocious adversaries, I shall briefly sketch for his guidance the main particulars in the following details which have given us this advantage:—

Dr. Dietl of Vienna, the physician of a large *allopathic* hospital, took the happy thought into his head of trying how inflammation of the lungs would deport itself, if he left it entirely to unsophisticated nature. Having done so in a large number of cases, he made the extraordinary discovery, for an Allopath at least, that nature was a vastly better doctor than he or any of his sect; but not only so, he also found that the mortality of this expectant method, as it is called, was very nearly as small as the homœopathic physicians had averred theirs to be. Now, granting the common allopathic assertion to be true, that homœopathic treatment is just *no* treatment, in other words, *expectant* treatment, it follows plainly, that the homœopathic statistics of inflammation of the lungs *must be correct;* for they nearly correspond with the expectant treatment, or no treatment, of Dr. Dietl. But where is Homœopathy then? say you. By no means extinguished yet; nay, more vivacious than ever. For here, in the first place, is settled, beyond appeal, the integrity of our homœopathic authorities. If they be correct in regard to inflammation of the lungs, as they *must* be, unless Homœopathy is *actively* injurious, which no one maintains it to be, they are correct in regard to other inflammations, where the difference of success in favour of Homœopathy, and against Allopathy, is not more startling than in the case of inflammation of the lungs, where the difference is *proved* to be in favour of Homœopathy, even supposing Homœopathy to be nothing. Next, the reader will find it proved also, that Homœopathy is *something;* for an examination of details enables us to affirm, that it cures inflammation of the lungs in a much shorter time than unassisted nature does; so that *it* cannot be merely unassisted nature too. Besides, it can be shown that there is a peculiarity in inflamed lungs which enables unassisted nature to save so many lives, which peculiarity does not exist in other inflammations; and hence we argue, that though we do not save many more lives from inflammation of the lungs than nature alone does, we save a vastly greater number from death by other inflammations than nature can do.

In the immediately following pages, also, the reader will find allopathic statistics compared with the homœopathic, and brought to the test of Dr. Dietl's experiments. I am not answerable for the awful contrast; the astounding facts are mainly from Allopathy itself, and Dr. Dietl has been appealed to (save the mark!) by Dr. Simpson, and others of his party, as an authority against us, but without entering into dangerous particulars. Allopathy may mourn with the stricken eagle, as she gazes on her wound, that she herself

"Nursed the pinion that impelled the steel."

As some cases of my own are introduced into the calculations which follow, I am induced to mention a circumstance here which further illustrates the reckless and dishonourable manner in which homœopathic statistics, and homœopathic physicians, are maligned. In my former reply to Dr. Simpson, I mentioned in a note that I had treated with success a number of cases of inflammation of the lungs. In the course of last spring, a lecturer in Edinburgh accused me to his pupils, (though not by name,) of having ascribed the death of one case, that was actually inflammation of the lungs, to organic disease of the heart, and thus he attempted to show that no confidence was to be placed in homœopathic statistics.

Will the reader believe that this malicious and false accusation was made in the face of the fact, that I had published that identical case three years ago, along with the cases adverted to in the following pages, and ascribed the death to *inflammation of the lungs*, which I regretted I had not seen my way to treat homœopathically, for that otherwise the event might have been different! The fact is, the case was one of very unusual difficulty, and puzzled Dr. Alison as well as myself, so that it properly belongs to no statistics.

Of M. Tessier, and his contribution to the homœopathic statistics, the following particulars are worthy of attention. This gentleman is physician to one of the ordinary public hospitals of Paris, and had, previously to his experimental inquiry into the practice of Hahnemann, been well known as an allopathic practitioner of most respectable attainments, to say the least of him. His homœopathic experiments on cholera, and inflammation of the lungs, issued in his becoming a believer in the homœopathic system. To his cases no objections have been made by the Allopaths, but such as are so easily and satisfactorily set aside in the following pages; indeed, the Allopaths have been sorely at a loss how to dispose of Tessier's experience, and the utmost they have attempted, though unsuccessfully, to do, has been to lower his success to about the level of their own. This attempt, had it succeeded, would have at least proved that Homœopathy was as good as Allopathy in the treatment of pneumonia; such are the perplexities and inconsistencies to which the desperate and confounded advocates of the falling practice are reduced. I think, then, it will be admitted that the accuracy of the homœopathic statistics, to be adverted to in this chapter, is unobjectionably guarantied,—a remark which does not apply to those of the other party universally, for Bouillaud is charged by his colleague, Grisolle, with the *suppressio veri*. But I shall take no exceptions to their statistics as they stand;

we can afford to give them a liberal drawback on the actual mortality of their practice.

What follows regarding pneumonia in this Chapter was published by me in much the same form in the British Journal of Homœopathy for October 1852. Dr. Simpson has taken care not to meddle with it, though he is well acquainted with the Journal.

In comparing the allopathic and homœopathic methods in the treatment of pneumonia, it is not my intention to enter at great length on the subject, or to bring together all or nearly all the statistical details that may have been more or less fully given on both sides. The task I have proposed to myself is much less laborious and extensive. I intend chiefly to examine in detail, as far as the recorded facts will enable me, a moderate number of cases from both sides; and I think that those I have selected for comparison will be found to present unobjectionable samples of the disease, its treatment, and consequences, under each system; there can be no objection at least on the ground that the homœopathic cases do not present as full a proportion of conditions usually regarded as unfavourable to recovery as any number of allopathic cases brought into comparison with them. I have, indeed, been at pains to discover accounts of allopathic cases that were unusually favourable for the happy issue of the treatment, and I have been successful in my search, having found them in treatises by Louis and Bouillaud. These with the examples from the practice of Drs. Walshe, Taylor, and Peacock, published by Dr. Routh, and those of Dietl of Vienna,* are all I have taken from allopathic authorities. The homœopathic side gives me no latitude for selection, for I know of no groups of cases published by Homœopathists, with the exception of the forty-one by Tessier, in his Recherches Cliniques, 1850, and the eleven by myself in the British

* Der Aderlass in der Lungenentzündung. 1849.

Journal of Homœopathy for 1850, which possess the condition which I regard as indispensable, on our side at least, of being a complete series of cases, from which none had been excluded or withheld from publication, that had occurred to the narrator between the commencement of his observations for the time, and the preparation of his treatise for the press. A few indeed of Tessier's earliest cases are not recorded, owing to the imperfection of the notes regarding them; but as they terminated favourably, their suppression is at least no objection to his contingent of cases, which may therefore be fairly regarded as commencing with the first that appears in his work. If the comparison about to be instituted between these allopathic and homœopathic cases shall be found to harmonize as to mortality with what we know of the groups of cases which are marshalled against each other on the grand scale, each containing many hundreds, we shall be entitled to conclude that the latter, had they been subjected to the same analysis, would have furnished nearly the same proportion of favourable and unfavourable conditions, as to age, sex, complications, &c., for these are the particulars which are supposed to influence more or less the rate of mortality under every treatment, and you cannot have the aggregate result in a multitude of cases, irrespectively of the conditions which produce a similar result in a smaller number. The same proportional results must be due to the same proportion of conditions, on the greater as on the smaller scale. If the mortality in Tessier's cases and mine be the same as in Fleischmann's, we may be certain that Fleischmann's cases must have closely resembled the others in all the essential particulars that are believed to bear on the mortality of pneumonia; for had he *selected* his cases, his mortality must have been less. The details of these other cases, therefore, will afford us a very safe ground for judging of the quality of Fleischmann's cases.

The most interesting part of this discussion, however, is

connected with another element which has been lately thrown into the controversy; I allude to the very remarkable statements of Dietl regarding the effects of a merely dietetic or expectant practice. I shall say of these statements at present only thus much, that they settle finally two questions; the fate of allopathic practice, in pneumonia at least, and the thorough, nay, on the principles of our opponents, the necessary correctness of the rate of mortality affirmed by Homœopathists as the result of their practice, even if, as is asserted, it be no better than doing nothing.

Before proceeding to the analysis of the cases on the homœopathic side of the question, I have a few words to say in reply to some of Dr. Simpson's* misrepresentations of Tessier's cases. Dr. Simpson maintains that one case that died of erysipelas, which began twelve days after the pneumonia was cured, and two that, he alleges, (though in reality only one, and he died three months after his pneumonia had been cured,) died of consumption before leaving the hospital, should be added to Tessier's mortality, because, according to him, these cases would be included among the deaths from pneumonia in the statistics of allopathic hospitals. We are not, however, about to compare the cases of Tessier with the crude returns of hospitals, but with the discriminating statements of individual physicians, who knew when an inmate of their hospital wards died of pneumonia, and when of some other disease that had no connexion with it; they, in common with Tessier, all speak expressly and intelligently of pneumonia, and of what they noted in their patients throughout that disease on to its termination, and there their business with every case ended in so far as the only purposes they had in view were concerned. If the allopathic physicians had told us all that happened to these patients weeks or months after their

* I substitute Dr. Simpson's name for Dr. Routh's in these passages, because the former has adopted the misrepresentations of the latter.

pneumonias were cured, no doubt they would have had to record casualties from erysipelas, or dysentery, or fever, or consumption, but then they would have treated of such under their proper titles, and not as casualties from, or during pneumonia. Dr. Simpson next objects to the admission into the number of successful cases treated homœopathically six that had been bled * prior to the commencement of the latter treatment, on the ground that the blood-letting must have benefited these cases, and thus disqualified them for bearing testimony to the efficacy of Homœopathy. Blood-letting, however, as we shall find from the researches of Dietl, so far from lessening the mortality of pneumonia, actually increases it; and when it does not do so, but appears to be of service, merely shortens the early stages of mild cases that would have terminated favourably of themselves. Besides, if the limited employment of a single allopathic expedient should be regarded as a ground for excluding these successful cases, the employment of other allopathic means in one of the cases that died, ought to be enough to exclude that case also from the homœopathic calculation; and thus the proportion of deaths would be further reduced, and Homœopathy would appear to be still more successful than Tessier makes it to be.

To proceed to the analysis, first of the homœopathic cases, and beginning with the question of

Age,—I find that among the 50 cases that were beyond the period of puberty, 25, or just one-half, were above 40 years old, and of these, 16 above 50 years old; while the average age of all the cases was 41 years. There was then an un-

* In one of these cases the bleeding was only by means of a few leeches, which in pneumonia must be utterly inoperative for either good or evil. It is *venesection* that is adverted to in the text as the deadly method. The six cases recorded by Tessier were not bled by him, but before they came under his care. Previous to his confiding in Homœopathy alone, he used to combine blood-letting with it; and he found that "the less he bled the more were the patients benefited after the administration of the minute doses."—P. 4.

usually great proportion of cases at the later periods of life, of which excess an estimate may be formed from the following larger statistics given by Grisolle: among 630 cases collected by him, 239, or three-eighths, that is 76 less than the half, were above 40, and above 50 there was little more than a fifth.

Sex.—The number of females amounted to 9,—about 1 in 5½, which is a smaller proportion than usual; for in the 542 cases of Briquet, Chomel, and Grisolle, there were 138 females, or about 1 in 4. This disparity is, however, of no real consequence, for the following reasons:—both Grisolle and Briquet conclude that the greater mortality which is acknowledged to occur among females affected with pneumonia, depends chiefly on the more advanced age at which they are liable to the disease; the excess therefore in point of advanced age, already noticed among the homœopathic cases, will counterbalance any advantage that may be presumed to depend on the smaller proportion of females; and it may be remarked, besides, that we have actually no evidence that pneumonia *of itself* is apt to be more fatal among females, as such, than among males. It is true a greater proportional mortality does occur among females, in allopathic practice, which is not entirely accounted for by their ages, but there is too much reason to believe, as we shall see in the sequel, that such excess of mortality among females, treated in the ordinary way, is actually due to the *practice*, and not to the disease apart from the injury done by the treatment; for females have generally less robust constitutions than males, and blood-letting would appear to be fatal in proportion to the number of the more delicate persons who are subjected to its operation.

Complications and Constitution.—In regard to local complications, and general deterioration of the constitution, I find that there were (exclusive of jaundice and pleurisy) 14 with complications, or about 1 in $3\frac{1}{2}$. The complications consisted of organic disease of the heart, chronic bronchitis, delirium tremens, pericarditis, acute bronchitis, and meningitis: besides those 14, in which local complications are specified, there were 8 others in which the complication is noted as enfeebled and deteriorated health, a state certainly as unfavourable in pneumonia as most of the chronic local complications are,—so that we have 20 cases of complication, or 1 in $2\frac{1}{2}$; a larger proportion than the worst of the allopathic groups present, and very much larger than some of them do to which I shall have to refer. The Homœopathic complications were chiefly chronic; and it would appear from Dietl's observations, that in allopathic practice acute complications are apt to abound, in consequence, as he thinks, of the tendency of the depleting measures to produce new inflammations. He supports this opinion by what he noticed after death in the bodies of such as had died under each of his three methods of treatment, blood-letting, tartar emetic, and the expectant plan. Among 17 of the first class, 7 presented complications with meningitis or pericarditis: among 22 of the tartar emetic class, only one presented acute complication (pericarditis;) and, of 14 that died under the expectant practice, not one instance of acute complication was found.

Affection of the upper lobe.—Among the homœopathic cases 10 examples of pneumonia of the upper lobe occurred. This is a smaller proportion than has been sometimes noticed in allopathic practice. Andral had 30 pneumonias of an upper lobe in 88 cases; and Grisolle's proportion has varied in different periods from a fifth to a third. The pneumonias of the upper lobe are believed by Louis to be more fatal because they are most liable to happen at the more advanced periods of life; so that the unusually great proportion of aged persons among the homœopathic cases will probably nullify the apparently more favourable condition of these cases as to the lobe affected. To show, moreover, how little the smaller proportion of pneumonias of the upper lobe accounts for the small mortality of the homœopathic cases, it may be mentioned here, that while, according to Sestier and Grisolle, the mortality of such cases in allopathic practice amounts to 1 in 4, or 1 in 5, in our homœopathic cases it amounted only to 1 in 10; and in that one case purulent infiltration of the lobe had occurred before the treatment was begun.

Double.—When pneumonia occurs in both lungs simultaneously, it is not surprising that the rate of mortality should be increased. One half of such cases die according to Chomel; Grisolle lost 7 out of 16. This, therefore, appears an important element in the quality of the cases, when a comparison is being made, such as I have now in hand. I admit that the number of double pneumonias among the homœopathic cases was less than appears to be common under the allopathic practice; but it would appear highly probable that the excess of double pneumonias found among the latter class of cases has some connexion with, and dependence on, the nature of the treatment. Thus Dietl, in 85 cases treated by blood-letting, had 10 double pneumonias, or 12 per cent., while, in 106 cases treated by tartar emetic, he had but 6 cases of double pneumonia, or less than 6 per cent., and in 189 cases, under the expectant treatment, there were only 11 double, or less than 6 per cent. Blood-letting, therefore, would seem to increase the proportion of double pneumonias. Bouillaud, who is a great bleeder, gives among his details, without being aware of this inference, what appears to corroborate the conclusion of Dietl; in 75 cases he had 18 double pneumonias, (he had one more than he expressly mentions.) No doubt some of these were double pneumonias before any treatment was used. This, however, was the case only in half of them; of the remaining 9 cases, 8 were bled one or more days before the first stethoscopic examination was made, and when it was made, the lung last affected was found in the earliest stage of the disease, as if it had begun but very recently, and after the bleeding was performed; in one case the pneumonia became double three days after the depleting practice was in full operation, the patient having been all that time in the hospital previous to the extension of the disease. Bouillaud had double pneumonias in the proportion of 24 per cent., and Grisolle, in the 1430 cases, collected from various allopathic authors, says the proportion was 18 per cent. In our homœopathic cases there were 5 double pneumonias, at the rate, therefore, of 10 per cent.,—or if we exclude one of the cases, because blood-letting had been employed before it fell under homœopathic treatment, there were but 4 cases, or 8 per cent. We shall afterwards notice Dietl's reasons for believing that blood-letting causes the more extensive diffusion of pneumonia, and I advert to it here as an additional ground (and he, too, views it in the same light) for the opinion that depletion favours the occurrence of double pneumonia. If such, then, be the case, allopathic physicians cannot plead the greater proportion of their double pneumonias as a reason why their cases cannot be justly compared with ours, for that disadvantage on their side appears fairly traceable to their injurious practice itself, which, of course, creates the evils that produce its greater mortality, and it seems this excess of double pneumonias among the rest.

Epidemic constitution affects the mortality of pneumonia, and chiefly in this way, that during influenza the pneumonias that are epidemic are unusually fatal, at least in allopathic practice. No such plea is set up on behalf of any of the groups of cases I am to compare with the homœopathic, and it shall not therefore be taken into account, although several of Tessier's cases occurred during such an epidemic.

Mortality.—Of our 50 cases 3 terminated fatally; the

proportion of deaths to recoveries being one to 17, or just 6 per cent. Of the 26 cases that were aged 43 years and under, only one died, and at the age of 43; none died of the 25 that were under 40. The others were aged respectively 58 and 60. Here, then, are 3 deaths in 25 cases aged between 40 and 70 years, a period of life when, according to Grisolle's extensive data, the mortality is at the rate of 23 per cent. in allopathic practice.

I compare with the homœopathic mortality as given above first the two groups of cases furnished by Louis. The first group, consisting of 78 cases, was mentioned in the *Archives Générales* for 1828, and in a reprint of the memoir, published in 1835, the author says in a note that he had excluded 46 other cases that had occurred to him along with these 78, *because the pneumonia in them occurred in unfavourable circumstances*, such as previous bad health, while of the 78 cases he says—"all were in a state of perfect health at the moment when the first symptoms of the disease began." Here then we have 78 *selected* cases of pneumonia, in persons in the most favourable circumstances, as to previous health, for the successful issue of the disease; and I might justly decline admitting such cases to a comparison with the unselected cases of the homœopathic group, in which many—about a third—were in bad health at the commencement of the pneumonia. This disadvantage will tell, however, all the more to the credit of Homœopathy, when it is known, that of Louis' 78 cases, 28, or nearly one-third, died! What makes the difference in the success of the two systems still more remarkable is, that Louis' cases were, in a large proportion, of an early age, and even the average age of the 28 fatal cases was only 49. That of the 50 that recovered was about 35.

The same author, writing in 1834, or 1835, says, that in the course of the 4 preceding years 150 cases of pneumonia had passed under his notice, but that he limits himself again to a selection of cases, 29 in all, who were, like the former group, "in excellent health at the moment when the first symptoms of pneumonia occurred." In this smaller selection he was much more fortunate, 4 only of the 29 having died, or 1 in 7, about 14 per cent.; but still nearly 2½ times greater than the mortality of the unselected homœopathic cases.

The treatment of the first group of cases consisted entirely of blood-letting; of the second, of blood-letting, tartar emetic, and blisters. Louis ascribes the less fatal results in the second group in some measure to the bleedings, though fewer, having been more copious at a time. But the whole quantity of blood drawn in these cases was less than in the others, and the facts to be quoted from Dietl appear to show that it is rather to this smaller loss of blood that the happier consequences should be ascribed, than to the manner in which the evacuation was performed.

Bouillaud's cases.—Pelletan, in the eighth volume of the *Mém. de l'Acad. R. de Médecine*, has published an account of 75 cases of pneumonia treated by Bouillaud, with the view of setting forth the advantages of his method of employing venesection, a method which is known as the *coup-sur-coup* plan of bleeding, in the course of which blood is abstracted daily for 4 or 5 successive days, in such cases as seem capable of bearing the loss.

Age.—In respect to age, these cases had the advantage of a considerably larger proportion at the earlier periods of life than occurred among the homœopathic cases. Of the latter, 25 cases, or one-half only, were below 37 years of age, while, of Bouillaud's cases, 46, or three-fifths, were below that time of life. Again, above 57 years old he had only 5 cases, while the homœopathic cases numbered 14 above that age. This disparity is important, for the mortality, according to Grisolle's large statistics of pneumonia, between the ages of 50 and 60, is not less than 27 per cent.

Sex.—Among Bouillaud's cases there were only 7 females, about 1 in 11 only, or $9\frac{3}{4}$ per cent.; while the homœopathic cases had 9 females, or 18 per cent. A disproportion of great consequence if it is true, as allopathic physicians assert, that the mortality of females is one-third greater than among males.

Seat.—Among Bouillaud's cases there were only 7 instances of pneumonia of the summit of the lung. This is at the rate of 10 per cent., while among the homœopathic cases the proportion was 20 per cent. In this respect, therefore, the advantage is again on the side of Bouillaud's cases, for the mortality of pneumonia of an upper lobe is ascertained by Grisolle to be nearly double that of pneumonia of other parts of the lung.

I have already said that Bouillaud had 18 cases of double pneumonia, or 24 per cent., while the homœopathic cases had only 5 examples, or 10 per cent.; and I have also already shown that the excess of double pneumonias among allopathic cases is to be ascribed to blood-letting, and that, not being an original disadvantage of such cases, but an evil consequence of the treatment, it cannot be pleaded in extenuation of the allopathic mortality.

Complications.—Of chronic complications, Bouillaud's cases had only one example—chronic bronchitis; the other complications, amounting to 10, were acute diseases of various kinds, chiefly of the bronchi and pericardium, and probably due in a great measure to the treatment.

Mortality.—Ten deaths occurred among the 75 cases, or 1 in $7\frac{1}{2}$, being at the rate of $14\frac{2}{3}$ per cent. Several of the cases are mentioned as being trivial, and treated with emollients merely, and three are noticed as having had no physical signs at all of pneumonia, and therefore were only conjectured to be cases of that disease. Notwithstanding these and the other favourable circumstances of those cases of Bouillaud, the mortality was more than double that of the homœopathic cases. Among the deaths, one, *not* included by the author in estimating the rate of mortality, occurred within 24 hours after the patient was admitted into hospital. A similar instance occurred among the homœopathic cases, and is expressly included by Tessier in his mortality. If either is deducted, the other should be deducted too.

Of the 75 cases of Bouillaud, Grisolle remarks, that in reality only 49 were treated in the heroic manner he recommends. Of these 6 died, or 1 in 8. The average age of these 49 cases was only 33 years, and when we take into consideration the fact rendered evident by the experience of Dietl, that the mortality of pneumonia at all ages, indiscriminately, when *no* remedial treatment is employed, is only one half so great as in Bouillaud's 49 cases, we shall see reason to regard the recoveries in those allopathic cases as due to the powers of young and vigorous constitutions, which resisted the fatal tendency of the blood-lettings.

Cases of Drs. Taylor, Walshe, and *Peacock.*—Dr. Routh, in his suspiciously inaccurate work, entitled—"Fallacies of Homœopathy," furnishes the particulars of these cases, and as he would give at least the most favourable view of them that they could honestly admit of,—that is, would take the utmost pains to display their disadvantages, and to find excuses for their mortality, I have the less hesitation in quoting the account of them from a work so little entitled to confidence, for I desire to contrast our homœopathic details with any that even such an opponent can venture to publish in favour of the system which he defends.

Age.—The ages are given of 126 cases, and of them 96, (Routh says 86!) or above two-thirds, were under 40 years old; while, in the homœopathic cases, only one-half was under that age.

Sex.—27 of the 140 were females, or less than a fifth, so that the proportion was nearly as in the homœopathic cases.

Complications.—The number of complicated cases is said to have been 62. Of these a large proportion, no doubt, consisted of acute diseases, as probably always occurs when blood-letting is employed freely. No specific statement is made regarding the proportion of chronic complications. We have seen that the homœopathic cases had, including the examples of chronic bad health and acute disease, 20 complicated cases, or two-fifths, being rather more than the proportion stated to have occurred in these allopathic cases.

Seat.—No details are given respecting pneumonia of the upper lobe. Among the uncomplicated cases, 14 instances of double pneumonia are said to have happened, being at the rate of 18 per cent.; a number must have occurred also among the complicated cases, but nothing is recorded of them. Enough, however, is mentioned to strengthen the inference, formerly adverted to, regarding the influence of the treatment in producing that fatal form of pneumonia.

Mortality.—The deaths amounted to 43, being rather less than 1 in 3, or above 30 per cent. From this enormous mortality I am quite willing to allow 10 deaths to be deducted, on the ground that they occurred among 17 cases of secondary pneumonia, that is, pneumonia succeeding fever, &c., of which we had no corresponding examples in the homœopathic cases. Notwithstanding the deduction, 33 deaths remain, 1 in every 4 cases, or above 26 per cent.! Of the complicated cases 32 died, or above one-half; while, of the 14 homœopathic cases complicated with known local disease, only 1 died.

Dietl's cases.—He gives three sets of cases, of which two were treated respectively by blood-letting, and by tartar emetic. By the former method 85 cases were treated, of which 17 died, or 20·4 per cent. By tartar emetic, in large doses, 106 cases were treated, and of them 22 died, or 20·7 per cent. There are no details respecting the ages, complications, sex, or parts of the lung affected, with the exception of what relates to the number of cases of double pneumonia. Of these, 10 occurred among the cases that were bled, or 12 per cent., and 6 among the cases treated by tartar emetic, or less than 6 per cent.

We have some very important and instructive details by Dietl, regarding the effects of venesection. His remarks are so strongly opposed to the employment of this practice, that we might be inclined to suspect him of a leaning to Homœopathy, did he not express himself as strongly opposed to it, and as "clinging more firmly than ever to the old standard," —a declaration that must have some strange and peculiar motive, considering the startling account he publishes of the evils of the common practice in pneumonia—evils which, on his own showing, must equally follow the employment of venesection in other inflammatory diseases.

Dietl left 189 cases of pneumonia to follow their natural course uninterrupted by medical treatment of any kind, taking care merely to restrict them to cool drinks and meager fare during the febrile period of the disease, and preventing them from moving about. The result was 14 deaths, being one in 13½, or only 7·4 per cent.! A result such as this cannot but be regarded as in the highest degree remarkable by all who have been accustomed to rely on medical expedients for the cure of serious, and especially acute inflammatory diseases. That the narrator of so striking a series of experiments has conducted them fairly, and given an honest account of them, cannot be doubted. He is not, as we have seen, an opponent of the established methods of treatment, and could have had no conceivable purpose of a sinister kind to serve by recording alleged facts that reflect so injuriously on the practice of that allopathic section of the profession of which he avows himself a firm adherent. At the same time, as he has unfortunately not furnished us with any information regarding the ages of the cases thus left to nature, and has said nothing of the proportion of females among them, of the number of complications, or of affections of the upper lobes, we are left in doubt as to whether the 189 cases may not have been accidentally more favourably circumstanced for a mitigated severity, and a happy issue, of the disease, than those cases are believed to be in which the usual proportion exists of the aged, of the chronically diseased, of the female sex, and of affections of the upper lobes. Still, even supposing these 189 cases to have been in a more advantageous condition than usual in one or more of the several respects adverted to, the amount of advantage cannot, in unselected cases, have been so considerable as very materially to affect the results. Accident may have helped to *increase* the apparent success of the dietetic or expectant treatment, and so the comparatively small mortality which followed that treatment, in these 189 cases, may not be a strictly accurate measure of the real superiority of the expectant over the ordinary allopathic practice; yet, let every reasonable allowance be made, and still the expectant method must by all candid persons be admitted to have presented, in the experience of Dietl, an amount of success unapproached in the published experience of any other allopathic physician of any country.

The first reflection suggested by these cases is, that we can now be at no loss to account for recoveries taking place under every variety of allopathic practice. The disease would appear to tend towards recovery in about 92 per cent. of those affected, unless disturbed in its course by injurious interference; and even when such interference has unhappily been practised, a very large proportion, notwithstanding, of those affected have such natural powers of resistance—so much of the vigour of youth, or of the toughness of hale old age, that commonly the number of recoveries cannot be lessened by more than an additional 10 or 15 per cent. That this explanation is just, is plainly proved by the circumstance, that the more vigorous, strong, and previously healthy the persons are who labour under pneumonia, the better is their prospect of recovery under the common practice, as well as under the expectant, the latter, however, giving even to such cases the more favourable prospect; while the more feeble, whether owing to age, sex, or previous bad health, die also of course in a much larger proportion under the allopathic practice than under the other. The common notion among allopathic physicians is, that in aged and feeble persons, in whom, as their phrase is, "there is no room for practice," the dietetic plan may do very well, but that it is far otherwise with the young and robust, who, it is said, demand energetic measures. That there is a great mistake on this matter is proved by the following facts:—assuming age to be a proximate indication of the degree of strength and robustness, we find from Dietl's work, that among the younger and more robust constitutions, in other words, among the patients under 40 years of age, the treatment by blood-letting lost 5 cases, which supposing 50 (the usual proportion) of the whole 85 cases to have been under 40 years old, gives 1 in 10, or a proportion of 10 per cent. of deaths during the 26 years above puberty, when pneumonia is presumed to stand the most in need of "active measures," and to be the most easily cured by them. Among the expectant cases only one death occurred under 40 years of age, and as the whole of these cases amounted to 189, the proportion under 40 years old would be 114, so that the expectant practice had one death in 114 cases at the most vigorous period of life, when allopathic evacuations, &c., are fancied to be so essential. In the same number of cases (114) the latter practice would have lost *eleven cases*, in other words, would have *caused* 10 more deaths than occurred when the cases were not subjected to any medical treatment. Above 40 years old, the depleting plan of treatment had also a larger mortality, 12 having died among the 35 cases, which, according to the usual proportion, must have been above 40 years, in the 85 cases; this gives us a mortality of 1 in 3, or 33 per cent. Among the 75 cases of the expectant class, which are presumed, according to the ordinary calculations, to have been above 40 years of age, 13 deaths occurred, about 1 in 6, or 17 per cent., about one-half the mortality of the other practice among the feebler class of patients—who certainly appear therefore to be proper cases for an expectant method, but not nearly such proper cases for that method, in its comparative superiority over the allopathic, as the young, strong, and vigorous are, among whom blood-letting—that active treatment—*is ten times more fatal than the dietetic plan is!*

Of the treatment by tartar emetic in large doses, I need only remark, that the mortality over the whole cases was much the same as under venesection, (such are the evil consequences of using indiscriminately, and in excessive doses, even a remedy which is *homœopathic* to some cases of pneumonia,) and that it was fatal in a smaller measure in the cases under 40 than venesection was; having lost 1 in 15, or between 6 and 7 per cent. below 40 years old, and 1 in 2½ or 36½ per cent. in the cases above 40.

In what we learn from Dietl of the tendency of pneumonia to recover spontaneously, and even in spite of any and every sort of injurious treatment, we have a sufficient explanation of the fortunate issue of so large a proportion of cases at the earlier periods of life, which allopathic writers, prematurely and needlessly as it now appears, have been accustomed triumphantly to appeal to in testimony of the virtues of blood-letting and tartar emetic. One death in 20 or 30 cases, between 20 and 30 years of age, has now and then been the happy result in the experience of some of these physicians, and more frequently, perhaps, among the athletic young men in military practice than in civil life. When it is more generally known, however, that without any medical treatment, the mortality is less than one per cent. among patients under 40 years of age, some other ground for the complacency of our allopathic brethren will appear to be reasonably required. It will, notwithstanding, always remain a remarkable circumstance, that even young and vigorous persons should be able to survive, in so large a proportion of instances, the simultaneous attacks of an acute inflammation of one of the most important organs of the body, large and repeated losses of blood, and the violent purgings and vomitings produced by excessive doses of tartar emetic.

Lest it should be suspected that the mortality exhibited in the comparatively small groups of cases, from allopathic and homœopathic practice, which have been contrasted in the foregoing pages, does not represent fairly the general rate of mortality from pneumonia under the two systems, I add the statistics on this point furnished on a large scale by allopathic and homœopathic hospitals. Taking Dr. Routh's statements on the subject, we find that among 783 cases of pneumonia, treated in homœopathic hospitals, the deaths amounted to 45, or 5·7 per cent.; while according to the same authority, among 1522 cases that occurred in the Glasgow Infirmary, the General (allopathic) Hospital of Vienna, and the practice of Drs. Walshe, Taylor, and Peacock, the deaths were 373, or 24 per cent. The almost exact correspondence of the mortality among the homœopathic cases on the large scale, with that among the 50 cases analyzed in the preceding pages, cannot fail to repel the insinuations which have been so recklessly made as to the admission into the homœopathic hospitals of only favourable cases. The 50 cases referred to are altogether unexceptionable in respect to the proportion of conditions usually esteemed unfavourable to recovery, and if they presented no greater a mortality than occurred among the 783 hospital cases, the fair conclusion is, that the latter must have been of the same mixed quality, pretty much in the same proportion, and not cases unfairly selected for the purpose of leading to a false impression of the superiority of the homœopathic practice. This conclusion is still further supported by a comparison of these 783 cases, with 189 dietetic cases of Dietl, a comparison which the Allopath will gladly accept, as proving, according to his notions, that homœopathy is no more than a merely expectant practice. Those cases of Dietl have been referred to, indeed, by Drs. Simpson, Routh, and others, as actually proving such to be the fact, while they have overlooked, in their zeal, another part of the same testimony which is altogether ruinous to the reputation of their own system. If the dietetic cases prove homœopathy to be merely an expectant practice, because the mortality among them was so nearly the same as in homœopathic hospitals, they prove at the same time, that allopathy is frightfully worse than its rival,—that it actually destroys from 13 to 17 per cent. of patients that would have recovered if treated homœopathically, or if left to the remedial powers of unassisted nature! On the supposition, then, that the homœopathic treatment was actually no other than a dietetic treatment, and granting, what no Allopath will deny, that the *deaths*, at least, occurred which are specified by the homœopathic authorities, and are not likely to have been magnified, the number of *bonâ fide* cases of ordinary pneumonia must, if calculated from the rate of mortality among the 189 dietetic cases, have been fairly and honourably stated by the homœopathic physicians, for the difference is only 1·7 per cent. of deaths in favour of the homœopathic practice;—the deaths under the dietetic treatment having been 7·4 per cent., under the homœopathic 5·7 per cent. We have thus, from an unexpected source, evidence, the most conclusive, of the substantial accuracy of the homœopathic records on the subject of pneumonia; evidence which ought to cover with shame those who have, without a shadow of excuse for their conduct, advanced charges against the homœopathic hospital physicians, painful to peruse, and disgraceful even to have conjectured.

I am quite prepared to admit that the results of Dietl's expectant treatment, completely destructive, as they eventually must be, of all confidence in the ordinary treatment of acute inflammations, ought to lower materially our estimate of the favourable influence even of Homœopathy on the *mortality* of pneumonia. To those who know the efficacy of Homœopathy in other inflammatory diseases, usually esteemed of the most dangerous kind, and have witnessed the power it has of controlling and cutting short the course of pneumonia, it cannot but appear remarkable that there should be so small a difference, in the rate of their respective mortality, between it and a merely dietetic treatment. The fact, however, is so; and I think good reasons can be adduced to show why it is so, while at the same time it can be proved that in acute inflammations, pneumonia not excepted, Homœopathy does possess an active, real, and positive remedial power of the highest importance. There is a speciality in pneumonia, which has been almost universally overlooked, on which depends, beyond all reasonable doubt, the remarkable capacity it displays of running spontaneously to a favourable issue in all but exceptional cases.

It is now twelve years since I incidentally pointed out, in a paper on the Anatomy of Pneumonia,* a peculiarity in the

* Monthly Journal of Medical Science, 1841.

effects of inflammation of the pulmonary air-cells—the true anatomical seat of pneumonia. On minutely examining the inflamed parts after death, it was not difficult to perceive that as the inflammatory exudation increased, the parts affected became gradually paler and less loaded with blood, until, on the inflamed cells becoming filled with the viscid substance, so much pressure was exerted on the blood-vessels, between the fibrous investment of the lobules on the one hand, and the exuded matter which distended the cells on the other, that the diseased portion of the lung became actually bloodless, or very nearly so, the deep red colour of the earlier stages of the pneumonia giving place to the straw or drab, or sometimes bluish gray colour that distinguishes completed hepatization.* As soon as this stage arrives, if the earlier stages of the inflammation be not going on in other parts of the lung, the pneumonia as an active inflammatory process is literally *put out*,—extinguished by mechanical force; for it is undeniable that an excess of blood, in vessels dilated beyond their ordinary size, is necessary to the existence of such a process. That compression is capable of producing the effect I have mentioned on the inflammatory process is well known from what has been observed of the consequences of bandaging in erysipelas of the extremities, and of "strapping" in acute orchitis. In neither of those diseases, however, are the facilities for an effectual pressure on the vessels at all to be compared with those which exist in the minute cells of the lungs, where every little mesh of capillary blood-vessels may be said to be exposed on all sides, and in detail, to the immediate pressure of the exuded matter in the air-cells, on whose surfaces they are spread; while counter-pressure is close at hand on the exterior of each cell, in the form of other distended cells of the same group, and on the exte-

* *i. e.*, Lung made solid by inflammation.

rior of every little lobule, or group of cells, in the form of the fibrous covering which they each possess.

This view of the effect of completed hepatization in suppressing pneumonia, is strikingly corroborated by the observations of Dietl, on the mutual relation of the general or febrile symptoms of pneumonia, and the completion of hepatization. "The fever and dyspnœa," says he, "increase with the continuance and progress of the exudative process, but decline in pneumonias left to themselves, as by enchantment, as soon as this is completed." (P. 71.) Again: "The febrile stage of pneumonia lasts in very few cases no longer than three days, in more from three to six days, especially in children; in most instances, however, seven to nine days; and extends to even eleven or thirteen days only when the pneumonic infiltration happens to be arrested in some measure." (P. 72.) And when narrating the subsidence of symptoms which in some cases of pneumonia (cases, it should be noticed, which, according to the plain tenor of his observations on the disastrous consequences of venesection, as a general remedy for pneumonia, must have been mild, of small extent, and in strong individuals) follow venesection, he says, "This improvement was in the majority of (such) cases permanent, so that the pneumonia appeared to be cured by a single venesection; or, in other cases, it was transitory, so that after 24 or 48 hours a getting worse or relapse began, which, however, by a second venesection was finally set aside. These unquestionable facts appear loudly to proclaim that pneumonia, in many cases by a first or second venesection, is cured in its first stage, and that its passage on to hepatization can be prevented. By physical examination of such cases, this, however, has appeared—that these apparently cured pneumonias almost never become stationary in this stage of mere congestion, but much more frequently pass very quickly into that of hepatization; so certainly, that within 24 hours not unfrequently a whole lobe, or even a whole lung, has become infiltrated. . . . We may conclude from this fact, that the relief in those cases must be ascribed not immediately to venesection, but to the quickly succeeding exudation, since by a constant law of nature, fever and dyspnœa of a regularly progressing pneumonia are almost instantaneously extinguished with the completion of the exudation." (P. 80.) While he has witnessed in cases of dietetically treated pneumonia the same speedy cessation of the fever and dyspnœa due to speedy hepatization, he says he has observed this happen in a greater number of cases after venesection, although in most cases it had no such effect. (P. 87.) Hence he concludes that venesection hastens the exudative process in the inflamed parts in certain cases of pneumonia, although in most cases it does not do so. (P. 81.) "Most cases of quickly cured pneumonia are therefore cases of rapid hepatization, the development of which is rather favoured than hindered by venesection." His conclusion is somewhat remarkable—"I believe, therefore, that venesection in many cases of pneumonia operates in an eminently homœopathic way, *i. e.*, it shortens the pneumonic process, while it forwards it." (P. 82.) A consequence which he believes to be produced by venesection acting on the constitution of the blood in the same way as the inflammation itself does, and thereby increasing the intensity of that state of the fluid on which the exudation depends.

Unfortunately this somewhat strange homœopathic remedy exerts the beneficial part of its influence on but a small proportion of pneumonias. Dietl does not tell us his proportion, but a strenuous advocate for venesection, Briquet, in detailing his experience of the rapidly favourable results which sometimes follow venesection, observes that this occurred in only one-fourth of his cases, *i. e.*, in 22 out of 87;

and he gives us a clue also to the reason, if not of its occurrence in them, at least of venesection being borne in such cases without injury—"three-fourths of these patients were of a strong constitution, and seven-eighths of them presented at the same time crepitant rattle with the bronchial respiration," that is, were in an early stage of the disease. In the great majority of the other cases of pneumonia that recovered, he acknowledges that the phenomena of the disease during the period that venesections continued to be practised either persisted unchanged, or commenced to diminish, as would certainly have been the case, judging from Dietl's experience of the expectant practice, had no venesection been performed, and fewer of the whole number, also, would have become progressively worse.

It would appear, therefore, that the prepossession in favour of venesection in pneumonia rests chiefly upon two grounds: 1*st*, On the suppression of the general symptoms speedily after venesection in a proportion of cases, although these are cases which, from the robustness of the patients, belong to the very class which we now know furnishes a smaller mortality when left to nature; the benefited cases therefore did not need venesection to prevent their dying, although from peculiar circumstances the disease in them was hurried through its febrile stage, and thereby made shorter, though not safer, by venesection. I may add to these the few cases in which pneumonia is stopped by venesection in its first stage, or stage of congestion, of which cases Dietl observes, "If in a very few cases the pneumonic process is arrested after powerful venesection in the stage of inflammatory congestion, yet this occurs *still more frequently under dietetic treatment*, so that we believe we ought to ascribe this circumstance with much more justice to the *originally limited and more insignificant intensity* of the pneumonic process, than to the influence of venesection." (P. 75.) 2*d*, On the foregone and hereditary conclusion that venesection was necessary in the general treatment of pneumonia, and consequently that the recoveries which took place were, in all severe cases at least, due to the venesection in a great measure; a conclusion which was not unnatural in the absence of actual clinical proof, that even in this formidable-looking disease recoveries would occur in a much larger proportion of cases had no such evacuation been employed.

The manner in which venesection proves injurious, and so often fatal, in the treatment of pneumonia, may be satisfactorily shown by the facts we now have in our possession. Formerly it might be argued with some plausibility, that the large mortality which occurred when venesection was a principal means by which it was sought to cure the disease, happened in spite of the remedy; for the best remedy in the hands of the best physician must occasionally fail to do good, as no human being can be so complete a master of the instruments he employs as always to wield them to the best purpose of which they are capable. This explanation will not now suffice, for it is placed by actual experiment beyond all question, that venesection destroys life in an appalling proportion of cases in which death would not have been the issue but for the employment of the supposed remedy. The strong and robust resist it for the most part, and happily recover, yet no contemptible proportion of them, and many of the weaker, whether owing to sex or age or morbid infirmity, are its unquestionable victims. The manner and circumstances of its operation in leading to this result are thus detailed by Dietl: "We cannot forbear this expression of our belief,—that venesection favours the spreading of hepatization, and favours it all the surer the oftener it is repeated, and the poorer the patient is in blood,—so that many pneumonias, both intense and extensive, were first pushed to their height by venesection—progressed and throve, so to speak, under the lancet." (P. 85.) And again, "In other cases we saw the hepatization proceed in pauses in two or three attacks, so that after the infiltration of a portion, the fever and dyspnœa ceased, the patient experienced the greatest relief,—the whole appeared to be ended. After the lapse of one or two days, however, the hepatization undergoing recrudescence, began to spread itself wider, until it affected a whole lobe or a whole lung, or even spread itself to both lungs, which sometimes first occurred after a second attack. These intermittent pneumonias happened almost exclusively in old and enfeebled persons, and as well under the dietetic as the venesection treatment, with this striking difference, however, that in the latter the second attack was much more severe, and the hepatization more rapidly extended, reached an extraordinary extent of surface, and that almost all the patients died; while, in the former, the second attacks proceeded much more calmly, the hepatization attained no such extent, and the most of the patients, even when the disease was very tedious and left indurations or wastings of the lung behind, recovered." At p. 88 he concludes, "that venesection favours the transition of red hepatization into suppuration, ... and that the resorption of purulent hepatization was not favoured by venesection, but that death often follows in the midst of it." "We have remarked the most extensive pneumonias, as well in private as in hospital practice, in the practice of others as well as our own, always to occur under the use of venesection." (P. 84.) "Of the patients treated dietetically, *not one died in consequence of the pneumonia alone;* or, what is the same thing, pneumonia left to itself is, of itself alone, proved not to be a fatal disease, but is so by being complicated with chronic disease." (P. 108.) "*By* *venesection seven fatal cases of uncomplicated pneumonia occurred*—one at 18 years of age, two at 40, two at 37, and two at 60; so that the deaths cannot be ascribed to the greater age." (P. 103.) "It cannot be doubted, therefore, *that venesection increases the mortality* of pneumonia as such, and the question occurs how? By the extension of hepatization over a greater amount of lung, the exciting of other acute exudative processes, especially pericarditis and meningitis,* and favouring suppuration, and the coagulation of the blood in the heart and great vessels." He adds to this catalogue of the evil consequences of venesection, "that it tends also to cause acute œdema (dropsy) of the lungs, which was more remarkable in the cases that died under venesection than under the dietetic treatment." (P. 105.) And that no sure ground exists for the selection of such cases as are likely to bear the venesection well, appears from this observation: "We have not unfrequently remarked that a single venesection, apparently well indicated, had, as consequences, striking sinking of strength, profuse sweat, miliaria, vibrating pulse, and a rapidly fatal termination." (P. 108.) After all this his conclusion will appear abundantly just: "That venesection has its certain and not unimportant share in the greater mortality of pneumonia." (P. 107.) Much more to the same effect as the preceding important and startling observations is scattered through the work, but the statements which have been extracted are sufficiently distinct and conclusive.

I proceed next to prove, that though, owing to the peculiarity referred to in the anatomy and consequences of hepatization, pneumonia is a much less fatal disease when left to nature than has been generally supposed; the success of the expectant method does not account for the small mortality under the homœopathic treatment. That it *does* is the con-

* Inflammation of the membranes of the heart and of the brain.

clusion of Dietl, a conclusion which is valuable, at least to this extent, that it admits the accuracy of the homœopathic statements as to the rate of mortality under the system, and the fairness with which the homœopathic statistics of the successful treatment of pneumonia are given by his fellow-citizen Fleischmann. For Dietl seeks no solution of the question by gratuitous and unmannerly insinuations regarding the candour and ability of the latter, the justice of whose claim to be considered a trustworthy physician he must have had opportunities of knowing, and does not dispute; as indeed he could not for another reason, that, regarding homœopathy as merely an expectant practice, he must admit it to be at least as successful as his own expectant treatment. A comparison of details would, however, have satisfied him that he greatly erred in his denial of active and positive virtues to the homœopathic method, and that its success is due to some other cause than that which favours the expectant plan—a cause calculated to produce still happier results. This truth is illustrated by the—*duration of the disease* under the different plans of treatment. The duration of the disease ought to be computed from the first symptoms of the inflammatory fever to the cessation of the local physical signs, or complete disappearance of the hepatization. And it is thus that Dietl proceeds in the analysis he has given us of the duration of pneumonia under the expectant and the allopathic treatment. When the resolution of the hepatization is not made the final particular in the estimate of duration, the physician is left to a somewhat arbitrary and uncertain criterion in fixing the period of cure, and is exposed to the temptation of under-estimating the length of time his remedies have taken to effect recovery. Louis tells us that he placed the date of convalescence "at the period when the patients have commenced to take some slight nourishment, three days at least after the cessation of the fever; the local symptoms not being yet dissipated in all the cases." Bouillaud adopts a still more questionable method, fixing the commencement of convalescence at the period when the characteristic signs of pneumonia and the fever have *almost* entirely disappeared, and when he had begun to give some "bouillons;" "as if," says Grisolle, "one had a right to regard as *cured*, patients in whom fever had not yet entirely ceased." Objectionable as both these methods are, yet as the French authors appear generally to adopt the course followed by Louis, I shall not conclude this part of the subject without comparing our results with theirs, as ascertained by their own mode of procedure. I have first, however, to advert to Dietl's averages, and to compare the homœopathic data with them.

He found the average duration of the cases treated by venesection to be 35 days; of those treated by tartar emetic, 28·9 days; and of those under the expectant method, 28 days. The whole duration of the disease, from the commencement of the fever to the complete resolution of the hepatization, is ascertainable in 43 of the 50 homœopathic cases. In a few of Tessier's cases the last report regarding the state of the lung is, that resolution was *almost* complete. To the duration of such cases I have added two days succeeding the final report, which is at least not too little. The average duration, then, of the disease in these 43 cases amounts to only 11⅝ days. This very remarkable result places beyond all rational doubt the claim of homœopathy to a high degree of active curative power in pneumonia. The cases under the expectant treatment lasted, on an average, 16 days longer than the homœopathic cases. Of the whole expectant cases, 36 (not much less than one third) were prolonged to between 30 and 60 days, while only 5, or less than one-eighth, of the homœopathic cases lasted beyond 18 days, and only once did the duration extend to 27 days. Lest it should be supposed that an average duration of 28 days is an incredibly long period for the duration of pneumonia, down to the period of complete resolution, it may be as well, by way of corroboration of Dietl's statements, to mention some particulars of 11 cases treated by Grisolle, according to the same plan. They were mostly young persons, the disease of small extent, and the attendant symptoms mild; so that cases more favourable to such rapid recovery as diet alone can achieve, could not be selected. M. Grisolle states that the *commencement* of resolution in these mild cases occurred towards the end of the second week—say, on the twelfth or thirteenth day, or after the hepatization had entirely disappeared in most of the homœopathic cases; and that some of the local signs of the disease persisted till between the twenty-second and thirtieth days. The author adds: "It results from the analysis of these observations, that in mild pneumonias, treated by emollients, the local symptoms of the malady, and especially the pain, have a very long duration, which has no proportion to the intensity of the fever and the extent of the disease. A circumstance equally remarkable is the slowness with which the pulmonary congestion is resolved, although it does not certainly extend to a great depth: one might remark, in fact, that there was an interval of nearly four days between the complete cessation of the fever and the period when the phenomena of auscultation *commenced to decrease.*" (P. 362.)

The facts which I have just adduced present not only a triumphant and irrefragable testimony to the positively remedial powers of homœopathy, but they likewise prove, I think, that it cures, and saves life, in a different way from that in which unassisted nature does in this disease; it tends to cut short the disease by *preventing* exudation, or restraining it within very narrow limits, both of extent and degree. Consolidation may indeed take place under homœopathic treatment, but that it does not consist in any considerable amount of exudation into the air cells, appears from the rapidity with which it vanishes. Within an average of four days after the cessation of the fever, the whole local disease was gone, whereas in Grisolle's mild cases, left to diet, the process of resolution had then only *begun*, and took from 11 to 17 days to be completed. M. Grisolle adverts to the hepatization in his cases, as if it amounted only to vascular congestion, or, what he considers the same, red hepatization; but complete hepatization is never *merely* vascular congestion, and he has no means of knowing, but by dissection, what the actual state of the hepatized part is. Besides, it is not in harmony with what we know of the state of inflamed parts elsewhere, to believe that intensely congested vessels should continue to afford signs of consolidation for four days after the fever had ceased, and should take so many days more to disappear. In these, as in Dietl's cases, (for he more correctly regards hepatization as almost synonymous with infiltration of the lung with exudation matter,) the local disease must have issued in distention of the air-cells with inflammatory exudation,—a condition which admits of being remedied only by the slow processes of absorption and expectoration. It is thus only that we can account for the very remarkable difference in the duration of pneumonias treated homœopathically, and of those treated by the expectant method.

Louis, and probably most other French physicians, as appears from the terms in which Grisolle refers to the practice of Louis, reckon the duration of their cases of pneumonia only down to the complete cessation of fever, and the capacity to receive and digest some more nourishing food than was previously safe. In 36 of Tessier's cases, the daily reports are such as enable us to ascertain the duration of his cases, according to this mode of reckoning; no data of the kind are furnished by my cases, as I allow nothing but fever-diet till the lung is nearly in its natural state again. The average duration of the 36 cases was 9⅑ days. Bouillaud makes the duration of his cases nearly the same, or 9⅓ days, but his colleague Grisolle reminds us that he did not wait till the fever was entirely gone, as Louis did, otherwise he ought to have made the average duration of his cases, even according to this objectionable method, from 12 to 14 days at least, and Grisolle adds, "I can give but an approximation to the truth here, because, as M. Bouillaud approaches the period of convalescence, he becomes *excessively sparing of details*." The average duration of Louis' two sets of cases, calculated according to his notion of the termination of the disease, amounting in all to 75, was above 18 days, or exactly twice the duration of the homœopathic cases.

It is evident that were the disease in those examples regarded as cured, as they ought to have been, only when the signs of exudation had entirely ceased, the actual duration of them would have been very much the same as those of Dietl under the depleting treatment; as it is, the facts furnished regarding them amply corroborate the statement of Dietl in this important particular,—that the duration of pneumonia, when treated in the ordinary way, is very protracted,—and display the superiority of the homœopathic method in a very striking aspect. I have said "in the ordinary way," because the 20 cases in Louis' second set, which were treated with tartar emetic, and other ordinary means, as well as venesection, lasted 18 days, or almost quite as long as the others who were treated only by venesection, so that the average given of the whole cases represents fairly what is to be expected under all the appliances of the ordinary practice.

Fever.—The duration of the fever, in Dietl's experience, was for the venesection cases, 11·1 days, for the tartar emetic cases, 9·2, and for the dietetic, 9·1. The duration of the fever in the first of these cases would appear closely to correspond with that of Louis' cases; for while 18 days was the duration of them down to the period when he thought it safe to give aliment, he says that this latter period was at *least* three days after the cessation of the fever, and we may presume that it was often several days more, which would leave us somewhere about twelve days as the average duration of the fever in his cases. In 43 homœopathic cases, the data are sufficient to enable us to determine the duration of the fever, and we find that the pulse in them was reduced to the natural standard, or below it, on the average in 8 days. This appears but a small difference as compared with the length of fever in the dietetic cases, but then it should be remembered that the homœopathic treatment was employed only during half the febrile stage, for the patients generally came under treatment about the fourth day of their disease. The subsequent part of the febrile stage was therefore shortened by a fifth part of the duration it had under the dietetic plan. Were the homœopathic treatment begun earlier, the result would doubtless be much more striking; and as an illustration of this, from a few cases, I find, that in 16 cases in which the homœopathic treatment was begun within the first 2 days, the duration of the fever averaged only 6 days. Besides all this, it is worthy of special notice, that the number of unimportant cases which are pushed, by venesection, rapidly on to complete hepatization, are, though they take a long period to recover perfectly, soon brought to the end of their febrile stage, and thus lessen the average duration of the fever in the whole cases, by means of an occurrence which is actually due to an increased activity of the local disease. Whereas, under homœopathic treatment, that accidental mechanical effect, which ensues on rapid and excessive exudation, is prevented, and the fever is less liable to be suddenly checked, though the whole course of the *disease* is greatly shortened.

With this analysis of the most important particulars of

pneumonia, under different methods of treatment, I draw these remarks to a close. I have compiled the facts with the utmost care and fairness. For some of the comparative results I was not prepared when I began the investigation, but I did not on that account the less faithfully record them as they successively emerged, and if each in its turn bears its unequivocal testimony to the efficacy of homœopathy, and to the serious evils of the common practice, the explanation is to be found solely in the details as I found them in authentic publications.

A single remark remains to be made, and although it does not bear on the further elucidation of the subjects treated of in the preceding pages, it is a plain and most important inference from some of them. The homœopathic hospital statistics, regarding the mortality of pneumonia, being proved to be correct by the evidence adduced from two sources, as narrated in the course of this chapter, the same hospital statistics regarding other acute inflammations, deemed not more dangerous than pneumonia has generally been supposed to be, are to be regarded as equally entitled to credit. The good faith and accuracy of the authorities having been demonstrated, in reference to what have been stigmatized as their incredible allegations regarding their success in pneumonia, a disease so deadly in allopathic practice, they are justly entitled to the benefit of that demonstration in respect to their *not more* extraordinary allegations as to the success of their practice in pleurisy, peritonitis, pericarditis, and other acute diseases.* Of all these inflammations, peritonitis is probably the most serious, and we have something like an admission of the alleged success of homœopathy in that disease, by an opponent of the system, who was an eye-witness of its operation in Fleischmann's hospital. True, says he, they cure

* Inflammation of outer covering of lungs, bowels, and heart.

peritonitis readily enough, but then their cases are, for the most part, only *tubercular* (scrofulous) peritonitis. I need not remind any professional reader, of respectable attainments, that *tubercular* peritonitis, when of any considerable extent, as it must be in many instances, is the most incurable form of the disease, (that which follows perforation excepted,) if indeed it is ever cured. Yet such an explanation of the homœopathic success as this, was actually made by a writer against homœopathy, in Dr. Forbes's Review, whose opinions and statements are even still quoted and referred to as authoritative by Dr. Simpson, Dr. Routh, and other allopathic controversialists! Even if we grant that, in a large proportion of such cases of tubercular peritonitis, the inflammation was sub-acute, and not extensive, the superiority of homœopathy, in the treatment of peritonitis, would be in no degree less manifest; for it is not pretended that tubercular peritonitis, even in its slighter forms, was not equally prevalent in the allopathic hospitals of Vienna, in which the proportion of deaths among cases of peritonitis is so much larger than in the homœopathic; indeed, the writer in question admits that he saw such slight cases only in an allopathic hospital!

It is altogether unnecessary, after the complete vindication contained in the preceding analysis of the various statistics of pneumonia, of the accuracy of the homœopathic statements regarding the success of homœopathic practice in that disease, to enter into any details in proof of the superiority of the same plan of treatment in other inflammatory diseases. Pneumonia has been regarded as an important and dangerous disease, scarcely inferior in gravity to any of the other common inflammations; it affords the largest statistical tables, on both sides, for the institution of a comparison between the claims of the rival methods of treatment; and a searching analysis of these statistics, along with the application to each class of the test of their respective *merits*, and to one class, whose accuracy has been ignorantly or maliciously impugned, the test of its *correctness*, afforded by the expectant practice of M. Dietl, has proved both the fidelity of homœopathic statements, and the vast superiority of the homœopathic treatment over the allopathic. The inference, from the proofs which have been adduced, of the correctness and fairness of the homœopathic records concerning pneumonia, which I am entitled to draw, as bearing upon the homœopathic statistics of other inflammations, is this, that they too must be regarded as correct and fair, for there was nothing known of the peculiarities of pneumonia, in reference to spontaneous recovery, prior to the researches of Dietl, that was not equally known regarding the other inflammations;* and as the former could not therefore be misrepresented by homœopathists, in order to meet a corroboration which they did not know was possible, but has been shown to be a fair and faithful record, *therefore* the other homœopathic records must be held to be equally fair and faithful, whether they shall meet with a similar corroboration or not. I content myself, then, with a simple notice of the results of the same treatment in other inflammmatory diseases, regarding which the homœopathic statistics are not more incredible than they were supposed to be in regard to pneumonia, prior to the proofs of their accuracy.

Among 299 cases of pleurisy the homœopathic practice in the German hospitals lost only 4, or 1 in 74; among 189 cases of peritonitis it lost only 9, or 1 in 21; while in these two diseases the allopathic mortality is from eight to sixteen

* With the exception, probably, of pleurisy, which has been generally believed to be frequently cured spontaneously, on the ground, that traces of pleurisy, long previously recovered from, have been often found in the dead bodies of persons who had never been treated for that disease. These traces, however, have usually shown that the attacks thus spontaneously cured had been of small extent.

times greater. The reason of there being this still larger comparative mortality under the allopathic system than under the other, in these two diseases than in pneumonia, probably is, that the allopathic measures have not in other inflammations the assistance of the *anatomical* peculiarities which enable cases of pneumonia to recover *in spite of* the injurious tendency of the treatment. Among 345 cases of erysipelas, there were only two deaths in the homœopathic hospitals; and a similar success attended the practice in membranous inflammations of the heart, and in dysentery. The records from which these facts are taken extend over a period of about fourteen years, a circumstance which obviates every objection that may be made on the ground of variable types of the several diseases in different years.

Allopathic writers, and Dr. Simpson among them, have lately begun to talk a great deal of the power of acute diseases to disappear of themselves. They have been forced to this by the undeniable recoveries under Homœopathy, which they desire to represent as no medical treatment at all. We, however, assert the same thing regarding acute diseases, and go a great deal farther in our assertions on the point than they do; for we contend that recoveries would be much more common in their hands than they are known to be, provided they would suspend their peculiar treatment, and leave such diseases to the less dangerous methods of nature alone. The justice of this opinion is amply attested by the statistics of pneumonia already given; and the continued inquiries that are now being made, by skeptical physicians of their own party, will, by and by, put us in possession of similar proofs in respect to other inflammations.

It is not in acute diseases of the inflammatory kind only that Homœopathy is superior to the common practice. But as I have already exceeded the space I had intended for the comparison of the two systems in the treatment of particular diseases, I must satisfy myself with the testimony of Dr. Forbes, the distinguished allopathic reviewer, in regard to this point. Alluding to Fleischmann's reports, he gives him the character of being a "well-educated physician," "of honour and respectability," says, "we cannot, therefore, refuse to admit the accuracy of his statements as to matters of fact," acknowledges the general correctness of his statistics of mortality among acute and chronic diseases, and of fevers he affirms—"the amount of deaths in the fevers and eruptive diseases is certainly *below* the ordinary proportion;" * although he explains this on the ground that Homœopathy does merely no harm, while Allopathy often does. We may take the liberty of denying the validity of the *explanation*, in so far as Homœopathy is concerned; but we are satisfied for the present with the admission of the *fact*, that the superior success is on our side.

I cannot pass from the consideration of medical statistics without a few remarks on each of two important points frequently adverted to by allopathic controversialists; and on both of which I have the fortune to agree with them. The first is, what I believe to be their just denial that the general statistics (including all the cases admitted) of their hospitals can be fairly compared with those of the homœopathic institutions. I entirely concur with them in thinking that the far greater proportion of incurable organic diseases that find their way into the large, old, allopathic hospitals, as into medical poor-houses for the incurable, places them at a disadvantage as to the class of cases subjected to treatment, when their mortality is brought into comparison with that of homœopathic hospitals. This much is due to fairness; but, at the same time, I strongly suspect that, although our mortality would be greater than it is if our hospitals had the

* British and Foreign Medical Review, 1846.

same proportion of incurable organic diseases as the allopathic have, the *difference* between the results of the two methods would be quite as great, if not greater, were the allopathic hospitals to have acute inflammations substituted for their excess of organic diseases; for it is only a *proportion* of the latter that die annually, though all of them must die within a few years.

The second point is, that the returns of one or two homœopathic dispensaries in this world of diversity are not faultless. They give what to me, as well as to our allopathic friends, appears an incredible proportion of *cures* of consumption. I do not know who presides over the Munich Dispensary, or the London Homœopathic Institution's out-patients; but if the reports are sanctioned by them, they must submit to be regarded as very incompetent persons in matters of diagnosis. I am not the defender of the errors of every medical man who chooses to call himself a homœopathist; and I have never thought that Allopathy monopolized all the apocryphal authorities and ill-informed physicians in the world. But while I dispute the accuracy of the reports which would make Homœopathy appear to cure consumption so readily, I am firmly of opinion that the only cures that are met with in practice are, when due to medicine in any degree, due to Homœopathy. It is chiefly as a homœopathic remedy that cod-liver oil acts, in the proportion of cases in which it acts beneficially, by dint of its minute quantities of phosphorus and iodine; and I have reason to think that Homœopathy has other remedies which are sometimes beneficial when that oil fails to be of service. I must not leave the reader to suppose that the homœopathic physicians adverted to above stand alone in their extravagant conceptions of the prowess of their art in consumption. M. Bayle, the allopathic writer on Digitalis, in the Bibliothèque Thérapeutique, has collected, from a number of the authors of his sect, 151 cases of that disease treated by digitalis,—of which they say 83 were *cured*, and 35 relieved. Does Dr. Simpson believe their assertions; and, if not, does he think that all *allopathic* statistics are monstrous fabrications or ignorant rhapsodies?

Lastly, Dr. Simpson most incautiously sneers at the statistics of the private practice of homœopathic physicians. (See p. 90 of the "Tenets.") Let him beware lest he provoke some of that body to constitute themselves a commission of inquiry into matters which had better remain as private as may be: Allopathy could ill stand such an investigation. As to the instance he refers to at Huddersfield, in connexion with cholera, the two gentlemen engaged in the conflict very plainly, I believe, gave each other the flattest contradiction, and it will always remain impossible for us to decide who was in the right; at all events, it has not been found that allopathic controversialists are usually trustworthy, certainly they are very far from being monopolists of credibility.

CHAPTER II.

Outline of the life and labours of Hahnemann; his parentage; early devotion to learning; medical education; relinquishment of practice from disgust at its uncertainty; distinction as a chemist; his first conception of the homœopathic law, and return to practice—Allopathy and Antipathy afford no hope to practical medicine—The *proving* of medicines the road to Homœopathy —First publications on a *new principle*, or the necessity of ascertaining the actions of medicines on the healthy—Persecution at Königslutter—Discovery of the prophylactic power of Belladonna—Proofs of its truth, and refutation of Dr. Simpson's objections.

No earnest or truth-loving man can peruse the facts recorded in the last chapter, without very seriously meditating on the state of medical affairs, or without the conviction that there is something fearfully wrong where both the public and the profession in general have been totally unsuspicious of error. These revelations are startling, and new to most of us, for we have been slow to believe the many solemn warnings of Hahnemann regarding the dangers and the many irretrievable evils, of the course usually pursued in the treatment of acute diseases. His language on the subject has been regarded as extravagant by many even of his own followers, and as the expression rather of his personal antipathies towards the practice of those who had loaded him with every imaginable abuse, than as the sober utterances of a man of deep and dispassionate thought, as well as of rare powers of observation: we may say now, with such evidences before us, that the half had not been told, that the warning voice of Hahnemann, strong as it is, is not half so loud as the occasion demands; and may well lament that while many of the medical guardians of life are wasting time on irrelevant trifles, and darkening counsel with words, thousands, yea, tens of thousands, are perishing that might be saved.* Medical men, by whatever orthodox name they distinguish themselves, cannot longer, without the deepest guilt, go on in a course of blind prejudice or indifference. Ignorance may be innocent when it is unavoidable; it is guilty when the means are at hand by which it may be exchanged for knowledge; and guilty just in proportion to the value of the knowledge which it excludes.

Having given in the preceding pages a sample of the benefits of Homœopathy, such as fully to justify the high estimate formed of it by its founder, and to establish his paramount claims to the lasting gratitude of mankind, I cannot be mistaken in supposing that a historical sketch of Hahnemann, and of the origin and development of his great discovery, will be welcome to such as take a genial interest in whatever relates to human worth, and is subservient to human happiness. I shall, therefore, devote this and the succeeding chapter to a narrative of his scientific life and labours.

Samuel Hahnemann was born in 1755, and ought, therefore, to be regarded as more a man of the last century than the present; a truth which is either forgotten, or kept out of view, by those who minutely criticise his knowledge and opinions, on some parts of medical science, by the standards of a succeeding age, remarkable beyond any other for the growth, and often for the beginning too, of whatever is held to be certain and of value to practical medicine, in physiology, morbid anatomy, organic chemistry, and physical diagno-

* From calculations founded on the reports of the Registrar-General, taken in connexion with the facts contained in the preceding chapter, it appears that in the United Kingdom there die, under the common treatment, in every ten years, about 20,000 cases of inflammation of the lungs alone, *that might be cured.*

sis.* His native place was the little town of Meissen, on the Elbe, near Dresden; and his parents, like those of many others who have risen to distinction in science, were in humble life; his father having been by trade a painter on porcelain. Hahnemann appears to have been at first destined for some lowly occupation, and to have been enjoined by parental authority to eschew the liberal studies for which he showed an early preference. But a love of knowledge being stronger in the boy than filial piety, he contrived means to evade the paternal injunctions, and by a midnight lamp, of his own secret construction, to gratify his intellectual longings when the household was asleep. "His aptitude for study," says his accomplished biographer, Dr. Dudgeon, "excited the admiration of his schoolmaster, with whom he became an immense favourite, and who undertook to direct his studies, and encouraged him to a higher order of study than what constituted the usual curriculum of a high-school. This did not please his father, who several times removed him from school, and set him to some less intellectual work, but at length restored him to his favourite studies, at the earnest request of his teacher, who, to meet the pecuniary difficulty, instructed the young Samuel until his twentieth year without remuneration."† He soon after began his medical studies at Leipsic, and it deserves to be noticed, to the credit of his youthful attainments, that he supported himself there by teaching French and German, and translating works from the English. From Leipsic he resorted to Vienna, where he enlarged his professional acquirements under the friendly direction of the once celebrated Dr. von Quarin, whose esteem he had the good fortune to gain, and who treated him with the kindness of a father.

* He was nearly seventy years old before the introduction of auscultation by Laennec.

† Hahnemann. An Introductory Lecture, by R. J. Dudgeon, M.D. 1852.

Having completed the orthodox curriculum, he graduated at the University of Erlangen in 1779, and appears forthwith to have commenced the practice of his profession. After some years of—as we may be sure, considering the man and his attainments—more thoughtful and intelligent experience than had often been exemplified in medicine, he wrote his first medical treatise, which gives the results of his professional labours in Transylvania, "and takes rather a desponding view of medical practice in general, and of his own in particular, as he candidly admits that most of his cases would have done better had he let them alone."* It would appear from his letter many years afterwards to the celebrated Hufeland, with whom, in 1808, he was on terms of intimate friendship, that after "an eight years' practice, pursued," as he says, "with conscientious attention," he had so "learned the delusive nature of the ordinary methods of treatment," as to be induced to relinquish his professional pursuits. His own words, descriptive of his views and feelings at this time, are as follow:—"It was painful to me to grope in the dark, guided only by our books on the treatment of the sick—to prescribe, according to this or that (*fanciful*) view of the nature of the diseases, substances that owe to mere opinion their place in the Materia Medica; I had conscientious scruples about treating unknown morbid states in my suffering fellow-creatures with these unknown medicines, which, being powerful substances, may, if they were not *exactly* suitable, (and how could the physician know whether they were suitable or not, seeing that their peculiar special actions were not yet elucidated?) easily change life into death, or produce new affections or chronic ailments, which are often much more difficult to remove than the original disease. To become in this way a murderer, or aggravator of the sufferings

* Dr. Dudgeon.

of my brethren of mankind, was to me a fearful thought—so fearful and distressing was it, that shortly after my marriage I abandoned practice, and scarcely treated any one for fear of doing him harm, and—as you know—occupied myself chiefly with chemistry and literary labours."* In chemistry his talents seemed to have found a field for their successful exercise, for, during several years prior to 1790, he published many articles on that science; among which are still remembered that on his valuable tests for ascertaining the purity of wine, and his treatise upon arsenic. To the value of the latter we have the testimony of the best writers on toxicology, among whom I may mention Professor Christison, who quotes Hahnemann's account of poisoning by arsenic, as no doubt the most graphic and accurate he could discover, and who cannot be accused of partiality. To his proficiency as a chemist, too, we have the tribute of Berzelius, one of the highest authorities in chemical science, though apparently of very mean information in medicine, who is reported to have said of him, "That man would have been a great chemist had he not turned a great quack."†

In 1789 we find him settled in Leipsic, and publishing his treatise on the only class of diseases he appears to have found amenable to treatment, although not yet suspecting that the cause of the exception was that the practice he recommended,

* Letter upon the Necessity of a Regeneration of Medicine, 1808. It may be worth mentioning that Louis, the eminent hospital physician of Paris, also forsook private practice, and went to work again at the public hospitals, in order to discover some means of practising medicine to better purpose. This happened, I believe, within the last thirty years.

† It was afterwards, however, remembered against him, when his name began to be distinguished in medicine, that he had mistaken borax for a new alkali, and had sold it as such. But it is not added by his enemies, that on discovering his error he hastened to correct it, and to refund the money he had received. Many a great chemist has made as great a blunder, and in more recent times too.

and which was but a modification of the customary method, was in accordance with the world-old, but yet unseen and unacknowledged law, with which his own name was by and by to be wedded, for better or worse, in all time coming. In this work he describes the manner of preparing and using his "soluble mercury," still known in Germany as "Hahneman's." In 1790 he translated Cullen's Materia Medica, and we may reasonably suppose the task to have had some influence on the current of his meditations, which, during this eventful year, set strongly in a direction from which they never afterwards swerved till the close of his long life. Working on the Materia Medica, he must have thought much and anxiously, as indeed he tells us he was now doing, on the possible ways of turning to the advantage of mankind the powers which so many substances in every kingdom of nature seemed beyond question to possess, of altering the actions and conditions of the living human frame. At this point it is that the mind of Hahnemann presents those features which distinguish the genius of discovery, wheresoever it has shown itself at work in its highest mood. It is a mistake to suppose that his first conception of the homœopathic law of therapeutics was suggested by the accidental observation of the similarity of the effects of Peruvian bark on his own person to the symptoms of ague, a disease for which that drug is a frequent remedy. He specifies that observation, in his letter to Hufeland, merely as having at that early period strengthened the idea he had previously conceived, on totally different grounds, of the probable existence of such a law. I shall presently allow him to tell in his own way the reflections which led him to anticipate the experimental proof that there is a homœopathic law in nature, by which the virtues of medicines and the processes of disease are adapted to one another, as they are by no other law, and in such a way and to such an extent as to make the powers which plants and minerals possess of altering the states of the body almost commensurate in their *healing* qualities with the vast diversity of corporeal disorders. But before doing so, I would direct attention to the fact, that in the manner of its first being thought of, the homœopathic law belongs to the category of probably all the great additions to science that were ever made. It is erroneously supposed by many who talk of the *inductive method*, that experiment, or the accumulation of details or particular facts, precedes the detection of great general principles or laws; but it would appear that neither in ancient nor in modern times has any such method been the instrument of great discoveries. "The process of Lord Bacon," says Sir David Brewster, "was, we believe, never tried by any philosopher but himself. As the subject of its application, he selected that of heat. With his usual erudition, he collected all the facts which science could supply,—he arranged them in tables,—he cross-questioned them with all the subtlety of a pleader,—he combined them with all the sagacity of a judge,—and he conjured with them by all the magic of his exclusive processes. But, after all this display of physical logic, nature thus interrogated was still silent. The oracle which he had himself established refused to give its responses, and the ministering priest was driven with discomfiture from his own shrine. This example, in short, of the application of his system, will remain to future ages as a memorable instance of the absurdity of attempting to fetter discovery by any artificial rules."* In another place he observes,—"It would be interesting to ascertain the general character of the process by which a mind of acknowledged power actually proceeds in the path of successful inquiry. The history of science does not furnish us with much information on this head, and if it is to be found at all, it must be gleaned from

* Life of Newton.

the biographies of eminent men. Whatever this process may be in its details, if it has any, there cannot be the slightest doubt, that in its generalities, at least, it is the very reverse of the method of induction."

Hahnemann, as we have seen, had in a great measure, if not entirely, withdrawn from practice some time towards the year 1790, in consequence of the dissatisfaction he felt at the uncertainty, general inefficiency, and frequent dangers of the ordinary method of practising medicine. But he was not, therefore, unoccupied with reflections on the healing art, and the possibility of discovering some better method than those in common use; and he has left us traces of the steps by which he was led to discover the surer and more effectual way of using remedies. And first, it is remarkable enough, considering the strange attempt that has been made of late to attach to Homœopathy the reproach of theological heterodoxy, that he places in the foreground of the sketch he has given of his meditations on the possibility of raising medicine from its low position, such conceptions of the bounty of God, and such reliance on His wise beneficence, as are striking no less for their lofty piety, than as the solitary instance in which a deep sense of the divine goodness proved to be the special incentive to arduous medical researches, and the starting point of a scientific voyage of discovery. Perhaps we are entitled to regard it in still another light—as the compass by which he steered, and as therefore the cause of his success. Having stated his sad experience of the methods of Sydenham and Hoffmann, of Boerhaave and Gaubius, Stoll, Cullen, and De Haen, he continues, "But perhaps it is in the very nature of this art, as great men have asserted, that it is incapable of attaining any greater certainty. Shameful, blasphemous thought! What! shall it be said that the infinite wisdom of the Eternal Spirit that animates the universe could not produce remedies to allay the sufferings of the diseases He allows to arise? The all-loving paternal goodness of Him whom no name worthily designates, who richly supplies all wants, even the scarcely conceivable ones of the insect in the dust, imperceptible by reason of its minuteness to the keenest human eye, and who dispenses throughout all creation life and happiness in rich abundance—shall it be said that He was capable of the tyranny of not permitting that man, made in His own image, should by the efforts of his penetrating mind, that has been breathed into him from above, find out the way to discover remedies in the stupendous kingdom of created things, which should be able to deliver his brethren of mankind from their sufferings worse than death itself? Shall He, the Father of all, behold with indifference the martyrdom of His best-beloved creatures by disease, and yet have rendered it impossible to the genius of man, to whom all else is possible, to find any method, any *easy*, *sure*, *trustworthy* method, whereby they may see diseases in the proper point of view, and whereby they may interrogate medicines as to their special uses, as to what they are *really*, *surely*, and *positively* serviceable for?"* "Well, thought I, as there must be a sure and trustworthy method of treatment as certainly as God is the wisest and most beneficent of beings, I shall seek it no longer in the thorny thicket of ontological explanations, in arbitrary opinions, though these might be capable of being arranged into a splendid system, nor in the authoritative declarations of celebrated men. No, let me seek it where it lies nearest at hand, and where it has hitherto been passed over by all, because it did not seem sufficiently recondite, nor sufficiently learned, and was not hung with laurels for those who displayed most talent for constructing systems, for scholastic speculations, and transcendental abstractions. . . . How, then, canst thou (this

* Letter to Hufeland.

was the mode of reasoning by which I commenced to find my way) ascertain what morbid states medicines were created for? . . . Thou must, thought I, observe how medicines act on the human body, when it is in the tranquil state of health. The alterations that medicines produce in the healthy body do not occur in vain, *they must signify something*, else why should they occur? What if those alterations have an important, an extremely important signification. What if this be the only utterance whereby these substances can impart information to the observer respecting the end of their being; what if the changes and sensations which such medicine produces in the healthy human organism, be the only comprehensible language by which—if they be not smothered by severe symptoms of some existing disease—it can distinctly discourse to the unprejudiced observer respecting its specific tendencies, respecting its peculiar, pure, positive power, by means of which it is capable of effecting alterations in the body, that is, of deranging the healthy organism, and—where it can cure—of changing into health the organism that has been deranged by disease! This was what I thought.

"I carried my reflections farther: 'How else could medicines effect what they do in diseases than by means of this power of theirs to alter the healthy body?—(which is most certainly different in every different mineral substance, and consequently presents in each a different series of phenomena, accidents, and sensations.) Certainly in this way alone can they cure.

"But if medicinal substances effect what they do in diseases *only* by means of the power peculiar to each of them of altering the healthy body, it follows that the medicine among whose symptoms those characteristics of a given case of disease occur in the most complete manner, must most certainly have the power of curing that disease; and in like manner, that morbid state which a certain medicinal agent is capable of curing must correspond to the symptoms this medicinal substance is capable of producing in the healthy human body. In a word, medicines must only have the power of curing diseases similar to those they produce in the healthy body, and only manifest such morbid actions as they are capable of curing in diseases!

"If I am not deceived, I thought further, such is really the case; otherwise how was it that those violent tertian and quotidian fevers which I completely cured four and six weeks ago, without knowing how the cure was effected, by means of a few drops of cinchona tincture, should present almost exactly the same array of symptoms which I observed in myself yesterday and to-day, after gradually taking, while in perfect health, four drachms of good cinchona bark, by way of experiment?"

Thus, the conception of the homœopathic law, and of the necessity of ascertaining the powers of medicines to alter the health by *proving* them on the healthy body, had manifestly preceded the "yesterday and to-day" of inquisitive experiment, as the first conception of the law of gravitation is known to have preceded the existence of the data required to make it provable. Abundance of experiment was yet to follow, unparalleled in its demands on patience, perseverance, and toil of mind and body; but, first, the records of medicine were to be searched to learn where accident had hit on the grains of gold that must exist even in that chaos. Accordingly, to chaos he next betook himself, with the pick-axe and shovel of his rare learning and discrimination, and ardent with hope as ever went gold-seeker in our days to California or Mount Alexander. In the works of his predecessors the "yield" was not enormous, so manifold were the alloys and impurities of polypharmacy; but specimens he got of the precious metal, of whose value they were as unconscious as the aboriginal Indian or Australian must once have been of the market worth of their yellow dust. Accidental cures of maladies whose symptoms resembled the effects producible on healthy persons by the drugs that had been given, sparkled here and there in ancient volumes, elsewhere dark as midnight. The discovery of some pure specimens of such accidental homœopathic practice of former days, and of others of doubtful character,* the result of his studies at this period, was subsequently published in his Organon. For he was far from holding, as many of his obtuse and ignorant detractors affirm, that medicine had been utterly ineffective for permanent good before his day. On the contrary, he expressly adverts again and again to cures in the highest degree remarkable, as having been performed by physicians in every age. What he laments, and with the most admirable acuteness and force of argument exposes, in several of his works, is the absence of any previous *rule* by which remedies, unquestionably serviceable at one time, can be made so with any degree of certainty at another: a defect which he shows to have arisen from the universal ignorance of the reason why, when they happened to be efficacious, they actually were so. It was to supply this fundamental want that he laboured: in order that men might have a principle for their guidance in the attempt to cure diseases, and no longer be successful by rare accident, or useless or injurious by pedantic ignorance.

In order to perceive the depth of meaning that lies in the passages we have quoted, and to discern the logical continuity of what seemed to Hahnemann the legitimate process of rea-

* There can scarcely be stronger evidence of the captious spirit, and the poverty of serious argument, with which Dr. Simpson attacks Homœopathy, than the fuss he makes about these dubious instances. As if it was of the smallest consequence to Homœopathy, though a single instance of accidental homœopathic cure could not be proved from the records of the dark ages that preceded Hahnemann.

soning on the subject, we need to place ourselves where he stood, and look at the field of medicine from his point of view. Medicines, by divine appointment, have powers, almost endless in variety, of affecting the healthy human frame: these powers must be there for some purpose, as every thing in nature has its use; if they are conferred with the design, not of adding to human woes, by means of human ignorance, but of lightening the miseries of this mortal life by means of human intelligence and human labour, (on which, in all else that concerns his well-being, man has been encouraged, indeed necessitated, to rely as the instruments of his temporal comfort,) there *must be* some other way of employing them than such as have failed almost utterly, in all time past, some surer foundation for medical practice than the shifting sands of pathological opinion concerning the *unknowable* essence of disease, than unsteady hypothetical theories of medicinal actions, or than the blind and senseless empiricism that acts it knows not why! Each and all of these may have hit occasionally on a happy expedient which has proved a cure, but accident is a miserable substitute for the surer method, which, "as God is the wisest and most beneficent of beings," must exist somewhere for the benefit of "his best loved creatures."

Anti-pathy, or the method which would proceed on the principle of *contraria contrariis curantur*, and prescribe medicines whose primary action is *opposed* to that of the diseased part, has been found in its operation temporary and palliative only, leaving the malady, (if it be not in its nature and degree fleeting and unimportant,) when the strong medicinal action is over, worse than it was before, and worse in proportion to the completeness with which it was silenced for the time; and all this owing to the reaction of the diseased living organs after the force that overpowered them had been spent. Witness, for example, the baneful effects of opium in habitual sleeplessness, when the dose has been large enough to reduce the resisting brain to a poisoned insensibility;—of purgatives in habitual constipation,—and the remaining small number of instances in which we have any thing that can be justly called an anti-pathic action. Besides, even were anti-pathy good, its employment to any considerable extent would be impossible, for the plain and sufficient reason, that *no opposite can exist* to thousands of the symptoms that disease presents, and it is by symptoms or sensible effects we must be guided, unless we are to lose ourselves again in ever groundless conjectures, and fanciful speculations, regarding that hidden essence of disease which makes its presence knowable only by its effects, while these tell nothing of its nature. The *absence* of a symptom or effect is not its *opposite*, and no opposite is conceivable for hundreds of different sensations, of altered appearances and secretions, and therefore we can oppose to them no *contrary* medicine,—except on hypothetical grounds, again, both of the disease and the remedy. Hahnemann knew all this, and therefore he had no hope from anti-pathy, and he was right. Nothing has been made of it to this hour, beyond what it always has been, and must be—*palliative, temporary, not curative.*

Nor was there better promise from Allopathy, or the method which would attempt to remove natural disease from one part by exciting artificial disease in another. This is essentially the system of counter-irritation applied to other parts than those which are diseased,—and though temporary checks may be caused by it in a few of the more important disorders, and though those which are unimportant, and naturally of short duration, may come to an end during the existence of the counter-irritation, as when blisters, or yet more violent applications, have produced inflammation of some part of the surface contiguous to the disease, the number of maladies is small in which it admits of being exemplified in this, its apparently most favourable illustration, and it is more than questionable whether, when recovery succeeds such counter-irritation, it is materially, if at all, the result of the artificial disease, in any considerable proportion of cases. In our own day it has been asked, by so decided an allopath as Andral, whether, in acute inflammations, blisters ameliorate the disease, by the exudation they cause to take place from the circulation, or increase it by aggravating the fever, and augmenting the inflammatory state of the blood; and Louis, another of the same school, questions their utility in one of the acute diseases, in which they are, perhaps, the most frequently employed, pleurisy,—which he is inclined to suspect is rather liable to be made worse by vesicatories applied to the chest. Allopathic applications of this kind, therefore, must have appeared to Hahnemann, also, as pertaining to the catalogue of dubious or hurtful expedients; and as the same estimate was still more applicable to allopathic *medicines*, his expectations from an allopathic method, even were it supposed to be practicable in the case of any large proportion of drugs,—which it obviously could not be without the aid of the everlasting theories and fanciful speculations regarding the nature of diseases, and the mode in which medicines acted, speculations infinitely more liable to be wrong than right,—must necessarily have been of the least satisfactory description. If so questionable in the simplest and most obvious form, how much more so, how uncertain and ineffectual must it have appeared to be in the obscurer and less manageable instances?

Several indirect operations of the allopathic remedies, besides those properly included under counter-irritation, were as well known in Hahnemann's time as in the present, and apparently as much employed. Diaphoretics, diuretics, purgatives, were all in vogue then as now, and if they are now employed with a discrimination that often prevents the injurious consequences that must have followed their administration in cases in which an improved pathology shows us they are calculated to do harm, they were still then as now justly open to the general charge of being merely temporary and palliative, capable, it may be, of removing some of the products of diseased action, by one channel or another, but not curative or capable of remedying the primary disease. In certain of these capacities they may be still properly employed, when the primary disease is incurable. Dropsy, for example, when a consequence of organic disease of the heart, or kidneys, may frequently, and can only, be lessened or removed, for the time, by the allopathic action of diuretics or cathartics,—but it will return when their action is exhausted, because it is a mere effect or symptom of another disease which is not remediable. When, however, dropsy depends on a primary disease that is remediable, Hahnemann justly condemns the allopathic palliatives which are directed against the removable effect, and leave the removable cause untouched. Besides all these objections to the allopathic method, as a method of *curing*, there remained this other, that the pathogenetic effects of drugs on the healthy body were, in the great majority of instances, of a description that *could* have no allopathic use. On this part of the subject I shall quote a passage from my letter to Dr. Forbes,* who, although an allopath, is a strong advocate for proving medicines on the healthy body, and recommends the task to the young hopefuls of the profession, whom he humorously designates "Young Physic."—"Suppose the task executed, and executed well, what can you gain by it, as allopaths, but some additional purgatives, emetics, narcotics, antispasmodics, diuretics, diaphoretics, and such like, of which you have a store already ample enough to melt the mammiferous creation from off the

* See British Journal of Homœopathy, 1846; and Homœopathy in 1851.

face of the earth, or to lull it into an endless sleep? I can understand how you may stumble on remedies for particular diseases, by trying drug after drug, as each comes to hand, on persons that are ill. This is the method that has been pursued for two thousand years, or thereby, and it has brought some useful remedies to light, of which some, probably the most, act homœopathically when they act with advantage. But what you can learn of the virtues which a medicine, tried on the healthy body, shall exert on the diseased, beyond its probable evacuating, and nauseating, and narcotising, and one or two other energetic influences, long since abundantly supplied, I am at a loss to conjecture. Will 'Young Physic,' then, allow all his pangs to go for nothing? was it for this that he has panted, and groaned, and writhed, and coughed, and spit, and sneezed, and bled? That he has endured headaches and colics, stitches and twitches, in every section of his frame, and so many a fac-simile more of the ills that flesh is heir to? Can he make no use of them allopathically, or antipathically: or must he be contented to let them stand as penances?

"Supposing he should try to turn them to some remedial account, what can he make antipathically or allopathically of such an effect of a medicine as a racking pain in his stomach, for example, or a fiery redness of the nose? Why, *allo*pathically, he can get up an artificial pain in his stomach, to remove a natural pain from his head or his feet; or he can set his nose in a blaze, to cure an erysipelas of his legs, on the principle that one fire puts out another. But will the cure not be as bad as the disease? Then, *anti*pathically, how will he manage to make a practical use of his voluntary afflictions? I can see how he may succeed, when his nose is disagreeably white, in striking the more becoming hue by a skilful administration of the reddening remedy; but I am at a loss for the useful employment of the pain in his stomach. The *opposite* of a painful is an agreeable sensation, and I know not an instance of a pleasurable feeling in the stomach playing an important part in pathology. Yes, there is one such. You will find it in the treatise of worthy Dr. Underwood on the diseases of children. The 'inward fits,' quoth he, 'are betrayed by a frequent and sweet smiling during sleep; the which is provoked by wind pleasantly tickling the stomach.' Now, for just such a dose of the ache-causing remedy as shall nicely strike the balance between a pleasure and a pain! What an opportunity for our infant Hercules, our young Antipath! to still the apprehensions of a fond mother, and disappoint the forebodings of the lugubrious nurse."

We have already seen that the *proving* of medicines on persons in health formed a prominent and essential part of Hahnemann's scheme for the advancement of practical medicine, and the considerations which have now been laid before the reader appear to show beyond dispute that such provings can be of little or no service to medicine on the allopathic or antipathic plan. Dr. Forbes is not the only allopathic physician who concurs with Hahnemann on the desirableness of medicinal provings. Dr. Forbes recommends the future cultivators of medicine "to reconsider and study afresh the *physiological* and curative effects of all our therapeutic agents, with the view of obtaining more positive results than we now possess."* Professer Forget of Strasburg had previously given the same advice at the Scientific Congress in 1842, the following deliverance having been presented to that body by the Medical Section over which he presided:—"The Medical Section is unanimously of opinion that experiments with medicines, on healthy individuals are, in the present state of medical science, of urgent necessity for physiology and therapeutics." And, indeed, so general is the feeling, however vague,

* British and Foreign Medical Review, 1846.

as to the consequences that may ensue to the healing art, of the propriety of having such provings, and of the discredit of not having them, that, in every allopathic work on the properties of drugs, their action on the healthy body is never, if possible, omitted. This is no small testimony to the sagacity of Hahnemann, who had so long previously descried the importance of such knowledge; and when it is acquired in a full and satisfactory manner by allopathic physicians, the result must be the general adoption of Homœopathy, partly because it will teach them to respect the scientific character of the first and greatest of provers, and partly because it will show them, by evidences of their own, that the remedies we use are *homœopathic*, or correspond, in their effects on healthy persons, to the phenomena of the diseases in which they are successfully employed. As yet the archives of the old methods are singularly deficient in information of the kind referred to; indeed, what does exist in them would deserve to be called contemptible, were it not ludicrous; for nothing is contemptible that can give even a *little* innocent amusement. Notwithstanding this defect, however, new medicines have been added to the old lists, and old medicines have become employed in new ways, and with occasionally better success, in ordinary practice, within the last twenty or thirty years. But the explanation of this is to be found in these very provings of Hahnemann and his followers, which those who thus profit by them affect to despise. Medicines get into good repute, through the practitioners of Homœopathy, for the treatment of various common disorders, and forthwith their virtues are quietly appropriated or *re-discovered* by the allopathic party, and their operation *explained* by some absurd or fanciful theory, and thus having cap and bells clapped upon them to conceal their true character, they are promoted (heartily ashamed of the honour) to the rank of orthodox drugs. Aconite, belladonna, nux vomica, arnica, are familiar instances of this indirect progress of ordinary medicine. One consoling reflection, however, is, that they won't be found very obedient to their strange masters, until *they* appropriate also the rules which the medicines have been taught to follow by Him who bestowed them on the world.

To proceed with our history, however: it is obvious that Allopathy and Antipathy affording Hahnemann no hope of advancing therapeutics to a respectable and useful position, he was shut up to Homœopathy, as the only remaining way that could be conceived for the employment of drugs, the only method that promised to give full effect to all the phenomena of medicinal provings on healthy persons. Conceiving, first, that medicines effected cures of disease "by means of this power of theirs to alter the healthy body," and by this *only*, —it follows, as a logical sequence, that since they cannot thus cure antipathically or allopathically, they must do so homœopathically; or in his own words, "it follows that the medicine among whose symptoms those characteristics of a given case of disease occur in the most complete manner, must most certainly have the power of curing that disease," if there is any meaning whatever in the multiplicity of effects which medicines can produce on the healthy frame, by the express appointment of the "wisest and most beneficent of beings." And thus was the idea of the homœopathic law reasoned out, before a single testing experiment was made. The first experiment, as we have seen, was made with cinchona bark, and the illustration it affords of the homœopathic action of medicines will be discussed in the sequel.

In 1792, Hahnemann, at the request of the reigning Duke of Saxe-Gotha, took charge of an asylum for the insane in Georgenthal, in the Thuringian Forest. "A cure," says Dr. Dudgeon, "that he made in this institution, of the Hanoverian minister Klockenbring, who had been rendered insane by a satire of Kotzebue's, created, we are told, some sensation; and, from the account he published in 1796 of this case, we find that he was one of the earliest, if not the very first advocate for that system of treatment of the insane by mildness instead of coercion, which has become all but universal. 'I never allow any insane person,' he writes, 'to be punished by blows or other painful corporeal inflictions, since there can be no punishment where there is no sense of responsibility, and since such patients cannot be improved, but must be rendered worse, by such rough treatment.' May we not then justly claim for Hahnemann the honour of being the first who advocated and practised the moral treatment of the insane? At all events, he may divide this honour with Pinel, for we find that towards the end of this same year 1792, when Hahnemann was applying his principle of moral treatment to practice, Pinel made his first experiment of unchaining the maniacs in the Bicêtre."

He did not remain long in his new charge; and we have traces of his temporary residence with his family in several places between 1792 and 1795, in which latter year he removed to Königslutter, where he remained practising his profession till 1799. Several new productions of his pen appeared during this period, including his *Friend of Health*, a popular miscellany, devoted chiefly to Hygiène; his *Pharmaceutical Lexicon;* his *Essay on a New Principle for ascertaining the Remedial Powers of Medicinal Substances;* and others on the absurdity of complex prescriptions and regimen, and on the treatment of fevers and periodical diseases. The *Essay on a New Principle, &c.*, was published in 1796, in his friend Hufeland's Journal, and is the first of his remarkable publications on Homœopathy. It may be read still with profit by the earnest inquirer into the methods by which physicians have endeavoured to improve their art. The true functions of chemistry and botany, in subserving the ends of practical medicine, are lucidly explained, and the limits pointed out with admirable judgment, beyond which they cannot go; while the importance of experiment with drugs is powerfully enforced. Having shown the narrow compass of the advantages to be derived from the two preceding methods, he continues: "Nothing remains for us but *experiment* on the human body. But what kind of experiment? *Accidental or Methodical?* The humiliating confession must be made, that most of the virtues of medicinal bodies were discovered by *accidental*, *empirical* experience, by *chance;* often first observed by non-medical persons.* Bold, often over-bold, physicians then gradually make trial of them.

"I have no intention of denying the high value of this mode of discovering medicinal powers—it speaks for itself. But in it there is nothing for us to do; chance excludes all method, all voluntary action. Sad is the thought that the noblest, the most indispensable of arts is built upon accident, which always pre-supposes the endangering of many human lives. Will the chance of such discoveries suffice to perfect the healing art, to supply its numerous desiderata? . . . . Sadly we look forward into future ages, when a peculiar remedy for this particular form of disease, for this particular circumstance, may, *perhaps*, be discovered by chance, as was bark for pure intermittent fever, or mercury for syphilitic disorders. . . . .

"When I talk of the *methodical discovery* of the medicinal powers still required by us, I do not refer to those empirical trials usually made in hospitals, where, in a difficult, often not accurately noted case, in which those already known do no good, recourse is had to some drug, hitherto either untried altogether, or untried in this particular affection, which drug is fixed upon either from caprice and blind fancy, or from

* See examples in the sequel,—Chapter on "Homœopathic Law."

some obscure notion, for which the experimenter can give no plausible reason either to himself or others. Such empirical chance trials are, to call them by the mildest appellation, but foolish risks, if not something worse." These remarks are not less applicable to the ordinary practice in our own day than they were in his.

The greater part of the essay is devoted to an exposition of the principle according to which, as he conceived, remedies that are homœopathic to the disease produce their effects, and to the notice of such instances as were then known of the pathogenetic action of medicines, and the homœopathic suitableness of this or that drug to various corresponding conditions of disease. For examples of the effects produced by drugs on healthy persons, he was even at this early period indebted in some measure to his own observation, showing how soon after his first perception of the homœopathic law he began to accumulate those stores with which he afterwards enriched scientific medicine. Among the medicines whose actions on healthy persons he had already made some progress in discovering, were chamomilla, arnica, millefolium, æthusa, belladonna, hyoscyamus, nux vomica, digitalis, ledum, palustre, arsenic, and camphor. He occasionally illustrates, besides, their homœopathic action as remedies, by particular instances of cure; and of the other medicines which he adverts to, he either tells how they had been useful on account of their homœopathic virtues in the hands of other physicians, or employed with advantage by himself on the homœopathic principle, from particulars concerning their action on healthy persons obtained from the incidental notices of authors; or he predicts from the same *data* that they will be found useful in certain disorders to which they seemed homœopathically suited. Learned researches, and experimental labours such as these, giving from year to year conclusions soberly drawn from premises carefully determined, and doctrines enlarging and becoming more definite as the observation of facts extended and became more precise, are not the characteristics of deceit, but the sure evidences of sincerity and a love of truth. In the essay on which I am now commenting, with the exceptions of the modest but firm announcement of his belief that medicines cure diseases by virtue of their power to excite *similar* diseases on healthy persons, and of the illustrations of that truth contained in books and furnished by his own experience, there is nothing advanced by Hahnemann that can be regarded as peculiar to Homœopathy as it now exists. There is no singularity in the manner of preparing the medicines for use, or in the doses in which they should be given; no evidence of a predetermination to start far away from his brethren in the profession, and to strike out a solitary path to fortune for himself; but much, on the contrary, that proves him to have been less intent on his individual fame, than on the clear discerning and propagation of important truths, and much that shows his desire that others should be partakers of all the knowledge and skill he himself possessed. Homœopathy, in its details, was to him, as it is at this day to his followers, a *progressive* science, for whose application to practice, while a very great deal was done by him in the course of the fifty years that he devoted his rare energy and genius to the study of it, much has been left for his successors to accomplish; and not, as its shallow adversaries suppose, a sudden contrivance that shot up into a mushroom maturity from the heated brain of an enthusiast, or the profligate heart of a charlatan.

One obvious inference from Hahnemann's views of the curative action of medicines was, that they should not be jumbled together in mixtures, pills, and boluses, whereof each, according to the custom of the old school, was made to contain several or many drugs, but that they should be given in the simplest form. This rule carried into practice, of course rendered the art of the apothecary, as it then existed, altogether useless to him, and he was under the necessity of preparing and dispensing his own medicines. The apothecaries of Königslutter were, therefore, easily incited by the physicians of the place, who had grown speedily jealous of the rising fame of their colleague, to bring an action against him for interfering with their privileges; for in Germany at that time the druggists were secured by law in the exclusive right of compounding physic. Hahnemann defended himself by the plea, that while they had indeed the sole right of compounding medicines according to the prescriptions of the physicians, every man, according to the spirit of the law, was at liberty to *give*, as he did, gratuitously, *uncompounded* drugs, which alone he employed. This reasonable argument was unheeded, he was prohibited dispensing his medicines, and thus his practice was of course forbidden at the same time.*

In 1799, the last year of his residence at Königslutter, he first conceived the idea that belladonna was a preventive of certain forms of scarlet fever. During the prevalence of an epidemic of that disease, he employed belladonna as a remedy for the first stage of the malady, in consequence of the similarity of some of the effects it produces to the early symptoms of scarlet fever. In a family of four children,

*On Hahnemann's rule of giving only a single medicine at a time, Dr. Simpson makes some choice remarks, indicative, as usual, of the greatest ignorance of the subject he writes about. Opium, says he, contains twenty-one ingredients, and yet homœopaths prescribe opium, while they pretend to give medicines singly. Opium, we reply, is a single medicine, because it has not been artificially compounded, and because it has been *proved* just as nature gives it; and *proving* bestows unity in the sense of showing what this natural compound can do, as distinguished from other natural compounds. *Proving* is the essence of singleness in Homœopathy: so that if opium, arsenic, and mercury, mixed together, were *proved* upon the healthy body, this artificial compound would thenceforth be a single medicine.

one was taking belladonna for some affection of the finger joints, when the epidemic disease invaded the household; and Hahnemann, having observed that she escaped while the others were seized with the malady, suspected that her exemption might depend on the influence of the drug she was taking. He had soon numerous opportunities of testing the correctness of his suspicion, by giving the medicine to many who were yet unaffected by the disease, in families which had others of its members ill with it, and the results satisfied him that belladonna had a protective power such as he had suspected. As it is of great importance that medical men should form a right opinion regarding the justice of this conclusion of Hahnemann, I shall lay before the reader the directions originally laid down by the discoverer of the prophylactic, and a summary of the experience which we possess on the subject at the present day. I say *we*, as including both sides of the profession; for it is not a little amusing, after all the abuse they heap upon homœopathic physicians for using a teaspoonful of castor oil, to find the allopathic practitioners making no scruple whatever to appropriate Hahnemann's discovery of the protective power of belladonna! So early as 1810, some allopathic practitioners in Leipsic "complacently recommended the employment of belladonna as a prophylactic for scarlet fever, as if they had just made the discovery," and without even adverting to the claims of the true discoverer, who was then practising in the same town. In 1826, Hufeland, the most celebrated of the allopathic physicians of his day in Germany, wrote an article in his journal on the *Prophylactic power of Belladonna in Scarlet Fever*, in which he honestly assigns the merit of the discovery to Hahnemann, and is said to have collected an overwhelming mass of testimony in its favour. Hahnemann did not publish on the subject till 1801, as he appears to have been very solicitous that there should be experience ample enough to prevent the possibility of mistake, and to determine the concurrent circumstances which were necessary to ensure the successful employment of the medicine, or the obstacles that might frustrate the attempt to render it of service. In the interval he appears to have furnished supplies of his prophylactic to a number of practitioners, in order that it might be tested by others as well as himself, and this he did originally without informing them of the name of the drug: and yet when he published his pamphlet on the *Cure and Prevention of Scarlet Fever*, eleven years after he first began his experiments on the subject, he remarks in the preface,—"Up to this period it is impossible that the corroboration of my assertion could be complete,"—a circumstance which he ascribes, in part, to the fact, that the medicine occasionally "fell into the hands of some who had neither the ability nor the good will to administer its solution in an appropriate manner," "to the hurry and inaccuracy of young doctors of the present day," and to the "little dependence to be placed on our private patients" in carrying instructions into effect. These, and other obstacles, have to this day left the question undecided in the estimation of many, and have led some to the hasty conclusion that belladonna has no power of protecting from scarlet fever. Among the most effectual means by which this last opinion may be at any time established to the satisfaction of the experimenter, is the unconscious using of another drug instead of belladonna; and that this has been the case with some cannot be doubted, for I learn from a gentleman of much experience in drugs, and who was some years ago assistant to the Professor of Materia Medica, that a collector of plants for the apothecaries having brought him a supply of *dulcamara* instead of belladonna, assured him, on being shown his mistake, that he was accustomed to regard the former (which is known by the name of woody nightshade) as belladonna (or deadly nightshade,) and that he had lately supplied one of the principal shops with a large stock of the one article instead of the other, and without any objection on the part of the druggist! How far this may account for the unfavourable results of some unpublished experiments in Edinburgh, I do not know; but it is curious, in connexion with the anecdote I have related, that this should as yet be the only city in which experiments made in an hospital for children have furnished results said to be opposed to the claims put forward on behalf of belladonna.*

Before adverting to the experiments made in Edinburgh, I shall adduce, from an article by M. Bayle,† a distinguished *allopathic* authority, the principal testimonies that have appeared on the subject in Germany.

"At the end of the last century, Hahnemann, having remarked that belladonna, taken in small doses, gave rise to a reddish eruption analogous to that of scarlatina, predicted that belladonna would be a prophylactic to this disease, according to the homœopathic principle that diseases are cured by medicines, the effects of which upon the organism are similar to the symptoms of those diseases.

"Notwithstanding some facts which seemed to confirm this hypothesis, it was only about 1812 that several physicians made methodic trials to confirm this point. But since that period to the time I now write, more than twenty-five practitioners have been occupied in establishing the preservative properties of belladonna against scarlatina. The epidemics of this disease having been frequent in the north of Europe, and often more fatal than the small-pox, the authors who

* I advert here to the unpublished experiments of Dr. Andrew Wood, adverted to by Dr. Simpson. We demand outspoken facts, details, not hole-and-corner whisperings.

† Bibliothèque Thérapeutique, t. ii. p. 583, *et seq.:* 1830.

have been occupied in verifying this point in therapeutics belong all to this part of the world.

"The following is a résumé of the different trials:—

"In 1812, a fatal epidemic reigned in the district of Hilschenbach, in the duchy of Berg; 8 persons died of it, 22 were ill. Schenk administered belladonna to 525 persons; 522 were preserved. The three who were attacked were a mother and her two children, who had only taken the medicine four times.

"Hufeland and Rhodius gave perfect immunity to all the individuals to whom they had administered this substance, in several very violent epidemics . . . . . Muhrbeck, at Demmin, (Western Pomerania,) obtained the same success during seven years, in which he had frequent opportunities of having recourse to this treatment . . . . Gumpert, physician at Posen, preserved his 4 children and 20 families, amounting to about 80 individuals; 2 persons were, however, attacked. In one the belladonna had only been used some days; in the other, the disease declared itself in the second week. Gumpert (senior) prevented the introduction of the epidemic into several villages, by administering the medicine continuously at the proper time. He remarked that in those where the epidemic had already appeared, the employment of this substance rendered the scarlatina very mild. In the district where he practises, the public have as much confidence in it as in vaccination, and the local authorities are ordered to furnish gratis this medicine.

"In the very fatal epidemics of 1817, 1818, and 1819, Brendt, physician at Custrin, made use of two preparations of belladonna. With one he preserved *all* the subjects: with the other he obtained the following results:—out of 195, 14 were attacked, and 181 preserved. The eruption was very slight among the small number of those who contracted the disease. One of the authors, whose observations are the best calculated to prove the prophylactic efficacy of belladonna, is Dr. Dusterberg of Warbourg. In three consecutive epidemics, this practitioner preserved from contagion all the individuals who made use of the remedy, although they were allowed to visit and keep company with the sick. He therefore regards this practice as certain a prophylactic as vaccination. To be more certain of his results, Dusterberg made a still more conclusive experiment; he chose, in each family submitted to the prophylactic treatment, a child who had not taken belladonna: *all the children* thus excepted were attacked by the contagion. Dusterberg adds, it is true, that several other children, who had only used the medicine for four or five days, were also attacked, but so feebly that the only trace of the scarlatina was the subsequent desquamation. . . . . In 1820, during the course of a very fatal scarlatina, Behr, physician at Bernbourg, gave the specific to 47 individuals; among these, 41 escaped the contagion, and 6 were attacked, but in an almost insensible manner. . . . . Twenty-three children, out of 84, were attacked with scarlatina in the Military Foundling Hospital of Halle, in Tyrol. Zeuch, physician to the establishment, gave belladonna to the 61 remaining; all were preserved, with the exception of one; and meanwhile the epidemic continued to rage in the environs of the hospital. . . . . Kunstmann found belladonna always efficacious, with the exception of one case; he, however, remained in doubt upon the subject, until the following trial confirmed his belief: he administered the remedy to 70 children of the Institution of Frederick, of which he is physician; 3 were attacked, 67 preserved. One other child, who had not been submitted to the trial was violently attacked. . . . ."* The whole number of persons who were submitted to the

* For the whole of Bayle's article on the subject, the English reader is referred to Dr. Black's *Principles and Practice of Homœopathy*.

preservative action of belladonna by the physicians referred to by Bayle amounted to 2027, and of these 78 were attacked with scarlet fever, while 1948 escaped in the several epidemics. He adds, "All authors, however, are not partisans of belladonna. Lehmann asserts that this medicine had no preservative virtue in the epidemic of 1825, at Torgo. According to Barth, two other physicians, Raminski and Tuffel, have also pronounced against it. We cannot justly appreciate the value of the opinion of these authors, because it is supported by no facts, and the disease has not been described. Could it not be possible that the affection treated by these practitioners was not the true scarlet fever, but rather the purple miliary fever, from which belladonna, according to Hahnemann, affords no immunity?"

I come now, then, to the Edinburgh experiments; and I ask, first, if the alleged unsuccessful trial of belladona in George Watson's Hospital, in 1851, was conducted according to the method prescribed by Hahnemann as that which was the best calculated to secure the preservative influence of the medicine? I am quite sure that the conductor of the trial, Mr. Benjamin Bell, made his experiments in perfectly good faith; for I believe, and I am glad to have an opportunity of saying so, that a more honourable and excellent man does not exist. But in so important a discussion as this he will, I am persuaded, pardon me for asking if he made himself acquainted, before he began his researches, with Hahnemann's instructions as to the proper dose, and the proper interval that should elapse between the successive repetitions of it? If he did not, why try the medicine at all: since there was no other discoverer of the alleged preventive power of belladonna than that same Hahnemann who also says that the dose ought to be very small, and ought not to be repeated above once in two or three days? I find on referring to Mr.

Bell's paper on the subject,* the following statement regarding the administration of the dose, and its effects:—"Upon the appearance of a second case of scarlet fever [in the hospital.—W. H.] the fifth part of a grain of the extract was given, morning and evening, to each of the boys. The dose was found, in a few days, to be too large, from the dilated state of the pupil and impaired vision which it occasioned in several instances. It was accordingly diminished," &c.—But how much? Not, certainly, to such an amount as *not* to injure the health of the boys; for it is added in another paragraph, "a *large proportion* of the boys who took the belladonna seemed to have more or less *furring of the tongue, impairment of appetite*, and other evidences of slight indisposition,"—Hahnemann having fifty years previously strongly represented to those who would make use of the preventive, that it must, in order to be a preventive, be given in extremely minute doses, so as *not* to injure the health. His instructions are, to give of a solution of belladonna nearly corresponding with the third dilution of his scale of potencies, a drop or two for every year of the person's age who is undergoing the prophylaxis, and not to repeat the dose, as a general rule, above once in 72 hours. His reason for giving such small doses may have been that the object to be attained is to produce as nearly as possible, and in the feeblest degree, a state of the system similar to that which precedes the very earliest period of pure scarlet fever, for which alone belladonna is a homœopathic cure after the disease has fairly begun. Of course, prior to the outbreak of *symptoms* of disease there must be latent preparatory processes going on; and so there must be also similar, latent, preparatory processes before the first effects of a drug, that produces corresponding

* Monthly Journal of Medical Science, 1851.

symptoms, become apparent. The belladonna, therefore, is to be given in such quantity as will meet the poison of scarlet fever at the very threshold, and keep it at bay. Large doses of the drug, by producing the ulterior effects of belladonna, abandon the vantage ground occupied by the smaller, and leave an entrance open to the contagious poison. The amount of injurious influence on the health of the hospital boys must have been considerable when the extract of belladonna was continued in very sensible doses for three months, at the end of which period it was that the last case of the fever occurred. Mr. Bell makes the following very sensible remarks on the subject; and it is surprising that the view he expresses did not induce him to reduce the dose below the injurious degree, or to suspect that he had not used the medicine properly:—"We cannot divest ourselves of the impression, that the continued use of a narcotic, for weeks together, even in small doses, [how small?] must be prejudicial to health, and that thus, while failing to defend the individual against infection, it may render him less able to cope with the disease when it really comes."

Having noticed the error into which Mr. Bell has fallen regarding the proper manner of conducting the experiment, it must be obvious that the preventive method discovered by Hahnemann was *not tried* in this instance; nay, it would appear, on the contrary, that a *large proportion* of the boys were thrown into a state of impaired health, which probably made them more susceptible of the power of the contagion than if they had been let alone. We are not informed how many of the cases of scarlet fever that occurred after the belladonna was given happened among those who had *furred tongue*, and *impaired appetite*, from the abuse of the drug; and we are of course, therefore, left to conjecture how far those whose constitutions were less susceptible of the injurious action of the belladona were protected by it from the disease. In the whole circumstances, however, taken in connexion with the experience of Hahnemann and his followers, we have a right to infer that, where the belladonna did *not* injure the health, but a very small proportion of cases of scarlet fever occurred, as in the numerous experiments I have quoted from Bayle's work; and that the less favourable results of Mr. Bell's experiments than of the latter are to be ascribed, in all probability, to the excessive quantity of belladonna that was given. This conclusion appears to be countenanced, further, by the previous experiments of Dr. Patrick Newbigging, another practitioner of the allopathic school, whose upright and gentlemanly character is a guarantee of the fidelity of his statements. After having had 22 cases of scarlet fever among 91 children, in George Watson's Hospital, in 1849, he began to give the belladonna, and though his doses were much the same as those with which Mr. Bell commenced, he ceased administering it after "more than five weeks" had elapsed, and thus did not continue it half the time that Mr. Bell had done before the last of his cases occurred. Dr. Newbigging had only three new cases of the disease among the 69 remaining children who had not yet had the fever when he began to give the medicine: and these three happened within four days from the first employment of the prophylactic. *All* Mr. Bell's new cases occurred during the *last two months* of his employment of the drug while the disease was still in the house; he continued, indeed, to use it a month longer, but the cases that continued susceptible, or had been made more susceptible of the action of the contagion, seem to have been exhausted in the two previous months. It is not unlikely, considering these facts, that, had Dr. Newbigging continued to give his preparation of belladona for six weeks longer, some more cases of scarlet fever would have occurred, as the drug began to tell injuriously on the health. As it happened, there were none after the first four days of its employment; and one reason of this may be, that his extract of belladonna was not so powerful as Mr. Bell's, for he says nothing whatever of injurious consequences having occurred, but concludes his interesting observations in the following manner:—Previously to his experiments, he says, he had no faith in the prophylactic, notwithstanding "the report made at the Orphan Hospital of Langendorf, in Prussia, in a family of 160 individuals, where belladonna having been administered, immediately on the occurrence of the epidemic, only two took the disease." But, he continues, "I should now consider it my duty to lose no time in making use of this medicine on the first appearance of this disease, and I would strongly recommend the same plan of practice to those of the profession who are connected with similar educational institutions."

That *some* of Mr. Bell's boys were protected by the belladonna, notwithstanding its excessive employment, will immediately appear to be in the highest degree probable, if not certain; and there is no inconsistency between this supposition and the other,—that those who were made ill by the drug were probably rendered more liable to the disease. The former conjecture is founded on a comparison of the proportion of cases of scarlet fever that occurred during Mr. Bell's experiments in George Watson's Hospital, with the proportion that occurred under Dr. J. D. Gillespie in James Donaldson's Hospital, where *no* belladonna was given. Dr. Simpson (I need not always repeat "as usual") shows profound and really astonishing ignorance on the whole of this subject. With the facts I have already noticed staring him in the face, and with the essay of Dr. Gillespie, and the others I have referred to, published in the Journal of which he is himself one of the conductors,—he utters this singularly erroneous sentence:—"We possess no positive evidence in favour of its protective influence; and we know it has entirely failed when tried under the most favourable circumstances;" and then he goes on to specify Mr. Bell's experiments as those which were made in these most favourable circumstances; conceiving that the number of his cases of scarlet fever after the employment of belladonna, was "a large proportion to be attacked in a single epidemic in such an hospital," putting preventives out of view. Among the boys under Mr. Bell's charge there were 57 who had not had scarlet fever previously, and, in the following summary, I exclude from consideration all who had had the disease before:—Of the 57, 22 took scarlet fever after the use of belladonna had been begun, or at the rate of 38 per cent. Among Dr. Gillespie's hospital children 100 had not had scarlet fever previously to the epidemic to which his observations relate, and of these 52 took the disease, no belladonna having been used, or 52 per cent. But this is not all. Dr. Gillespie observes that, besides those which were included under one form or another of fully developed scarlet fever, there occurred "a number of milder cases, probably caused by the same contagion, but where the symptoms were not sufficiently marked to warrant their being ranked among any of the ordinarily received classes of the disease." This is a statement of much importance, especially when it is considered that the epidemic in Donaldson's Hospital was of almost unexampled mildness. Supposing that 7 or 8 cases of sickness, not included among the 52 of ordinary scarlet fever, were, notwithstanding, "caused by the same contagion," we shall thus have 60 per cent. of the children affected by the fever poison, and we are entitled to conclude that, had the epidemic been of the usual severity, the number of decided cases would have been considerably greater than it appears to have been. But neither is this all; for there were peculiarities in the circumstances of Donaldson's Hospital at the time this epidemic occurred, and there are in that institution, besides, certain arrangements which are at all times singularly favourable to obstructing the progress of contagious diseases among its inmates. It possesses accommodation, we are told, for 300 residents, but at the time of the epidemic it contained only 123 children, and 26 adults. Spacious apartments, such as this hospital possesses, thinly inhabited, afforded most unusual facilities for dispersing contagious effluvia, or diluting them to a degree which must deprive them of the power of acting on persons who are but little disposed to be affected by them; and some of the children, we are bound to conclude, from what we know of the advantages of fresh air and good ventilation, must have escaped the disease for that reason. Added to all these important circumstances, there was still another most unfavourable to the diffusion of the disease, thus described by Dr. Gillespie:—"The accommodation for the sick in Donaldson's Hospital cannot be too highly commended. It reflects much credit on the governors who suggested, and on the architect who planned the arrangements. The whole of the upper story of the back of the building is appropriated to that purpose, being farthest removed from the various dormitories and class-rooms. All access to it is completely prevented, save by two stair-cases, one for the boys, the other for the girls, the doors at the foot of which can be kept locked if necessary." It was for this reason partly that Dr. Gillespie did not employ belladonna, for he says, "had belladonna been administered, the experiment would not have been decisive without allowing the healthy children to mingle freely with the infected; but as great facilities were afforded for keeping them entirely separate, such a procedure would not have been warrantable." According to this very sensible view, therefore, some of the children must have been preserved from the disease in Donaldson's Hospital, with its great facilities for preventing the spread of contagious maladies, who would have been affected with scarlet fever in other institutions not so wisely constructed. The plain inference from all that has been said is surely this, that, at the very least, double the proportion of cases of the fever would have occurred in Donaldson's Hospital, where no belladonna was used, that occurred in George Watson's, where belladonna was used, *were it not* for the much inferior virulence of the fever-poison, for the very much larger space the children had to occupy, and for the very complete arrangements for the separation of the sick,—advantages which are declared to have been enjoyed by the former institution. Nor let it be forgotten, in estimating the value of the prophylactic, that George Watson's Hospital had the smaller per centage of fever cases, *notwithstanding* that the medicine was administered in doses that are admitted to have impaired the health of a considerable proportion of the children,—*not* in the manner recommended by the experience of Hahnemann, but in a manner which he expressly warns the physician to avoid.

I think, then, it will be admitted by every reader capable of thinking rationally, and of speaking candidly, that we have a very good case indeed in favour of our belladonna; and that not the weakest part of it is founded on what Dr. Simpson calls very justly, though without seeing to what his superlative is really applicable, "Mr. Bell's *excellent* paper in the Monthly Journal of Medical Science for August 1851." And the reader will perhaps do us, of the despised party, the justice to think that we don't, after all, neglect "Medical Science" so very much as our conceited opponents would have him to believe, and that we know, at least as well as some who rate themselves very highly indeed, how to bring truth somewhat triumphantly out of the clutches of those who would smother it if they could. That belladonna always protects from scarlet fever, or will protect from all forms of it, neither the discoverer of its powers nor any of his followers have ever asserted. And in this respect Hahnemann has the advantage of Jenner, who would allow no possibility of an exception to the universality and the permanence of the protective power of vaccination against small-pox; and congratulates his country "and society at large on their beholding in the mild form of the cow-pox an antidote that is capable of extirpating from the earth a disease which is every hour devouring its victims." No one now entertains either of these opinions of Jenner, yet no one abuses him or contemns his discovery, because he held extravagant notions on the subject. He is not called quack and cheat, because small-pox occurs pretty often after vaccination, and is still common where vaccination is even rendered imperative by law.

So far was Hahnemann from asserting that belladonna was always a preventive of scarlet fever, that he expressly states that he is not aware if his preservative would have the power of averting attacks of a particular form of the disease which distinguished some of the epidemics of 1800. He thought these were different from the pure scarlet fever, which alone he regarded as capable of being prevented by belladonna. Some of his disciples appear to have overlooked this fact; and among them Dr. Elb, who is specified by Dr. Simpson as one of the "more rational homœopathic physicians" who have, according to him, "given up the idea" that belladonna is a prophylactic against the disease. Dr. Elb, however, says nothing of the kind. He gives some account of an epidemic of extraordinary virulence, or of a "malignant character," and not therefore of the nature of the ordinary or "true scarlet fever." Death occurred, he says, in most cases on the third day, in rarer cases as early as the first; and of his whole experience of the powers of belladonna he makes a statement which proves that in that epidemic the grounds he had for forming an opinion were not extensive. He speaks only of "cases having come before him," how many he does not say, in which the children who had taken belladonna had remained unaffected, while "just as often" others took the disease in an unmitigated form, who had been taking belladonna for several weeks previously. The "just as often" goes no further, of course, than the instances of escape, and these, for aught we know, may have been very few; so that the whole experiment is inconclusive, as to the power of belladonna having been ineffectual even against a type of the malady, for the averting of which we have no right to suppose that Hahnemann himself would have believed it adequate. Nor does he utter a single expression to warrant the assertion of Dr. Simpson, that he had given up the idea of belladonna being capable of protecting against scarlet fever of the more ordinary kind. If Dr. Simpson believes Dr. Elb to be one of "the more rational homœopathic physicians," whose mere belief, expressed in vague general terms, and without the details which alone ought to give weight to an opinion on medical subjects, is so authoritative with him as he pretends, is he prepared to accept as equally authoritative the assurances of the same person, that he found calcarea, in one of the gravest forms of the disease, fulfil his expectations "in the most brilliant manner," because as Dr. Elb avers, "of all the children to whom I gave calcarea I did not lose one:" or his high estimate of the utility of zinc in another very dangerous form of the malady, "the effect of which," he says, "exceeded my expectation; for not alone in isolated cases, but in all where

I employed zinc, I had the happiness to save the apparently dying child?" These allegations are from the same "rational" homœopathic physician who made the other regarding the belladonna, and we have precisely the same amount of proof in reference to the former as to the latter, and the mere authority that is good for the one is equally good for the other.

CHAPTER III.

Hahnemann settles in Leipsic in 1810—Poverty and abuse the attendants on his devotion to medical reform—His numerous Essays on Homœopathy, and on speculative systems in medicine, &c.—Publication of the *Organon* in 1810—Small-pox and vaccination as illustrations of homœopathicity among diseases—Dr. Simpson's gross misrepresentations of Hahnemann on this subject—Dr. Mühry and Dr. Willan—The substantial accuracy of Hahnemann's statements regarding small-pox—Remarkable errors of Dr. Simpson—Measles and hooping-cough—Dr. Simpson charges Hahnemann with *falsehood*—Proofs that the charge is untrue—Publication of the *Pure Materia Medica*, &c.—Persecutions at Leipsic—Hahnemann obliged to leave it in 1821—Residence at Cœthen—Publication of his *Chronic diseases*—The *Psoric doctrine* shown to be an *allopathic* doctrine—The *itch*-doctrine not a doctrine of Hahnemann at all—The *Psoric* doctrine substantially correct—Proofs from Willan, Budd, &c., &c.—Removal to Paris in 1835; his death in 1843.

RETURN we now to Hahnemann, who has no doubt been waiting all this time with such impatience as immortals feel at the tardy movements of those who are still cumbered with their load of clay. Driven from Königslutter, as we have seen, by the jealousy of his *brethren*, he journeyed with his family to several places in succession, and found a resting-place in Leipsic in 1810, where he remained till 1821. In the course of his eleven years of a somewhat unsettled life, he found time for the composition of some of his finest essays; for his mind appears never to have reposed in idleness, or to have been discouraged in its onward search after truth by the many hardships he had to encounter. It is but justice to one of the brightest and bravest beings that ever adorned our profession, to ask the reader to pause and to reflect on the circumstances of Hahnemann's lot and occupations at this period of his life. Many suppose that he was cheered on the path he took, if not by the plaudits of his professional contemporaries, at least by the abundant offerings of a public grateful for real or fancied benefits. Nothing can be farther from the truth. In 1803, at the mature age of forty-eight, Hahnemann who was styled by Hufeland,* in 1801, "one of the most distinguished of German physicians," was without a fixed residence, and in absolute poverty. For years he had been spending his strength in seeking to improve his profession rather than his circumstances. With talents and knowledge that could not fail to have enriched him, had riches been his aim, in the trodden path of medical routine, he deliberately preferred the contempt, oppression, and privations which dogged him year after year in the course which he believed to be that of truth and duty. Writing in 1828, he says of himself and his labours, "I have paid no regard either to ingratitude or persecutions in the course of my life, which, although toilsome, has not been without satisfaction on account of the grandeur of the end which I had in view." How many of his modern detractors would have taken the like course at the call of conscience, under the like discouragements and sacrifices?

Among the works which he published in the period referred to, I cannot regard that on *The Effects of Coffee* as a favourable specimen of his lucubrations. No doubt he appears to have drawn his conclusions on the subject from the abuse of that substance; an abuse which is probably seldom practised among us; yet making every allowance on this point, it is surprising that he should have thought coffee capable of producing so many serious chronic disorders as he has ascribed to it. One only apology can be found for him,

* See his Journal, vol. v. 1801.

and I think it is an apology of some weight. How was he to account, in the state of medical science of that day, for the origin and the obstinacy of many constitutional diseases? Some abuse, some contamination of the living substance; from one source or another, there must be; and he was apparently shut up to the conclusion, that it was to be found either in the excessive comsumption of this foreign drug, for (drug it is,) or in the taint derived from *psora*, the supposed constitutional evils of which were undoubted in his time; nay, were acknowledged in what was "an old medical dogma" before Hahnemann was born. Our modern unlearned, with the Professor of Midwifery in their van, seem never to have heard of the psoric doctrine of chronic diseases but in connexion with the speculations of Hahnemann. It is nevertheless an *allopathic* doctrine, that existed, and was entertained by the most eminent allopathic physicians, long before he saw the light; and not only so, but he was even slow of accepting it, and preferred the nicer, if not the wiser, hypothesis regarding the abuse of coffee, to account for much that his predecessors had ascribed to the itch. I shall in the sequel adduce the allopathic claims to this once favourite hypothesis.

Strikingly in contrast with this hasty production are his two tracts, *Æsculapius in the Balance*, and *The Medicine of Experience*, published in 1805 and 1806. They contain a still further development of his own views, and masterly criticisms of the pedantic fooleries and inevitable evils of the common practice. I know no works in medicine of their antiquity for a moment to be compared with them for acute observation and just reasoning, and none of any age that deserve better to be thoughtfully perused by the really earnest physician. The latter of these two essays was the last of his communications to the ordinary medical press; it appeared in Hufeland's Journal, the principal organ of the medical public of that day in Germany. His writings had now brought on him so much abuse and persecution from the followers of the old methods, that Hahnemann withdrew from this time forward both from their periodicals and their society. In 1808 and 1809, he wrote several papers for a magazine of general literature and science, and among them were his admirable treatise *On the Value of the Speculative Systems in Medicine*, and his beautiful *Letter to Hufeland*, "whom," says Dr. Dudgeon, "he never ceased to love and esteem, though in every respect he was a much greater man and finer character than the Nestor of German medicine, as Hufeland was called."

In 1810 he published the first edition of his *Organon of Medicine*, which contained a fuller exposition of his doctrines than any of his previous writings, and in its last edition is to be regarded as expressing his maturest conclusions on the art and science of Homœopathy. As I propose to discuss the homœopathic law, the provings, and the doses, in a separate part of this work, I leave them untouched in this place; and stop for a moment or two to notice only one point, which cannot be so easily introduced elsewhere. Hahnemann, in his endeavour to illustrate the homœopathicity of means of cure to the diseases cured, cites from the relations apparently subsisting in some instances between two successive diseases, —the one of which was followed by the permanent removal of that which had pre-existed,—examples which he thought might be regarded of one disease curing another homœopathically, that is, because of its *similarity* to that other. Among these examples he gives the case of small-pox in its relation to cow-pox, which he thus describes:—"Small-pox coming on after vaccination, as well on account of its greater strength as its great similarity, immediately removes entirely the cow-pox homœopathically, and does not permit it to come to maturity; *but, on the other hand, the cow-pox when near* *maturity does, on account of its great similarity, homœopathically diminish very much the supervening small-pox, and make it much milder, as Mühry (in Robert Willan on Vaccination) and many others testify.*" I have put the latter half of the quotation in italics, because it contains a different proposition from that contained in the other half,—a proposition which is now universally admitted as generally true, and the only proposition given by Hahnemann on the authority of "Mühry (in R. Willan on Vaccination) and many others." Dr. Simpson, in order to make an occasion for attacking Hahnemann's veracity and learning, arrests the attention of his readers on that part of the quotation which asserts what nobody questions. Thus he says, "And, first, let me observe, that, in the above paragraph, Hahnemann refers as his authority to Mühry in 'Dr. Willan on Vaccination.' In the celebrated work of Willan, to which Hahnemann refers, I do not find the name of Dr. Mühry."* When I had read thus far, I was instantly reminded of the celebrated fable of the frog and the ox; in which it is related that the former, (*Rana obstetricians?*) swelling herself out, in order to rival the envied magnitude of the other, burst herself in the effort. Dr. Simpson collapses under a similar catastrophe; for Hahnemann referred to Mühry's translation of Willan, which exists under the following title, "Willan über die Kuhpocken Impfang, aus dem Englischen, mit Zusatzen, (with additions,) von G. F. Mühry." So much for the authority of Mühry's Willan, on a point respecting which *all* are now agreed. Next, for the other half of the paragraph from Hahnemann. Dr.

* He adds in a note, that possibly Mühry's name may occur in some French or German translation of Willan. But that his remark in the text is intended to raise a suspicion of Hahnemann's honesty, I have reason to conclude, *for Dr. Simpson has employed it in private with that view*, as I have been informed by one to whom he made that use of it. He cannot, then, complain of the exposure given above.

Simpson accuses Hahnemann of perverting the "facts and deductions" of *Willan*, while he professes to be giving them as they occur in Willan's work. At p. 158, Dr. Simpson's words are—"The very authority, Dr. Willan, to whose work Hahnemann unscrupulously refers his credulous readers in support of his views, gives facts and conclusions most flatly and avowedly contradictory of these very views." Now, in reply to this disgraceful accusation, the reader will observe, first, that Hahnemann *never refers to Willan at all*, but only to "Mühry and many others," and even their authority he adduces in support of quite *another proposition* than that contained in the former half of the paragraph. In the second place, the *English* edition of Willan's work does actually contain statements, which, so far from being "flatly and avowedly contradictory" of Hahnemann's views, *are decidedly in favour of them*, though Hahnemann does not advert to Willan's statements on the subject, but speaks apparently of experience of his own, which Willan's observations tend to confirm. Thus, on the very same page of Willan's work from which Dr. Simpson quotes what he supposes will serve his purpose, but which has no bearing whatever on the point at issue, Dr. Willan says, "The variolous and vaccine fluids, inoculated about the same time, *do* restrain the action of each other on the human body, so that, in some cases, the *vaccine vesicle* is smaller than usual, and has a very slow progress; in other cases, the areola is scarcely perceptible; while, in others, it is large but premature!" showing, beyond all question, that the cow-pox was to a great extent superseded; or, as Hahnemann averred, is not permitted "to come to maturity," as cow-pox does when unchecked. The "immediately" of Hahnemann, supposing it to be a correct translation, of course cannot have been meant to be taken literally. Some time must elapse before the small-pox can produce its modifying influence on the cow-pox, though it may immediately *begin* to do so. So far, then, as Willan's remark goes, it is thoroughly favourable to the tenor of Hahnemann's argument; and, no doubt, had Hahnemann been referring to Willan's authority, and not to what he had seen himself or learnt from another, (possibly Dr. Mühry,) he would not have made more use of Willan's experience than was justified by Willan's expressions, even had he been capable of such dishonesty, for the translation by Mühry had placed it in the hands of all his contemporaries. The well-known cases reported by Willan, in which small-pox pustules rose within the border of vaccine vesicles, the vaccine having *preceded* the variolous disease, are still more in favour of Hahnemann's views. The best example of this occurrence is mentioned in Willan's Reports on the Diseases of London. He says, "In an adult female, at the Inoculation Hospital, the casual small-pox appeared six days after the vaccine disease had been inoculated, the *two* variolous pustules arose within the circumference of the vaccine pock: when these were maturated, fluid taken from them on the point of a lancet, and inoculated into another person, produced the regular small-pox: at the same time, fluid taken from the vaccine pock, at a little distance from the supervening (small-pox) pustules, gave the vaccine disease in its genuine form, without any eruption." (P. 315.) Alluding to the drawing of a similar case, as given in Willan's work on Vaccination, Dr. Simpson says, "It represents not only the small-pox unable to overcome and annihilate (as it homœopathically *ought* to do) the cow-pox upon the same individual, but it shows it to be unable to do so even when the small-pox pustule is developed *in the very same portion of skin as the cow-pox pustule.*" P. 156.) Now, what actually happened in these cases? Why, just this express confirmation of Hahnemann's doctrine, that the stronger poison, invading a portion of skin *previously* occupied by the vaccine disease, *did* destroy the vaccine disease over so much of the surface as the small-pox pustules required for their development; for within the border of the vaccine disease a spot or spots occurred where vaccine matter was no longer produced, but only the small-pox matter; which is the plainest confirmation that can be of Hahnemann's dogma, in reference to homœopathic *diseases*, that "the stronger morbific potency, when it appears, does, on account of its similarity of action, *involve exactly the same parts* of the organism that were hitherto affected by the weaker morbid irritation, which consequently can no longer influence the system, but is extinguished." This passage is actually given by Dr. Simpson, in connexion with the preceding cases, to show how absurd were Hahnemann's doctrines, and yet it is positively the only rational inference that can be drawn from these very cases. And he adds, "In the instance to which I refer, the small-pox, or stronger morbific power, as Hahnemann declares it to be, did not extinguish the weaker morbific power of the cow-pox, even though situated on the same structure, and though developed in *identically and precisely* the *same* limited spot of skin as the (vaccine) disease," &c. Now, what can any one say to this precious sentence, but that it displays the most extraordinary obtuseness or the grossest perversity? The two diseases did *not* occupy *identically and precisely* the same spot of the skin, for the small-pox *took* a portion of it *from* the pre-existing cow-pox, and obviously *because* it was the *stronger* morbific power, for if it was the *weaker* it could not!

While it is quite true that small-pox does not always materially interfere with the progress of the vaccine disease, for reasons which are as yet inexplicable in some cases, yet it is certain that it does so often enough to justify Hahnemann in adducing the relation between these two affections as illustrations of the homœopathic law among diseases. Even were he as entirely wrong, as he is manifestly right, in this and most of the other instances he mentions of homœopathicity between *diseases*, the error would be of no earthly consequence, in the estimation of those entitled to give an opinion, to his doctrine of homœopathicity between *remedies* and the diseases they cure; for the latter can be tested at pleasure by experiment, and *has been* tested by millions of experiments, which have left not a shadow of doubt as to its truth in the minds of those who have honestly set about the inquiry.

The next instance on which Dr. Simpson condescends, as an evidence of Hahnemann's absurdity and falsehood, (for he does not mince matters in accusing the venerable dead,) is that of measles and hooping-cough. Now, granting that Hahnemann was wrong in supposing that measles, in the experience of Bosquillon, proved a protection against hooping-cough, the error is not worth a straw as an objection to Homœopathy. "The measles," says he, "bears a strong resemblance in the character of its fever and cough to the hooping-cough, and hence it was that Bosquillon noticed, in an epidemic where both these affections prevailed, that many children who then took measles remained free from hooping-cough during that epidemic. They would all have been protected from, and rendered incapable of, being infected by the hooping-cough, in that and all subsequent epidemics, by the measles, if the hooping-cough were not a disease that has only a partial similarity to the measles," &c.—(Organon, p. 1500. Upon this passage Dr. Simpson makes the following commentary:—"Hahnemann adduces as his authority for the truth of his assertion, the evidence of a distinguished French physician, Bosquillon, the translator of the works of Cullen. Unfortunately, however, for Hahnemann's veracity, the author he thus refers to as his authority in the matter, (exactly as in the preceding case of Willan,) does not state what Hahnemann alleges he states."—(P. 160.) He next quotes the passage from Bosquillon to which Hahnemann refers, and which is to the following effect:—Having said that epidemics of measles often precede hooping-cough, he continues, —"From this one might suppose that it has, like the matter of measles, a particular attraction for the mucous glands, and that the two maladies have some affinity. They are, however, independent of each other, and the contagion is different; for many persons have been seen who have been attacked with measles, to *escape the hooping-cough*, and others to acquire this last, *although they have formerly had the measles;* which proves that the generation of the morbific matter is different in the two diseases." Now, I should like to know what there is in Hahnemann's reference to this passage that deserves the monstrous imputation of falsehood. Bosquillon says that he saw *many persons who took measles escape hooping-cough*, and Hahnemann says nothing more on Bosquillon's authority than "that Bosquillon noticed, in an epidemic where both these affections prevailed, that many children who then took measles remained free from hooping-cough during that epidemic," which is precisely what Bosquillon says of epidemics he is supposed to be referring to as having been observed by himself. Bosquillon gives no *explanation* of the exemptions from hooping-cough, after measles, to which he alludes, and Hahnemann *never says* that he does. The explanation is Hahnemann's, the alleged facts are Bosquillon's; and the former, right or wrong, regarded these facts as explicable by the partial similarity between measles and hooping-cough; while he asserts, moreover, just as Bosquillon does, that though many escape hooping-cough who have had measles, *others do not*, a circumstance which he accounts for on his own principles, without any reference to Bosquillon's opinions at all! And yet, without a shadow of excuse, he is deliberately accused of falsehood. If there be *falsehood*, and I leave the reader to settle that point to his own satisfaction, it certainly does not lie with *Hahnemann*.

The minor point however remains, namely, whether measles does or does not protect any persons, for any time, from hooping-cough. Of course Dr. Simpson, "and many a nurse," know, what everybody knows, that hooping-cough occurs after measles, and sometimes along with it. That is not the question; Hahnemann says nothing at variance with that universal experience, but everything that is in harmony with it. The real question is,—Does measles prevent hooping-cough from occurring in any considerable number of cases during the same epidemic season? *That* is what Hahnemann answers in the affirmative; and I venture to say, that neither Dr. Simpson, nor any nurse in Christendom, is prepared to prove that he is in error! I do not maintain that Hahnemann is right, for I do not know that he is; but, on the other hand, Dr. Simpson, and the nurses, cannot *informedly* maintain the reverse, for they don't *know* that he is wrong!

After this lengthened exposure of a very extraordinary degree of artful misrepresentation on the part of the "Tenets," the reader will not be surprised to learn that, in the *addenda* to so peculiar a strain, the same spirit of cunning detraction and distortion keeps up a running accompaniment of "false notes." I can give but a single example. Hahnemann, among the illustrations of the homœopathic law to be found among diseases in their action on one another, mentions ophthalmia (inflamed eyes) as very liable to occur in the course of small-pox; and therefore it is, says he that Dezoteux and Leroy *cured* cases of chronic ophthalmia by the inoculation of small-pox. A very fair conclusion, as I think. Dr. Simpson, in reference to this and many similar instances, without telling his readers the real and special grounds of Hahnemann's view of the reason that such cures followed the small-pox, adduces the local diseases that were thus cured, with a sneer at their *similarity* to *small-pox*. It was not to the *eruption* of small-pox that they were ever compared, but to the frequent accompaniments to the eruption, which the *same poison* was capable of producing. But I must stop here, though I could fill a volume with exposures of the calumnies and misrepresentations which occur on every page of the medical apocrypha.

"With a wide-spread reputation," says the biographer of Hahnemann, "he now re-entered Leipsic, where a crowd of patients and admirers flocked around him, and the flood-tide of fortune seemed at length to set in towards him. Professor Hecker of Berlin wrote, in 1810, a violent diatribe against the *Organon*, which displays more wrath and untempered hostility than wit or good-breeding, and was replied to in a masterly style by young Frederick Hahnemann, who undertook the defence of his father; for the latter treated all attacks, whether on his character or his works, with silent contempt; though it could not be said he viewed them with indifference, for there is every reason to believe that the poisoned shafts of envy and calumny rankled in his soul, and communicated acerbity to a disposition that was naturally overflowing with love to his fellow-men. Hecker's attack was the signal for numerous others of the same nature, written with greater or less ability, and with more or less fairness; but it would be wearisome to recapitulate even the titles of the articles and pamphlets that issued from the press, intended by their authors to crush the presumptuous innovator." They had not that effect, however, either on him or his system, for He who rules the raging of the sea, and prescribes its bounds, equally governs the wrath of man, and curbs it with His fiat, "thus far, no farther shalt thou go." Hahnemann, then, steadily held on his course; and in 1811 published the first volume of his *Pure Materia Medica*, which contained the results of the provings or experiments he had made on himself and his friends, with a number of medicines, together with the symptoms he had gathered from the records of poisoning by the same substances. At this time he meditated founding a college and an hospital, with the view of training young physicians to the practice of Homœopathy; but failing of the means, he satisfied himself of the more attainable object of giving a course of lectures on the new science. In order to qualify himself legally for this purpose, he had to comply with a regulation of the Faculty of Medicine, which required a thesis to be written and defended by those who aspired to lecture on medical subjects. He chose for the theme of his essay, *The Helleborism of the Ancients.* The thesis was written in Latin, and contains an elaborate medico-historical dissertation on the employment of white hellebore, by the ancient Greeks and Romans; in the course of which, by many learned references, he proves the identity of their plant with our veratrum album, and details its various effects and uses as recorded by the Greek and Roman writers of antiquity. I have the authority of one of the ripest scholars of this country for stating, that this thesis is remarkable for the display of "extensive reading in the ancient authors, and not only those more immediately connected with his own professional pursuits, but also in the classical writers of antiquity;" and, intimate as the gentleman to whom I refer is with some of the most learned physicians of Europe, he adds, "I know very few medical men possessed of the same amount of learning." His was no mere lexicon learning, which enables the really ignorant or half-educated to acquire among the vulgar the fame of erudition in Greek or in Hebrew, when they barely know the alphabet of either; but the learning of the hard student and the man of genius, for Hahnemann, as Dr. Forbes justly admits, "*was* a man of genius and a scholar." I should like to be present when the medical faculty of St. Andrew's or Aberdeen gets such a thesis to criticise from some despised follower of Hahnemann; as I should like to have been, were it not for the present penalty of old age that the enjoyment would have demanded, when Hahnemann defended his thesis before the faculty of Leipsic. "This thesis," says Dr. Dudgeon, "he defended on June the 26th, 1812, and it drew from his adversaries an unwilling acknowledgment of his learning and genius, and from the impartial and worthy Dean of the Faculty a strong expression of admiration. When a candidate defends his thesis, he has what are called opponents among the examiners, who dispute the various opinions broached in the thesis; but the most of Hahnemann's opponents were so polite as to confess they were entirely of his way of thinking, while a few who wished to say something for form's sake, merely expressed their dissent from some of Hahnemann's philological views. This trial, which his enemies had fain hoped would end in the exposure of his ignorance of the shallow charlatan, proved incontestably the superiority of Hahnemann over his opponents, even on their own territory, and was a brilliant inauguration of the lectures which he forthwith commenced to deliver to a circle of admiring students and gray-headed old doctors, whom the fame of his doctrines and his learning attracted round him." From among the numerous disciples who now resorted to him for instruction, he chose some to assist him in his labour of acquiring a knowledge of the powers which medicine possesses of altering the health of the human body, for the use of his prospective publications on the *Materia Medica.* While residing at Leipsic, from 1810 to 1821, he gave various valuable essays to the world, besides a second edition of the *Organon*, and five more volumes of medicinal provings.

The jealousy of the allopathic physicians of Leipsic did not remain very long in abeyance, and they gave expression to their feelings in the same magnanimous way as their colleagues had done at Königslutter and other places. The apothecaries, as usual, were made the instruments of their persecution, but the arrival among them of the celebrated Austrian Field-Marshal, Prince Schwarzenberg, who went to

Leipsic in order to place himself under the medical care of Hahnemann, his life having been despaired of by the practitioners of the old school, interrupted for a time the progress of their designs. Their chagrin at the improvement which the prince's health experienced for a time may be as easily conceived as their subsequent satisfaction when he died, of the organic disease which even Hahnemann could not remedy.

So inevitable an event was, of course, as in similar circumstances it still is, the signal for a general outcry of pretended indignation against the new practice; and the apothecaries, taking advantage of the impression industriously propagated among their ignorant fellow-citizens, that Hahnemann's method had hastened if it did not actually cause the death of the illustrious patient, had now little difficulty in procuring an injunction against his dispensing his own medicines. "Hahnemann could not write prescriptions for his medicines seeing that the privileged apothecaries did not keep them, and could not be trusted with their preparation, as they were his bitterest foes. His practice was therefore gone, and though he was urgently advised to dispense his medicines secretly, yet he had too great a respect for the authority of the law to act contrary to the verdict of those whose business it was to enforce it, even though he believed that they had misinterpreted its spirit; nothing was left for him, therefore, but to quit Leipsic, a town which was now endeared to him by many pleasing associations connected with the spread and development of his great reform; and his fatherland, Saxony, now offered no place where the most illustrious of its sons could live in peace. Under these discouraging circumstances, the reigning Prince of Anhalt Cœthen, who was an ardent admirer of the system, offered Hahnemann an asylum in the tiny capital of his tiny dominions, and accordingly to Cœthen Hahnemann proceeded in

1821. It must have been with a heavy heart that he left Leipsic, the goal of his youth's ambition and the scene of his manhood's triumphs. It must have cost him a pang to leave that dear fatherland which he loved with that longing ardour that the Swiss bears to his Alps. To exchange the busy commercial and literary capital of northern Germany for the lifeless and dismal little town of a petty principality was but a sorry exchange indeed. . . . Though Leipsic has now the honour of containing his bronze effigies, and though Leipsic's magistrates and municipal authorities joined in the inauguration of Hahnemann's monument in 1851, this will hardly suffice to efface the stain of bigotry and intolerance that attaches to the town and its authorities by their expulsion of the greatest of Leipsic's citizens in 1821.*

At Cœthen he remained till 1835, leading a life of still greater retirement and devotion to study, than that by which he had been always distinguished. He seldom left his house except to visit his patron when he required his services: the many patients who repaired to Cœthen, in order to receive his advice, visited him at his own residence; and his only walks were in his garden, which, he used to observe, "though very narrow was infinitely high." During his sojourn in this place of refuge he published three successive editions of the *Organon*, as well as a second and a third of his *Materia Medica*, and numerous articles in the literary journal formerly adverted to. In 1828 one of his most celebrated works, *Chronic Diseases, their Peculiar Nature and Homœopathic Treatment*, made its appearance. In this publication he gave forth his opinions on the ancient doctrine of *psora*, as a constitutional taint to which a vast variety of the most important, chiefly chronic, diseases owed their existence. So far was he from claiming the credit of being the originator of this pa-

* Dr. Dudgeon's Biographical Sketch.

thological doctrine, that he adduces, in support of his own decision in its favour, nearly *a hundred allopathic* authorities, his predecessors, as having more or less explicitly declared their conviction of its truth, or given examples in illustration of it. It is ignorantly sneered at by Dr. Simpson, and the many who take up the cuckoo-cry of derision against everything that Hahnemann taught, as the *itch-doctrine* of the homœopathists, whereas it is neither an itch-doctrine in a candid and intelligent sense, nor is it a peculiarly homœopathic doctrine. "I call it psora," says Hahnemann, "with the view of giving it a general designation;"* and that he did not regard it as *synonymous* with, or limited in its meaning to, *the* itch, every one knows who has perused his treatise on the subject. One sentence of his is sufficient of itself to settle this point, and to leave those who have so industriously misrepresented his opinions utterly without excuse. "I am persuaded that not only are *the majority of the innumerable skin diseases* which have been described and distinguished by Willan, but also almost all the pseudo-organizations, &c., &c., with few exceptions, merely the products of the multiform psora." (P. 13.)

Like Milton invoking Urania, Hahnemann might say, in reference to the *psoric* hypothesis: "The meaning, not the name, I call;" and the meaning he plainly and expressly announced was this, that the majority of chronic diseases that appear as palsies, asthmas, dyspepsias, consumptions, headaches, epilepsies, vertigoes, &c., &c., are due to a morbid matter (or miasm, as he termed it) existing in the body; the same as that which, when it comes to the skin, produces the almost numberless varieties of eruptions known as scaly diseases, leprosies, milk-crusts, scald-heads, ringworms, itch, pustules, and the like. Psora was an ancient term used almost indiscriminately for every diversity of chronic, and almost every

* Maladies Chroniques, t. i. p. 11.

kind of acute, cutaneous disease; and no term appeared more convenient as a "general designation" for the radical malady of which all these local diseases, both internal and external, were occasional expressions or developments, than that which already, for ages, had associated with it the idea of constitutional taint (dyscrasia,) that might show itself in operation on the surface, or indicate its activity within by the throes of some hidden organ. Dr. Simpson is heartily welcome to rescue his protégé, the itch-insect, from the society of so many fulsome maladies, since he has taken a fancy to that comely production; and, when he does, the psoric hypothesis of chronic diseases will remain substantially *one of the most incontrovertible doctrines even in modern pathology*. This is not the occasion,—any reasonable space will not admit of it,—on which to discuss this doctrine completely and satisfactorily; but I throw down the gauntlet before the Professor of Midwifery, and challenge him to argue the point, were it only for the honour of his sect, if he believes them to be committed to the rejection of the psoric hypothesis. But they are not committed to anything of the kind. The psoric hypothesis, *essentially as held by Hahnemann*, *was* held by his allopathic predecessors; *is* held by his allopathic successors, and *among them only, as an* ITCH-*doctrine*, and *must* be held in some degree by every medical man of common sense and common information.

It *was* held by his allopathic predecessors: take an example from a work that was published before Hahnemann was born, by Frederick Hoffmann, who laid, as we shall see in another chapter, "the basis of the pathology at present taught in the schools of medicine."* After adverting to the occurrence of pains in the joints on the cessation of ulcers in the legs, he adds, "We have known, likewise, atrocious pains of the

* Thompson's Cullen, t. i. p. 197. 1832.

joints suddenly removed on the occurrence of psora or itch (psora vel scabic) having the character of white lepra. For, whilst shifting of the morbid matter from internal to external parts is very beneficial; on the contrary, what turns from the external to the internal parts is most pernicious." * Having said, again, that "the true, proximate, and immediate cause of these evils," which he describes as pustules, itch, papulæ, &c., "is nothing else than an impure, viscid, and acrid serum," (Hahnemann never was so minute,) which is proved to be virulent and violent, "because almost all the most serious and deadly diseases, both chronic and acute, and these the most firmly rooted in the system of nervous parts, may be relieved on the matter being expelled, according to the habit of body; and on the contrary, the matter being repelled to the interior parts, the same diseases may be excited:" he adds, "Experience itself teaches this truth; for innumerable observations of the most credible authors exist, which record that spasmodic asthma, inflammation of the joints, gout, and many other dieases, have been removed on the appearance of itch (scabies,) and, on the other hand, have arisen on the ich being suppressed." † Among the many "other diseases" which Hoffman ascribes to the itch, throughout his *Opera Omnia*, are epilepsy, amaurosis, hematuria, consumption, rickets, hooping-cough, apoplexy, rheumatism. Though he often employs the term *scabies* (itch) in designating the disease, which was thus the frequent source of those serious maladies, he did not, any more than Hahnemann by the equivalent term *psora*, mean to specify a particular kind of skin disease, but one or other of the many eruptions to which the surface was liable. Thus, he speaks of a *psora* or *scabies* like white lepra (Lepra alba;) so that in fact almost any chronic skin disease

* Opera Omnia, t. ii. sect. 2, cap. viii.

† Opera Omnia, De Pustulis, &c.

was *psora* or *scabies* with him, as with the older writers in general. Let the above suffice as a specimen of Hahnemann's hundred allopathic authorities for the *psoric* hypothesis. I have given Hoffmann merely because I have his works at hand.

Next, the psoric doctrine *is* held by the *allopathic* successors of Hahnemann. Schönlein, the allopathic professor of pathology and therapeutics in the University of Berlin, in a clinical lecture on a case of organic disease of the heart with dropsy, delivered himself thus:—"What is the cause of this affection? On looking backwards, we find no other complaint than the itch. Latterly, the admission of consequences of the itch, that *old medical dogma*, is not only become dubious, but has been abandoned and turned into ridicule. Among the *older physicians*, we particularly notice Autenreith, who wrote a masterly treatise on this subject, *so that it was remarkably impudent in Hahnemann to pretend that he was the first to point out the consequences of the itch.* . . . I must confess that, according to my own observations, and to those of many other physicians who deserve the fullest confidence, *I have no doubt whatever about the existence of consequences of the itch.*"* The work of Autenreith, to which reference is made in the preceding passage, as containing an anticipation of Hahnemann's doctrine regarding psora, has the following very explicit declaration on the subject, showing how completely the psoric hypothesis owes its parentage to Allopathy:—"The most formidable, and, in our country, the *most frequent source of the chronic diseases* of the adult, *are the itch eruptions*† badly treated by sulphur ointment, or by other active greasy applications. I have so often seen the misery which the itch occasions to the lower

* Lancet, 1844, p. 211.

† "Kratzauschläge." See his treatise. Tübingen, 1807.

classes, and to those who follow sedentary occupations; and I see it daily in such a manifold and melancholy aspect, that I do not hesitate a moment to declare it loudly as a subject worthy of the observation of every physician, and even of every *magistrate*, who lays to heart the health of those committed to his care." This is sufficiently decisive, and curious too, considering the recent attempts to palm the *itch*-doctrine on Hahnemann. Schönlein *claims it for Allopathy*, and, with the ignorance which is universal among allopathic writers who would depreciate Hahnemann, accuses the discoverer of Homœopathy of arrogating to himself the discovery also of the *itch*-doctrine, though he expressly refers to nearly a hundred *preceding* authors in confirmation of his own views regarding it. Schönlein's lecture is curious in another respect. The discrimination of *a particular disease*, which should be distinguished as *itch* from all other skin diseases, by its *insect* (or rather arachnid) more especially, is entirely a modern accomplishment; indeed, as a general attainment, it is but a very few years old, and *was not recognised at all by Hahnemann;* perhaps it was even unknown to him that the itch could ever be so distinguished, notwithstanding that the insect had long been ascertained to occur in connexion with an eruption on the skin. By the term *psora*, Hahnemann did not mean the special disease which Schönlein and his contemporaries discriminate as *the itch*, but without distinction scaly, papular, and tettery, eruptions of all kinds. It is plain, therefore, that the *itch*-doctrine is a *modern allopathic one*, and by no means the doctrine of Hahnemann, which is, on the contrary, the *psoric*-doctrine. Dr. Simpson must, therefore, keep his itch to himself; we have nothing to do with it, and never had, in the same sense as modern Allopathy has a right to it. Hahnemann, indeed, in treating of the primary form of psora, which he regarded as contagious, probably to account for its extensive prevalence, adverts to an eruption of vesicles or pustules distinguished by *itching*, (when there is an eruption at the outset, which, however, he holds not to be always the case,) but as that is a symptom common to *the itch*, and to many pustular eruptions, as well as in a very excessive degree to the vesicular *eczema*, it affords no evidence whatever that the skin disease he speaks of as the primary form of cutaneous psora was the same as that which we now distinguish as the itch. The presence of the *Acarus or Sarcoptes scabiei*, termed the *itch-insect*, is now generally held to be the distinctive characteristic of the itch; and Hahnemann, knowing nothing of the essential part it plays in that disease, cannot be regarded as having necessarily referred to what is now called itch, especially when we remember how closely eczema often resembles itch —the insect being put out of view. What makes this remark entitled to more weight is the fact, that *eczema* may be *contagious*, as well as the scabies or itch which it so closely resembles. Mr. Erasmus Wilson, in his work on Skin Diseases, admits this fact, although he limits the action of the eczematous matter which excites the disease in another to mere non-specific irritation. (P. 171.) And still farther to show that Hahnemann's observations did not refer specially to the *itch*, as distinguished from itching vesicular and pustular diseases in general, it is worthy of being noticed, that the minute doses of sulphur he recommends as having been successful in the cure of the primary eruption, are incapable of curing *itch* with its insect, though they do cure *eczema.*

One important point in which Hahnemann's views of psora differed from those of his predecessors was this, that while they regarded internal diseases as producible only when the psoric matter was *driven in* from the surface of the body, he thought that the constitution might be elsewhere seriously disordered by the "miasm," while the skin was also affected, and that it was not *necessary* that the skin should ever be affected, though it generally or often was. The "miasm," once ensconced in the body, might, in this opinion, act anywhere according to circumstances, internally or externally; though of course when its principal operations were conducted on the surface, the more deeply seated parts enjoyed comparative repose. His psoric doctrine, therefore, was almost identical in its principles with the modern *dyscrasic* pathology, which recognises a *morbific admixture*, taint, or poison of some kind, as the cause of a great many chronic diseases. Indeed, there is at present a *mania* among physicians on this subject. Almost every disease is now being traced to morbific matters and animal poisons in the blood. The *solids* of the body are, in the estimation of some pathologists, and these of no mean note, the mere creatures and appendages of the fluids, and are all but utterly deprived of any other standing in health or disease, than as the field on which the fluids execute their *devoirs* when they happen to be sound, or perform their dyscrasic ebullitions when they are diseased.

The reader who is curious on the subject will find some very ingenious arguments and speculations by Professor Paget and Dr. W. Budd, in support of the doctrine that a morbid material in the blood is the cause of many diseases of the skin, bones, joints, arteries, &c., not always ascribed to such a source.* Dr. Budd, after expressing his opinion that this morbid material produces skin diseases by entering into union with portions of the cutaneous tissue, says, that the morbid matter is liable from various causes to be repelled from the surface, and, in consequence, to produce various disorders in internal parts. In confirmation of this latter statement, he refers to Willan "On Cutaneous Diseases" for illustrative instances, and gives the following interpretation of the occurrence:—"That the peculiar morbid matter of the disease,

*Medical Gazette, 1850; and Medico-Chirurgical Transactions, 1842.

which was before detained in the part affected, and held in union with it, being now suddenly loosed and set afloat in the general circulation, has become free to fix on internal organs, or, circulating anywhere with the blood, to affect the system at large."* But it is not only from the skin that he believes the morbid matter to be subject to repulsion. It may be from deeper-seated parts likewise, as from the tissues of the joints in gout, as he refers to "repelled gout" as explicable on the same principle as that which is expressed in the above quotation. Finally, *repulsion* of the morbid matter is not more essential to this pathology of the allopathic school, than it was to the similar pathology of Hahnemann. In the estimation of Dr. Budd and others, important internal organs, such as the aorta and other arteries, and the lungs, may become the seats of the most serious diseases by the morbid matter attaching itself to them in the first instance. It is thus that Dr. Budd, as others had done before him, accounts for the atheromatous patches on the interior of blood-vessels: it is thus that Baumes and others in later times, as Bordeu and Pujol before, explain the occurrence of pulmonary consumption; and it is thus that the origin of the many local diseases which are included under the name of scrofula is explained, as, by Pujol, when he says, "The slow but destructive poison which gives birth to scrofula, attacks indifferently all parts of the human body;" and by Müller, who is said by Dr. Tyler Smith to suppose "that struma (scrofula) is produced by the presence of an acrid or irritant principle in the liquor sanguinis" or blood. Here, then, we have all the essentials of Hahnemann's psoric pathology in the doctrines of his allopathic contemporaries or successors. The *only* difference (contagion excepted) between him and them being this, that what he, in general terms, alludes to as dependent

* Medico-Chirurgical Transactions, p. 111.

on *a* morbid matter in the body, they seem to regard as due to several. The difference is, however, more in appearance than reality, for the term *psora*, by which Hahnemann's hypothesis is designated, is extremely indefinite, and seems never to have been employed expressly to distinguish any one special morbid condition; while all that he says of his psoric miasm may, without any violence to his pathological or practical doctrines, be understood as said of several, or even many miasms. The only *essential* particular in the psoric pathology is the recognition of *morbid matter*, *materies morbi*, of some kind or kinds, as the *constitutional taint*, or dyscrasia, on which chronic diseases depend for their manifestation, their obstinacy, and their liability to recur after being apparently removed; and it is of no consequence whatever to the general doctrine whether the matter be single or manifold.*

Without believing that the modern doctrinal pathology of the allopathic physicians to whom I have referred is correct in every particular, or in reference to every disease to which they have extended it, I am prepared to contend that it is just in the main, and *must* be held by every well-informed and observant physician. In saying so much in favour of this modern pathology, as held by allopathic physicians, I say, in effect, that I believe, and am prepared to show, that Hahnemann's psoric doctrine is, in the main, just, and that it must be held by every intelligent physician.† For Hahnemann's

* Hahnemann appears to have believed, indeed, that the *psoric miasm*, or morbid poison, is *not* single; for he speaks of it as contagious in its primary form, and not contagious in the multiplicity of its secondary forms.—*Chronic Diseases*, p. 67.

† I do not, of course, include in the above affirmation respecting Hahnemann's psoric doctrine, his opinion that the *materies morbi* of so many chronic diseases as may be reasonably held to depend on a *materies morbi*, or morbid matter, in the body, always originates from contagion. It *may* in some instances; but it is not necessary to the general principle of a dyscrasic patho-

doctrine differs in no one essential particular from theirs, and has no more to do with the *itch* than theirs,—nay, much less; for Schönlein specifies the *individual disease*, now distinguished as *itch* by its insect, as capable of causing internal diseases, which Hahnemann *never did.*

I need not enlarge upon the proofs of the general soundness of this pathology, both Hahnemannic and Allopathic, because I believe that no one worthy of being argued with will dispute it; at least I shall wait until it is disputed by any respectable opponent. The kind of facts, however, on which the doctrine rests, I may briefly notice. First, then, they are analogical; as, for instance, when eruptions on the skin or internal diseases are produced by the reception of poisons or medicines into the body, as mercury, arsenic, lead, iodide of potassium, and a multitude of others. These are examples in which morbific substances are known to be introduced into the body, and the disorders which arise as a consequence are too familiar to admit of any doubt as to their being caused by those substances; while, in some instances, the *presence* of the morbific agent is detected, by chemical means, in that part especially which is the chief seat of the medicinal disease. Secondly, the facts are such as to admit of no question that a morbid matter, of the nature of an *animal poison*, and not merely drugs or inorganic poisons, is the cause of disease, as when blood is transfused from a diseased animal into a healthy one, and, in consequence of its containing a morbid matter, produces diseases in the latter. And, thirdly, the facts which remain, if less pointedly and indubitably proofs of a morbid matter being the cause of the diseases to which they relate, than those direct evi-

logy, or to any practical bearing of the doctrine, that contagion should play a part in it. All that Hahnemann says about contagion, and the primary form of the psoric maladies, is mere hypothesis, derived apparently from a supposed analogy to syphilis, and is the only really weak part of his doctrine.

dences are which have just have been noticed, are far more satisfactorily explained in accordance with the doctrine which the latter serve to establish than with any other. Examples of this last class are the cases in which the sudden disappearance of eruptions from the surface has been followed by serious and even fatal internal disease. Willan records an instance in which repelled nettle-rash was fatal, and mentions, among others of a similar kind, the case of a girl affected with lepra, who had the eruption repelled by drinking cold water while she was overheated, and in consequence became affected with "a perpetual disposition to vomiting," which resisted all remedies, and ceased in about eight months only to be replaced by convulsions of the limbs and body, which remained unmitigated after several months of treatment. There are probably few practitioners who have not had occasion to remark equally or even more severe consequences to follow the repulsion of chronic eczema of the scalp, and one or other of the forms of strophulus which affect infants. Of the latter, Willan observes:—"If it be by any means suddenly repelled from the surface, diarrhœa, vomiting, spasmodic affections of the bowels, and often general disturbance of the constitution succeed; but on its reappearance those internal complaints immediately cease." . . . . "On these remarks," he adds, "a necessary caution is founded, not to expose infants with the eruption upon them to a stream of cold air, nor to plunge them into a cold bath, the most violent symptoms and even fatal consequences having occasionally resulted from such imprudent conduct." * A single additional instance from the same author is worthy of being quoted, as it illustrates the doctrine of Hahnemann on the agency of a psoric poison in producing internal disease independently of the primary occurrence of an eruption. Treat-

* On Cutaneous Diseases, pp. 20, 178, 402.

ing of Lichen agrius, he says of a female who was ultimately the subject of it:—"During the year 1793, she had often complained of pains in the head and stomach, with a sense of depression and faintness. These symptoms were occasionally troublesome to her till the spring of 1794, when they were suddenly relieved by an appearance of numerous red, tingling papulæ on the arms and wrists. . . . At the beginning of the year 1795, in a severe frost, the eruption assumed a pustular form . . . . The ulcerations succeeding them were partially covered with blackish scabs, but continued to discharge a watery fluid for several months, and did not wholly heal till the end of the year. Since that time she has been affected with pains of the limbs, headache, languor and indigestion. These complaints are, from time to time, removed, in consequence of the appearance of papulæ on the arms and other parts of the body," &c.*

By the time that the work on Chronic Diseases was published, Homœopathy had a goodly number of professional disciples, among whom a diversity of opinion prevailed regarding the soundness of the psoric hypothesis. Twenty or thirty years ago, *solidism*, or the doctrine which regards disease as primarily and peculiarly an affection of the properties of the living tissues, was generally, if not universally the pathology of physicians in every country of Europe. It had succeeded, and gradually supplanted, the *humoral* pathology of former times, and some of the followers of Hahnemann had difficulty in entertaining the conception involved in the revived psoric pathology, that chronic diseases, which they had been accustomed to consider as affections peculiar to the solids of the body, depended in any degree upon so moveable a substance, as Hahnemann's doctrine supposed to be so essential an element of disease. The *facts* to which he appealed in

* On Cutaneous Diseases, p. 45.

support of his views, they of course knew to be unquestionable, but they had been accustomed to interpret them on a different principle, and to ascribe to the agency of the nervous system, in particular, what the resuscitated doctrine referred to a fluctuating miasm or poison. To this day, homœopathic physicians remain divided on the subject of the psoric hypothesis; but I have no doubt that, in proportion as they reflect upon it more, in connexion with a close observation of the phenomena of disease, they will come to be more and more at one in regarding the doctrine, whether they shall continue to distinguish it as the psoric, or shall learn to know it by a different name, as essentially sound and indispensable to just conceptions of the requisities for successful practice. Many of the allopathic party, as has been shown, have embraced pathological opinions that are almost identical with the psoric doctrine, and the general tendency of pathology in the present day is so strongly towards *humorism*, that the risk is of physicians running to such extremes on the subject as to forget that man possesses "an animated nervous frame," as well as a "chemical mixt," in his constitution.

In 1831 the cholera invaded Germany from the East: "And on its approach," says Dr. Dudgeon, "Hahnemann, guided by the unerring therapeutic rule he had discovered, at once fixed upon the remedies that should prove specifics for it, and caused directions to be printed and distributed over the country by thousands, so that, on its actual invasion, the homœopathists and those who had received Hahnemann's directions were fully prepared for its treatment and prophylaxis; and thus there is no doubt many lives were saved, and many victims rescued from the pestilence. On all sides, statements were published testifying to the immense comparative success that had attended the employment of the means recommended by Hahnemann before he had seen or treated a single case. This one fact speaks more for Homœopathy and the truth of the law of nature on which the system is founded, than almost any other I could offer, viz.: that Hahnemann, from merely reading a description of one of the most appallingly rapid and fatal diseases, could confidently and dogmatically say, such and such a medicine will do good in this stage of the disease, such and such other medicine in that; and that the united experience of hundreds of practitioners in all parts of Europe should bear practical testimony to the accuracy of Hahnemann's conclusions."

In 1835, Hahnemann had reached the patriarchal age of eighty, and his long and noble life was therefore wearing towards its close. He had now been a widower for five years, having lost the faithful partner of his indigence and his plenty,—the sharer of his persecutions and his honours, in 1830. There was one act more of his life-drama to be accomplished which his friends had not anticipated: he became the spouse of Mlle. Melanie d'Hervilly, who bore him off, in his old age, as her captive, to a new sphere of occupation, and a new style of existence. She had procured for him, from M. Guizot, the permission to practise in Paris; and in that gay capital the recluse of Cœthen tasted, ere the curtain fell, some of the pleasures of society, though in the moderation that was consistent with his previous character. And there he died, on the 2d of July, 1843, at the age of eighty-nine; full of years, it is plain, and if not full of honour in the estimation of the world at large and of his own times, not the only instance of humanity committed to the tomb observed of few, though destined in after ages to dignify the spot where its dust reposed.

A word or two more on a single point in his intellectual constitution, and I leave this greatest of physicians to the candid consideration of the reader. I refer to that characteristic of the German mind which makes intellects, adapted perhaps more than any other to the successful exploration of whatever is profound in philosophy, or difficult in science, impatient of ignorance even where knowledge is impossible, most eager and enterprising often where the darkness is thickest and the ground least secure, where it has, in short, to trust to the wings of venturous conjecture more than to the solid footing of observation, for reaching the goal at which it aims. That Hahnemann possessed this intellectual peculiarity is certain; that he exercised it seldom is equally true. That it led him into some mistakes is possible enough; that it was of essential service to him in his discoveries need not, and cannot, be denied. Without it, the homœopathic law would have flitted through the world a "viewless spirit," doing good rarely and by stealth, its mission unfulfilled. Without it, the extreme attenuation of medicinal bodies, needful for their general utility as homœopathic remedies, would have remained undiscovered; for it must have been speculation, sprouting from some "seed-corn" of fact, that shot so far away above all former experience to the conception of the "infinitesimal," the proof of which was to be leisurely inquired into by experiment. In what particulars it *mis*led him, is not so easily determined or agreed upon. I would say, though many homœopathic physicians will dispute the opinion, that it misled him in the "dynamization" hypothesis, or that which holds that medicines, by being triturated and shaken, acquire an increase of potency on each successive dilution. This doctrine, as I think, is inconsistent with the results of observation, and lands its disciples in contradictions,—it did so even to Hahnemann. Being a mere *explanatory* hypothesis, however, it imposes no necessary restrictions on practice, because physicians will, of course, use the potency which is adapted to the requirements of each case of disease, irrespectively of hypothetical explanations of the reason why one potency acts better than another. The difference of opinion which still exists among us regarding the soundness of this doctrine of dynamization is some evidence of the difficulty there must be in arriving at a correct decision on the subject; the reason of which I shall notice in another chapter.

If the mental tendency to which I have been adverting, has misled Hahnemann in any of his doctrines, we have but to apply the principles he himself so strongly inculcates, in order to arrive ultimately at a correction of the error. Nothing is more remarkable in his writings than his earnest appeals to observation as the only test of accuracy in medicine; his denunciations of every method of practice that is not founded on the truths of experience; and the contemptuous manner in which he regards theories, speculations, and systems, which cannot be shown to be facts, as the assumed guides to the employment of remedies. Let his followers obey his injunctions, and take nothing on trust, even from Hahnemann himself, but try every doctrine by the test of observation and experiment.

CHAPTER IV.

Eleven notable charges against Homœopathy—Hahnemann's change of opinion; his treatment of Allopathy; his morbid anatomy; his erroneous notions of the moon; the character of some of his disciples; erroneous estimate of him by Dr. Mure; Homœopathy countenanced by great folks and by the clergy; Homœopathists don't agree in every thing; Homœopathy not universally adopted; Homœopathy is witchcraft; Homœopathy is avarice.

In the sketch I have given in the two preceding Chapters of the history of Hahnemann and of his doctrines, I have limited myself to an account of some only of the principal particulars of both, and have reserved for a separate part of this work the consideration of his provings of medicines, the doses employed by homœopathic physicians, and the homœopathic law. Before proceeding to the discussion of these topics, I shall advert to some points which are paraded by Dr. Simpson, with so much apparent urgency as to warrant the belief that the view he takes of them must be regarded by him as of essential consequence to the success of his efforts to damage the credit of the homœopathic system.

It appears,—1*stly*, That Hahnemann, during more than half a century of very prolific authorship, of ever-increasing experience, and more ripening views, was not uniformly of the same opinion on some of the obscurest and most difficult subjects within the reach of human thought and observation.

2*dly*, That he was so notable an exception to the rule that is observable among physicians, as to write very smart things against the doctrines and customs of those who differed from him, and to extol in very confident terms what he regarded as much wiser and better.

3*dly*, That he was not profoundly acquainted with a department of the anatomical science which was still in its infancy when he had reached the ordinary extreme of human longevity.

4*thly*, That on some matters *not* peculiarly or exclusively connected with Homœopathy he was actually so unlike every other human being of his day as to hold opinions that are now very questionable, if not plainly erroneous.

5*thly*, That he and his system, differing in this respect from every other physician and practice, have disciples whose zeal is a good deal more prominent than their knowledge and discretion.

6*thly*, That Hahnemann and Homœopathy are not and never were "divine," but unquestionably finite, mundane, fallible, and therefore, because totally dissimilar to other physicians and their methods in this particular, quite beneath the respect of reasonable mortals.

7*thly*, That Homœopathy, in violent contrast to Allopathy, has been and is patronised by men of rank and literary eminence, and—most awful of all—"clergymen."

8*thly*, That homœopathic physicians are not all of the same opinion upon all homœopathic subjects,—a defect which the unanimity of their allopathic brethren renders disreputable and glaring.

9*thly*, That in some countries Homœopathy has but a few adherents, while, with the grossest violation of consistency, in others it has a great many.

10*thly*, That Homœopathists have trokings with "spirits," and deal in witchcraft, while it is becoming better known every day that the "regular" doctors are no witches.

11*thly and lastly*, That Homœopathists, in contempt of the custom followed and enjoined by their allopathic colleagues, universally, add to the misfortunes of the already too unfortunate and pitiable sick, by selling their advice for filthy lucre.

I cannot defend Hahnemann, his system, and his followers, from all of these serious imputations. I am afraid that on some of them they must accept an unfavourable verdict, and be thankful if they can "get by hanging," that utmost ambition of a certain notable character when in equally suspicious circumstances. Almost all I can do for them, in this part of their trial, is to take "a chance of decision in their favour," on some of the counts in the indictment, by an appeal to the jury on the score either of bad examples in their youth or evil company in their maturer years, for I acknowledge that I have, generally speaking, "no case" of a better kind.

On the first charge I have nothing to say in mitigation of sentence. Hahnemann pleads guilty, and offers no excuse; the plea of early ignorance and later wisdom being rather an aggravation of the offence. It is quite true, indeed, that changes of opinion are common among gentlemen on the other side; but such examples are so extremely bad that I doubt whether any man in his senses would venture to pretend that they had any influence upon him. He must be naturally excessively wicked who would not rather be disgusted and deterred from evil ways by such examples. I shall shock the reader, I know, but I must give him an opportunity of judging of this matter. "The same truth," says Dr. Forbes, "as to the uncertainty of practical medicine generally, and the utter insufficiency of the ordinary evidence to establish the efficacy of many of our remedies, as we stated above, has been almost always attained to by philosophical physicians of experience, in the course of long practice, and has resulted, in general, in a mild, tentative, or *expectant*, [that is, no medicine—W. H.] mode of practice in their old age, whatever may have been the vigorous or heroic doings of their youth." (Brit. and For. Med. Rev.) As an instance in point, of a very notable kind, I may state, that Sir Benjamin Brodie recants, in the last edition of his work on the joints, some of the chief practical directions he had laid down thirty years before. Sir Benjamin's delinquencies are exemplified in the following quotation, from his remarks on diseases of the spine:—"In the early part of my professional life, I was led to follow the practice which was then very generally adopted, of treating caries of the spine, by means of setons and caustic issues, one on each side of the diseased vertebræ. A more prolonged experience has satisfied me that, in the very great majority of cases, this painful and loathsome mode of treatment is not only not useful, but actually injurious. The observations which I made on this subject formerly, with reference to scrofulous diseases of other joints, are equally applicable to cases of scrofulous diseases of the spine. For many years past I have ceased to torment my patients who were thus afflicted in this manner, and I am convinced that the change of treatment has been attended with the happiest results." (P. 346, *anno* 1850.)

Dr. Simpson, in his eagerness to place Hahnemann in the same list with Dr. Forbes, Sir Benjamin Brodie, and "philosophical physicians" in general, is very strong on the change that took place in his opinions as to the permanency of the benefits which resulted from the homœopathic plan of treatment he recommended in his earlier publications. In ten or twelve years' time, it appears that Hahnemann had ample opportunity of ascertaining that, in many chronic cases, the ordinary homœopathic remedies produced only a temporary restoration to apparent health, and that, after a time, the patient who once laboured under symptoms of chronic disease was seized, either with a return of the same ailments, or with others assuming the same chronic character, in a word, was subject to relapses of chronic sufferings of some kind or other. It took him some years to ascertain this unhappy tendency, and to discover that he had been premature in announcing that a *cure*, in the radical and permanent sense, was the speedy and common result of *any* sort of homœopathic treatment in all kinds of disease. Had he been less earnest than he was, he would have kept quiet upon this subject; but being unusually candid and single-minded, he made no scruple of announcing his mistake when he had become fully aware of it. In his *Chronic Diseases*, published in 1828, he tells us that he had ascertained the fact just referred to, and had been occupied for twelve years in discovering the reason of so perplexing an occurrence, and the means of obviating it. The explanation he gives is what has been referred to in considering the psoric hypothesis in the last chapter. The sufferings of chronic diseases, in a large proportion of cases, are, according to that doctrine, held to depend on the existence of a morbid poison in the bodies of those affected, and they were, moreover, held by Hahnemann as capable of being removed for a time by certain medicines, which were homœopathic to the symptoms that they manifested in the occasional outbreaks of disorder caused by the morbid poison; but as these medicines did not cure the condition on which the morbid poison itself depended, the local ailments which it was capable of producing were liable to return, either in the same form as they had previously presented, or in some different form, and even in a different place, after the temporary relief afforded by medicines, which, though *homœopathic*, were not also *antipsoric*, that is, capable of curing the psoric state of the body, as well as the occasional manifestations of it. In his treatise on *Chronic Diseases* and psora, he affirms that the medicines which many chronic internal diseases require for their permanent cure, must be such as are both homœopathic to the sum of the symptoms which are present, and selected from among those that are ascertained to have the power of curing the *psoric condition* from which these symptoms spring. He enumerates twenty-two medicines which have this virtue, as ascertained by their homœopathic relation to the psoric eruptions on the surface. Whether the greater permanency of their curative effects in chronic diseases is really or always due to their *antipsoric* powers is another matter.

On the second charge, Homœopathy must also bow to the jury-box, and admit that "two blacks," or any number of blacks, professorial or otherwise, never can make a white. On the third, I have no better apology, for Hahnemann was, of course, as accountable for the scarcely avoidable ignorance of any thing deserving the name of correct views of morbid anatomy in his old age, as for knowing so little of chloroform since his demise; and even if he had, when three score and ten, begun to entertain better opinions, if he avowed them, he would fall under the condemnation due to No. 1. On the fourth charge, I have something to urge on behalf of the accused. Hahnemann, in recounting the effects produced in the proving of a certain medicine, noted down, (for he thought every thing, however minute, especially if new in the experience of the person affected, worthy of being noted, were it only for future more extended inquiry,) that symptoms apparently due to the medicine became aggravated "at the new moon." Possibly he was wrong in thinking that the moon had any thing to do with the aggravations, a point I leave to Baron Reichenbach, Professor Gregory, and others intimate with the "Od" force; but as in Hahnemann's early days the moon was generally thought to be a very influential personage, he may be pardoned for connecting a new moon with certain symptoms he noticed to be simultaneous with her appearance. It is little more than fifty years ago that a favourite pupil, as Dr. Thomson says he was, of the celebrated Cullen, published a succession of treatises on the influence of the moon in certain diseases; and in reviewing one of his works on the subject in 1795, the then Professor of the Institutes of Medicine in the University, instead of sneering at him as a fool, styles him "both learned and ingenious;" and acknowledges that he had proved, by his "numerous facts," that something of the nature of lunar influence on fevers did occur in Bengal, though he does not think it "by any means ascertained" "that this arises from a general law of sol-lunar influence extending over the whole globe."* It would be to no purpose to go farther back for proofs of a general belief among physicians that the moon has an influence on diseases. The great Hoffmann believed it, and yet his other opinions are not thought absurd on that account. I need not add, that if a man might believe that the moon could affect the symptoms of ordinary diseases, without his authority on other subjects being necessarily scouted, he might believe the same regarding the symptoms of *medicinal* diseases, and still have a claim on our courtesy and respect. And still farther to show that, even if Hahnemann was wrong about the moon's influence on medicinal dieases, the error does not in the least invalidate his practical precepts as a physician; let it be remembered that no opinion is more firmly rooted among farmers than that the moon influences the weather, while Arago and other men of science maintain that she does no such thing; yet we do not doubt the practical wisdom in their calling of those who adhere to the ancient notion.

In regard to the fifth charge, that Homœopathy is not destitute of indiscreet disciples, the unfortunate accused has scarcely a word to say. She admits that she is most culpable in this respect, and blushes when she contrasts Dr. Mure, Mr. Everest, and some others, both reverend and lay, with the many truly wise and immaculate persons who follow her aged rival. But still she desires mitigation of punishment on the

* Med. Com., vol. xx. p. 180.

score of bad example. Dr. Mure certainly puts her to shame with his *Pediculus Capitis*, and she acknowledges that she was hasty in admitting him into her company with such an attendant. Yet what could she do? Before receiving him, she considered whether there were any precedents for such abominable things as he wanted her to countenance, and she found that Allopathy, both ancient and modern, made no scruple on the ground of decorum, as to what or whom she consorted with. Privately she tried to ascertain what *musk* and *castor* were, and in what doses Dr. Simpson and his friends gave them to their dainty feminine patients. She remembered Virgil's allusion to the one—"Virosaque Pontus Castorea"—and did not think it by any means a proper substance for physic; and she bethought herself also of the celebrated Hoffmann's edition of the other, as a second-hand something (bad enough when fresh and original) that was not to be thought of in civilized society, and never to be expressed but in a dead language,—"Attentione dignum curiosumque est," says he, "quod moschus odore suo privatus, *in latrina si suspendatur, suavem suum odorem iterum acquirat;*"* and being thus refreshed is a particularly fine medicine. Beside a scruple or a drachm of either, the billionth of a grain of the Patagonian pediculus rises into a bonne-bouche for the most fastidious taste.

Castor and musk perfume and adorn the *armamentarium* of modern Allopathy, and, therefore, might amply excuse her homœopathic rival for adopting the pediculus, even though it had no personal recommendations. But Allopathy is so incessantly pluming herself upon her antiquity and her noble antecedents, that her opponent was very willing to inquire if the family history, so full of all imaginable glories, would not be a still better authority for her closing with Dr. Mure

* In Hoffmann's notes to Pharm. Spagyricæ, p. 166, by P. Poterus, whose Materia Medica he adopts by his notes and commendations.

and his offspring. Hoffmann seemed a communicative personage, and though all but a contemporary of Hahnemann, and therefore not likely to be so exquisite in physical matters as some of the more immediate descendants of Apollo, his modern renown gave a certain weight to his authority that made him appear at once a suitable person to apply to. The late Professor John Thomson, in his Life of Cullen, gives Hoffmann a distinguished place among medical philosophers; and as I am about to cite a few samples of the opinions and practices of that celebrated physician, I naturally desire to enlist the good opinion of my readers in his favour, lest, not entirely concurring with him on some minor points, they should rashly condemn, as a fool or charlatan or pick-pocket, the great founder of modern pathology, and one of the most voluminous and learned writers of the last century on the medicinal peculiarities of the common or old school; for these reasons, I say, I shall bespeak for him the most worshipful consideration of the reader, by two or three extracts from the eminent biographer I have mentioned, in proof of the great sagacity and singular services of the illustrious Allopath,— "The great and prominent merits of Hoffmann," says Dr. Thomson, "as a medical philosopher, undoubtedly consisted in his having perceived and pointed out more clearly than any of his predecessors, the extensive and powerful influence of the nervous system, in modifying and regulating at least, if not in producing all the phenomena of the organic as well as of the animal functions in the human economy, and more particularly in his application of this doctrine to the explanation of diseases." (P. 195.) " . . . He employed all the powers of his capacious mind, and his extensive learning, in borrowing from anatomy, and from natural philosophy and chemistry, whatever could tend to elucidate the study or improve the practice of medicine. His writings, in six folio volumes, form an immense storehouse of theoretical and practical knowledge, collected from his own observations and reflections, and from all the treasures of ancient and modern learning." (P. 199.) "The ideas with regard to the nervous origin of diseases, which pervade the numerous writings of Hoffmann, and which he has explained and illustrated in a very distinct and luminous manner in the fourth and fifth chapters of his Therapeutics, where he treats of the genealogy of diseases, and of the sympathies existing between the different parts of the nervous system, form the *great basis* of the pathology *at present taught* in the schools of medicine."* (P. 197.) I have put a few of the words of my distinguished predecessor in italics, because it is of consequence that the reader should mark very particularly the relation subsisting between the excellent Hoffmann and modern physic, in order that he may understand me when I beseech him not to think all medicine a delusion and a snare, invented merely to gull the community and enrich the profession, should he find occasion to differ from the great medical philosopher in some of his views and customs. I hope and believe that no right-minded and charitable person will think less of the nervous system, or of clear-headed Hoffmann—who "amply realized the expectations expressed by Leibnitz," when he said in a letter to him, "you appear to me to be one of the few who are at particular pains to speak of things the meaning of which is understood"† —merely because he was not, what Hahnemann is required to be, altogether destitute of any trace of boundary to his intellectual and scientific perfections.

The first specimen I shall give of Hoffmann and Allopathy (that wonderful system which, like a Chinese stripling, always presents itself so venerable with traditionary associations, that the "vast age of the race and name overpowers

* Life of Cullen, by John Thomson, M. D., Professor of Medicine and General Pathology in the University of Edinburgh, vol. i. 1832.

† Life of Cullen, p. 197.

the sense of youth in the individual") is the remarkable cure of an itchy Dominican friar. A contumacious *psora* had tormented the reverend father for six years, in spite of many physicians, till at last Poterus set him to eat vipers with a little salt; and the doctor tells us that, during the summer, above 150 of them having descended into the friar, "his skin being renovated, he became quite another man, and he who before looked a particularly old person, was made young again, stronger than before, and fitter for every thing."* At p. 151 of the same ingenious volume, he gives directions for preparing the aqua or water of crabs, earthworms, frogs, and frog-spawn; which, I may mention—in order to let people into the secret of that invaluable experience of so many centuries which our allopathic friends always thrust into our upstart faces—were respectively found by the "capacious mind" which meddled with "things, the real meaning of which is understood" to be admirable† in inflammations, (like the lancet and tartar emetic,) bites of mad-dogs, stone in the kidneys, consumption, worms of children, (the earth-worms did *their* business—a kind of Isopathy, therefore, like bugs for bug-bites,) hemorrhages, erysipelas, gout, and burns, not to mention others that are not mentionable.

At p. 152, we are introduced to something still more philosophical, and more conclusive of the soundness of the ancient foundations. But here I am at a great disadvantage, and feel almost as if I must shut the book, and leave Dr. Simpson to crow by himself. For while he, with little violence to decency, can give in plain English the worst therapeutic ravings of the most harebrained homœopathist (so-

* Supplementum, p. 126.

† "Radically cure," and "wonderfully benefit," are the judicious phrases expressive of their action.

called,) I dare not do the same with the allopathic bill of fare, without sending my imaginative readers to their scent-bottles and snuff-mills. What can I make in English of the *Aqua stercoris animalium*, or *De oleo excrementorum*, or *Facultas stercoris humani?* I can't venture to translate. Suffice it to say of these things, "the meaning of which," as Leibnitz says, "is understood," that they are so offensive as to be better left in their classical dress. But I may translate some notices of their indubitable virtues, in order to do homage to the foundations and antecedents of that modern experience which has grown so naturally out of the good old stock, and preserves so strikingly the family features.* I shall give the unmentionables their due, each in succession, under the signs of No. 1, No. 2, and No. 3.

Under No. 1 it is mentioned generally, that so and so "possess wonderful and excellent virtues;" the stercus gallinarum being capital in the colic, that of swallows having anti-epileptic energies, especially when flavoured with anodyne flowers; that of the peacock, with a little spirit of wine (to keep it down,) always manifests (semper exstitit) "specific virtues against diseases of the head, giddiness, and epilepsy." Under No. 2 it is said, "in . . . many secrets are hidden, as is proved by a multiplied experience," and special mention is made of its power over the jaundice, malignant as well as benign tumours, and pestilential buboes. These external diseases are overpowered by poultices *ex stercore humano vel vaccino;* for he, the considerate Hoffmann, naïvely admits, that the oil from the former is so abominable that *he could not easily get it given internally.*

Under No. 3 there is an opening sentence which I must submit to the learned:—*In animalium excrementis, mirum*

* An allopathic physician of eminence, not a hundred miles from this, uses "cow-tea" (which is neither milk nor beef-tea) in *diabetes.* A rude attempt at Homœopathic practice!

dictu quam rara et perfecta remedia reperiantur; et ut ab homine omnium principe exordiar, in humano stercore mira vis latet, in viscerum obstructionibus aperiendis. This is what may be termed the solid foundation of Allopathy. It has a fluid foundation, too, by virtue of which it claims rule by sea as well as land; but I cannot trust the account of it, in somewhat too transparent Latin, to my page. However, the meaning "is understood."

After all this there is a positive insipidity in the *Extract of mummies*, *Precipitate of human blood*, and *of the human skull*, of *frogs*, *vipers*, *worms*, *gems*, and *pearls*, and *the oil of human fat*—all of which are duly celebrated in the same fundamental volume, between pages 159 and 173. It is needless to say that the cures they work were wonderful, and the allopathic experience they imparted as sound as any from that day to this—Dr. Dietl, Dr. Forbes, Sir Benjamin Brodie, and "philosophical physicians" in general, being witnesses to the fact.

As to the sixth count in the series, the non-divinity of Homœopathy and its founder—notwithstanding the assertions to the contrary of the enthusiastic and ridiculous Dr. Mure —the charge is frankly confessed to be but too true. The gentleman I have just mentioned, with unpardonable impropriety, terms Hahnemann "a messenger from heaven," and the Rev. Mr. Everest pretends that the Scripture injunction to the Apostles to "heal the sick and cleanse the lepers," admits of a modern application to the practitioners of the healing art. Dr. Simpson thinks both of them in the wrong, —the clergyman especially, on the ground that he is guilty of a false interpretation of a passage in the sacred writings, —which, of course, no allopathic clergyman was ever known to be. All the divine honours and heaven-descended blessings of medicine unquestionably belong to Allopathy; and if any one doubts the fact, let him hear what Allopathy says herself on the subject. The great organ, interpreter, and lawgiver of allopathic physic, the British and Foreign Medical Review, not content with the apotheosis of any single individual, puts all the members of all the Colleges of Physicians, and all the graduates of all the universities, (invidiously omitting the surgeons,) into the supernal calendar. "The physician," quoth the oracle, "cannot but be impressed with the dignity of his pursuits; he cannot conceal from himself *that his mission is to ameliorate the 'primal curse;' that he is the* SPECIAL messenger of Providence to suffering man." But this is not all—the lofty estimate which Hippocrates entertained of allopathic doctors is complacently appropriated thus: —"It is impossible to peruse the ethical portions of the Hippocratic writings without *feeling their moral grandeur.* In the book 'De Medico' it is asserted, that the truly philosophic physician is *godlike;* using the identical term (ισοθεος) applied by Homer to Machaon, and adding, 'that *indeed he differs little from the gods.*'"* That this tolerably modest opinion is endorsed by the reviewer in the name of his clan is obvious, for he speaks of "moral grandeur," as pictured in the sentence which he quotes; while immediately afterwards he rather boggles at the elevation to which Menecrates of Syracuse would raise them, when he maintained that physicians "ought actually to be worshipped as gods." This, unlike the former, to which no objection is made, is a glorification "carried even to a ridiculous excess;" but whether it is declined because of its pagan idolatry, or the unsubstantial quality of its emoluments, we are left to guess. That it may possibly be for the latter reason, is rendered supposable by the next sentence, which tells how Philip of Macedon taking Menecrates at his word, instead of giving him food and fees, "offered him incense"—about as acceptable a donation to

* No. xxxvii. 1845, p. 122.

the allopathic father of a small family, as the smell of the gold waggishly proffered to the ill-used homœopathic doctor. The reviewer, three years later, favours us with his opinion of Dr. M'Gowan's tract on Medical Missions, and in the course of his article expresses opinions identical with those of the Rev. Mr. Everest, so much objected to by Dr. Simpson when coming from a homœopathic divine. He says that every practitioner must take a deep interest in the missionary tract, "because, if truly Christian, he must see that the medical missionary is therein *more closely assimilated to the founder of his holy religion than any other*."* And then he quotes from Dr. M'Gowan, in proof of this statement, a sentence which goes the full length of Mr. Everest's heretical interpretation:—"It is his province to assuage human suffering in all its varieties and aggravations, and, in imitation of the Saviour, 'to heal all manner of diseases.'"

For my own part, I must say that I think all introduction of scripture language and allusions into professional publications objectionable. It is rarely done with good taste, never, I suspect, with good effect, and I cannot remember an instance in which it does not issue in extravagance. Even in sermons, the mixture of Christianity and medicine has, to my mind, an ungainly, laboured, infelicitous appearance,—the repulsiveness of incongruity, when the attempted combination becomes particular,—the coldness of commonplace when it endeavours only to be general. But there are graver objections still; and as I have wandered into theology accidentally, in this place, I shall say all that I mean to say now, instead of reserving the theological aspect thrust upon a medical controversy for a more elaborate and, I believe, unnecessary dissertation in a separate chapter. The graver objections to the mingling of Christian and medical subjects,

* British and Foreign Medico-Chirurgical Review, 1848, p. 2.

which I have referred to, are these,—that professional works which all medical men may require to peruse, are thus apt to be the vehicles of unsound religious opinions, rendered doubly dangerous by being diffused among important scientific truths; and that names which ought never to be uttered without reverence, and doctrines which should never be specified without solemnity, are liable to become bandied about amidst the acrimonies of disputation, and made the weapons of personal or party hatreds.

The former of these objections has its illustration on either side of this medical controversy, but not, I think, of so dangerous a description on the side of Homœopathy as of its rival. Dr. Mure's parallel between human and divine things is too great an outrage upon good taste and common sense to be perilous to any one—even to a fool; while his work is necessary to no one, and has probably no medical wisdom to gild its allegorical absurdities. Dr. Simpson errs in saying he is blasphemous; he is simply disgusting.* The Reverend Mr. Everest's medico-religious philosophy, fanciful and erroneous as it is, is merely *his* philosophy; has no other existence than in his published sermon; and no sanction but that of a board of hospital managers, who probably never heard it, of a zealous private gentleman in an after-dinner speech, and of a weekly homœopathic journalist, who praised it before it was printed. Dr. Simpson is wrong when he says it contains *Hahnemannic* theology, and he knows that he is wrong, for he inadvertently quotes from Hahnemann a sentence which contains the expression of an opinion and an experience the *very opposite* of the principal peculiarity of the sermon; and

* As the impression which Dr. Simpson seeks to produce upon his readers is, that Dr. Mure is the founder of a new sort of religion made up of Christianity and Homœopathy, I may state that he is in reality a very devoted Roman Catholic, whose orthodoxy in the faith of his Church is unquestioned, however heretical he may be as to taste and judgment.

not only so, but the notions of Mr. Everest are as little allied to homœopathic doctrines and practices as they are to the allopathic. I presume that allopathic physicians admit the imperfection of human bodies, their proneness to constitutional distemper, their influence when disordered upon the thoughts and feelings of the mind, and the capacity of that influence to be lessened or removed by appropriate physical treatment. Mr. Everest goes, indeed, a degree or two farther, but it is in the same direction, and no farther than he may be followed as easily and consistently by an allopathic as by a homœopathic physician, who is inclined to speculations regarding mind and matter that are more ingenious and bold than consistent with Scripture and experience. There is nothing peculiar to Homœopathy in the philosophy of Mr. Everest, and, but for Dr. Simpson's resuscitation of it, it would have been forgotten long ago.

On the allopathic side the case is very different. I approach it with hesitation, because it appears to me too serious to be quietly allowed to drop, once the attention of the many excellent and Christian men, who are allopathic physicians, is pointedly directed to it. The few instances which I think it necessary to adduce of error, bearing upon theological matters, from the allopathic writings, are extracted from the same influential review to which I have already adverted. I do not desire to charge the conductors of that publication with a deliberate intention to sap the foundations of Christian belief, or to inculcate doctrines which they know to be at variance with Christian precepts, but simply to show that valuable records of medical science, when religious subjects are permitted to mingle with them, are liable to become objectionable and unsafe, as vehicles of error on the most important of all concerns, whether from the thoughtlessness or the theological peculiarities of their authors. Having reviewed one of the works of the infidel Fichte, the writer, carried away probably by inconsiderate enthusiasm, observes, "The truly spiritual Christian cannot fail to recognise in the doctrines and precepts we have quoted some fundamental Christian verities; and *not the less Christian* because translated from modern German *instead of ancient Greek*."* Of course Christian verities are Christian verities, whether they are translated immediately from the ancient Greek of Scripture, or from the reflections of Scripture wisdom contained in the moral or religious writings of Christians. But I venture to say that a dozen of quotations with less of Christian truth in them and more of human mysticism and conceit cannot easily be selected from modern German, than those which are presented by the reviewer as on a level with the verities of *that ancient Greek*, whose authority Fichte's reveries would supersede.†

"Having established his faith," says the reviewer, "on broad and comprehensive principles, the medical practitioner can hardly become sectarian;" and one reason that should weigh with him probably is, although not specially adduced as such, that "frequently the sectarian practitioner is the least learned and skilful; *for the time that he devotes to his religious exercises and public services is necessarily taken*

* British and Foreign Medico-Chirurgical Review, 1848, p. 10.

† Those who may peruse the article on "Medical Ethics," referred to above, in the Review, are cautioned against being misled by the frequent mention of "revelation," "Christianity," "inspiration," &c., in an apparently devout manner. In the sense put upon such expressions by a disciple of Fichte, there can be nothing that resembles the meaning in which they are employed by those who are regarded as Christians in the ordinary and orthodox acceptation of the name. Fichte's "inspiration" is the possession of what he calls the "divine idea," and it is such as any and every man may possess in the same manner and of the same kind, if not in the same degree, as the inspired writers of Scripture, and even their Divine Master, did. Fichte's "revelation," too, may be any man's, who attains to so common a thing as his "divine idea." It is needless to say what his "Christianity" is, and what the founder of Christianity was in his estimation.

from that which ought to be devoted to his studies." (P. 13.) Let these examples, from the many that might be quoted, suffice to indicate the sort of influences that may accompany medical teachings, if all who conceive themselves wiser than their brethren in matters of religion are to be encouraged to infuse their religious opinions into their medical works. I lay no special charge of an aptitude for objectionable views on theological questions against allopathic writers. If the practice shall become general among medical authors, of mixing their notions of Christianity with medicine, I do not doubt that the evils of it will be abundantly and equally apparent on both sides. The second of the objections which I mentioned as applicable to medico-religious discussions needs no elucidation from me; it will be found painfully illustrated in the work of Dr. Simpson.

The seventh charge accuses Homœopathy of being supported by men of rank, literary eminence, and clergymen. Such personages are said by our opponents not to be always the best judges of what is worthy of belief and patronage; and as this is a very unanswerable argument against any system which they may support, Homœopathy here makes a resolute stand, and declares that the objection is a great deal more applicable to her rival than to her. The Pope and the Archbishop of Canterbury, Mr. Macaulay and Mr. Dickens, my Lord Aberdeen and my Lord Chancellor, (not to mention the highest head in the realm,) are all allopaths, and the fact proves two things: Firstly, in accordance with Dr. Simpson's line of argument, it shows very plainly that Allopathy is the merest quackery, for persons of the several classes referred to have chiefly patronised the most absurd delusions, such as St.-John-Longism, Perkinism, and Stephenism. Was it not the Parliament of England that gave £5000 for Mrs. Stephens' specific; and does not the Parliament of England—with its Lords Spiritual and Temporal, and its Commons—at this moment countenance and maintain the principles and practice of Allopathy? Secondly, their adhesion to Allopathy, while it proves the absurdity of that system, also proves their own. For has it not been shown that Allopathy, with its lancet and other lethal weapons, destroys a large amount of human life; and is it not confessed by one of the allopathic authorities,—"That in a large proportion of the cases treated by allopathic physicians, the disease is cured by nature and not by them;" and "that in a lesser, but still not a small proportion, the disease is cured by nature *in spite* of them; in other words, their interference opposing, instead of assisting the cure?"* It is obvious, then, that the medical system which has the greatest *following* of the aristocracy, the literary people, and the clergy, is always the worst; and, reciprocally, that adherence to Allopathy may be regarded as a proof and instance of "the follies of the wise." On the other hand, Homœopathy avers that when the minority of such eminent classes in the community are witnessed among the supporters of some great movement, the presumption is that it is a movement in the right direction. It was thus not long ago in regard to such political questions as parliamentary reform, the corn-laws, and free trade; and it was thus with the practice of vaccination, which was countenanced by non-medical personages, such as the Prince of Wales, the Dukes of York and Clarence, Lords Egremont, Hervey, Aylesbury, Ossory, and others, at a time when its great advocate, Dr. Jenner, had to contend with the prejudices and calumnies of his professional brethren, as we have now to do with those of ours in defence of Homœopathy.

In the eighth place, Homœopathists are accused of not being unanimous on every point of their practice, and every doctrine of their system. Now this is unpardonable, con-

* Dr. Forbes, in British and Foreign Medical Review, 1846, p. 258.

sidering that their opponents are unanimous on every thing in theirs. To give some fair samples of the allopathic harmony,—Mialhe maintains that alkalies cure diabetes, Bouchardat is "unanimously" of opinion that they do not, but make it worse; Haygarth, Percival, and others, recommend mercury in water in the head; Abercrombie *concurs*, in the following terms:—"Its reputation seems to stand on very doubtful grounds;" Dr. M'Adam recommends mercury in *peritonitis*, thus, "as soon as a salivation is established, we have generally found the symptoms become much mitigated; and our experience accords with that of Dr. Gooch, who remarks, that whenever the gums were affected in this disease, the patients invariably recovered," (Cyc. of Pract. Med.,) with which Dr. Alison's extensive experience coincides in these terms:—"When its action on the mouth has been excited in the course of acute internal inflammations, we have not only been very generally disappointed of seeing improvement of the symptoms immediately follow that change, but are constrained to add, that we have more frequently seen an aggravation of them," (*same* work, p. xcvi.;) of Digitalis, Pereira says, "Dr. Withering stated, that this medicine more frequently succeeds as a diuretic than any other, and that if it fail, there is but little chance of any other remedy succeeding. My experience, however, is not in accordance with Dr. Withering's," (p. 1211;) of iodine in goître, observes the same author.—"Dr. Copland observes, that of several cases of the disease which have come before him since the introduction of this remedy into practice, 'there has not been one which has not either been cured or remarkably relieved by it.' I much regret, however, that my experience does not accord with this statement," (p. 241;) Dr. Dundas states, that if quinine be used at the commencement of continued fever, in doses of ten or twelve grains, every two hours, the disease will be arrested "in the great majority of cases." Dr. Bennett has tried this method in the manner recommended by Dr. Dundas, in two cases of typhoid, and in four or five of typhus. "In none of the cases," says he, "notwithstanding the physiological action of the drug was well marked, did it in any way cut short the disease, or produce on its progress, as far as I could ascertain, any amelioration whatever," (Brit. and For. Rev., 1852;) Dr. G. O. Rees writes a pamphlet in commendation of lemon-juice in acute rheumatism,, and Dr. Fuller and his reviewer in the Edinburgh Monthly Journal come to this favourable conclusion about it, "the latest of all (remedies) in the field, like many others that have gone before it, lemon-juice, appears, when weighed in the balance of experience, unworthy of the panegyrics which have been bestowed upon it." (January, 1853.) Yet why be tedious with instances of a unanimity which is not, and never has been, denied? let the great allopathic reviewer, Dr. Forbes, sum up the argument in his own graphic way. "This comparative powerlessness and positive uncertainty of medicine is also exhibited in a striking light, when we come to trace the history and fortunes of particular remedies and modes of treatment, and observe the notions of practitioners, at different times, respecting their positive or relative value. What difference of opinion,—what an array of alleged facts directly at variance with each other,—what contradictions,—what opposite results of a like experience,—what ups and downs,—what glorification and degradation of the same remedy,—what confidence now,—what despair anon in encountering the same disease with the very same weapons,—what horror and intolerance at one time of the very opinions and practices which, previously and subsequently, are cherished and admired." (Brit. and For. Rev., 1846, p. 258.) Whosoever is desirous of enlarging his memoranda of particulars on this curious subject, is recommended to take notes from the first chapter of this work on blood-letting and tartar emetic in pneumonia,—on the former *remedy* in acute rheumatism, as unanimously concurred in by Bouillaud, Hope, Latham, &c.; on mercury in pericarditis, by Graves, Latham, and Taylor; on the various estimates of calomel in croup; on all that has been written on all manner of diseases, treated in all manner of ways,—from consumption down to sore throats, and from the royal touch to the last invention—grease-rubbing.

To balance this enormous unanimity Dr. Simpson has produced *six instances* of apparent disagreement among homœopathic practical writers! Now, we have about 400 medicines, more or less fully proved; and multiplying these by only as many varieties of disease, and the product, by some 2000—the probable number of homœopathic physicians,—and we have three hundred and twenty millions of particular opportunities of disagreement, with an actual number of *six*, or about one in fifty-three millions! We may go a figure or two higher still in estimating the opportunities afforded by Homœopathy to disagreement among its disciples, by multiplying the last product by *thirty*, the ordinary number of dilutions of each medicine. We shall have then nine thousand six hundred millions of such opportunities, which, divided by six, gives a proportion of one disagreement in sixteen hundred millions of instances, or occasions, on which difference of opinion is possible. I hope there are a great many more in reality, for, much as unanimity is to be prized in some things, so very great a concordance of opinion as Dr. Simpson charges us with, would argue a common level of powers of observation, and degree of experience and knowledge, which would be anything but flattering to some of us, considering what the average level of mankind is. Dr. Viettinghoff, however, seems so far behind the rest of us that he never heard that bromine (an ingredient of our remedy for croup, spongia) produces plastic exudation in the first air-passages, and is therefore *homœopathic to membranous croup*, as we should have concluded it must be,—considering how easily croup is cured by spongia,—even though we had no provings on animals to show why it is so. Dr. Fleischmann's exclusive preference for phosphorus in pneumonia is easily explained; for surely there is room for mistake in the way of over-estimating the capacities of a drug in the course of a practice which was so successful as his, when allopathic physicians all over the world have fallen into the monstrous error of attaching value to a *remedy* in the same disease, which actually destroys life to the extent of twice as large a number as die of it when left to nature! Similar explanations apply to other instances adduced by Dr. Simpson.

In the ninth charge Homœopathy is accused of being but partially diffused over what is obligingly termed the civilized world. In regard to the extent to which Homœopathy is countenanced, there is, however, a diversity of statement among its opponents. At one time their men-of-straw witnesses are made to testify that Homœopathy has very few adherents in such a place, (no matter where, the evidence will accommodate itself to the circumstances of any locality or occasion,)—that it is in very bad odour among certain sensible aborigines,—that, in fact, its hospitals are deserted, and its doctors starving. By and by, as the exigencies of the argument demand, it must be sworn to as having a great many followers, for quackery always has a multitude of dupes, and Homœopathy must be shown to have that distinguishing mark of the genius to which it belongs. Well, I shall meet them on both views of the case, one at a time, and try whether either will answer the purpose intended. First, then, Homœopathy has very few disciples at such a place, or anywhere, and consequently it must be humbug, it must go down. We have all heard of the anecdote of the eminent physician, Dr. Mead, and the quack doctor. Dr. Simpson gives it, and I may give it too. "A man of good education had become a quack, and had a booth in one of the most frequented streets of London. He calculated on the weakness and credulity of mankind, and made a most fortunate speculation. Mead, regretting that an intelligent man, capable of advancing truth, should degrade himself to such a trade, advised him to abandon it. 'How many men a-day,' said the quack, 'do you think pass through this street?' 'Perhaps 20,000,' said the doctor. 'And how many of these do you suppose possess the right use of their senses and a sound judgment?' 'Five hundred.' 'The proportion is too great,' said the quack. 'A hundred, then!' 'Still too many.' At last they agreed to reckon them at ten. 'Let me alone, then,' said the quack; 'let me levy on these 19,990 *fools* the tribute which they owe me, and keep the ten to yourself.'" This pet anecdote, the great and undeniable truism of the profession, the almost solitary pleasantry that the good old school will listen to on the subject of quackery, is, therefore, entirely against Dr. Simpson and his friends on the argument before us. The moral of the story is, that true worth and professional capacity are disregarded by the great mass of the public, who will pass by your really competent man with his head full of knowledge and his pockets empty, and flock in crowds after the fashionable quackery of the day. Numbers are all, according to the oracular tale, on the side of charlantry and its absurdities; and Homœopathy being, with Dr. Mead, in the minority, is your only true science. The voice of philosophy, too, both ancient and modern, is for once on the same side with that of Allopathy, as uttered in its grand illustrative anecdote. Seneca and Sir William Hamilton alike condemn the crowd, and by implication give the palm of excellence to the lesser party. I have quoted a passage to the point on a like occasion before, but it will bravely bear repetition. "Why," says our illustrious Professor of Logic, "should a multitude afford any presumption in favour of the opinions which it espouses? On the contrary, '*argumentum pessimi turba est.*' The height of a crowd is no higher than the highest man in it. This is true, both physically and intellectually. But in a crowd intellectually there is even a tendency to bring down the higher minds to a lower level; for all experience shows, that men under the sympathy—the mutual Mesmerism—of numbers do enthusiastically in a body what, had they been left to their individual judgment and responsibilities, many of them would have ridiculed or condemned."* Allusion is here made to the intellectual stature of the highest man, in that sense, in the crowd, as forming the utmost height of the crowd itself. The observation is so just, that we may well pause a moment to ask what the intellectual eminence of the medical multitude is that decry Homœopathy? Is there a man so high among them that his simple decision ought to weigh anything in the estimation of those who like an opinion in science to have experience on its side? We must, in so far as the British empire is concerned, let the unbiassed foreigner—the Parisian Academy of Medicine—answer the question. A few months ago, there was not a British physician thought worthy of a place in that respectable body. Since then Professor Simpson has had the fortune to be elected a foreign associate.† Still the question

* The mention of Sir William Hamilton suggests to me his prediction regarding the practice now supported by the minority:—"Homœopathy and the Water-Cure are now and here (in Edinburgh) *blindly* anathematized as heretical; in the next generation, it is not improbable, that these same doctrines may be no less blindly preached as exclusively orthodox. Such is poor human nature! Such is corporate—such is medical authority."—*Discussions, &c.* p. 638. We prefer our present more honourable position, and hope he may prove wrong.

† I am so far from thinking this distinction a disproportionate tribute to the value of chloroform as a means of preventing pain in natural or surgical operations, that I would have applauded the bestowal of the same honour on

remains unanswered—Is there in the crowd a physician entitled to decide, *ex cathedra*, from his pride of place, as a man of scientific and intellectual stature, on a question which he has not specially and practically examined?

But enough of this argument—now for the other. Homœopathy has a great many followers, says Dr. Simpson on the other tack, and therefore it must be quackery, for quackery has always a numerous retinue; St. John Long had it, &c., &c., &c. Softly, good doctor. Are you willing to be tried by the same test? Are you much run after or not? I know nothing on the point beyond what everybody appears to believe; and if everybody is right, and if Homœopathy be quackery because it is so popular, pray, what are you? Surely not a ——! I will not suppose it possible. You will see, though, that this argument won't stand inspection a whit better than the other. Let us all conclude then, in common civility and common sense, that the vulgar argument from numbers leaves the matter where it found it.

Although, as we have just seen, no argument can be legitimately drawn against Homœopathy or Allopathy from the numbers, whether great or small, which may have embraced either, it may be allowed me to ask, Has Homœopathy had fair play in the world? To judge from Dr. Simpson's objection to Homœopathy, on the ground that its medical votaries are not yet so very numerous as a system with such pretensions ought to have, if it is sound, those who know nothing on the subject may suppose that it has had opportunities for its growth fairly and impartially conceded to it. But the objection reminds one, who does know something on the subject, of the tyranny of Pharaoh towards the Israelites when they sojourned in Egypt, whose "tale of bricks" must be

Drs. Keith and Matthew Duncan, for their share, as joint experimenters with Dr. Simpson, in the important discovery of so considerable an improvement upon ether.

forthcoming though the supply of straw was withheld. Our "bricks" have multiplied under so many cruel disadvantages, that the real wonder is that they are so many and so true, and *not* that they are not more numerous, or that one or two of them should have proved to be false. Protestantism flourishes not in Tuscany, political liberty in France, free-trade anywhere but in England;—yet does any protestant of the "liberal party" doubt therefore the excellence of his religion, his personal freedom or his cheap bread? I trow not; and for the same reason which checks the growth of other good things, viz., discouragement by persecution and bad laws the limited number of professional Homœopathists in some countries, is not to be employed as an argument against the fitness of their system to take the first place in medicine wherever it is free to follow its native tendency to rise. Only thirty-three years ago, as we have seen, its illustrious founder was virtually banished from Leipsic by laws which bestowed exclusive privileges upon the allopathic apothecaries. Since that time, slow concessions have been made in favour of the new method, by state regulations, in some parts of Germany. I do not know that it is even yet emancipated in all parts of that country; certainly, ten or twelve years ago it was not so.* But supposing that it is now free, the stigma of illegality has been too recently removed for all traces of the reproach to have vanished; and medical men in general are too much the slaves of opinion, stand too much in cowardly awe of one another, and of their patients, to take the manly position they ought to take, and as some among our-

* I observe that persecution still continues in Germany. The "Magdeburg Zeitung" of 5th April last, contains the following:—"The homœopathic physician, Dr. Kallenbach, was this day officially expelled from this town in consequence of the Sanitary Board laying a complaint against him on account of his large practice. He has removed to Bockenheim in Electoral Hesse: Kallenbach was body-physician to the late Elector of Hesse."

selves to my certain knowledge had begun to take when the coming blast of obloquy sounded ominously in their ears, and warned them to retreat. Though legal impediments may not exist, it does not follow that Homœopathy has fair play. The avenues to preferment even in this free country are still closed against the disciples of this medical reform, or rather regeneration. The old Sarums of a passing system are still too numerous among universities, and colleges, and hospitals, and military boards, yea, even among poor-law guardians and other parish patrons—who dispense a scanty dole to the too generally needy and anxious practitioner of medicine—to be readily defied. The incubus of old and stiff institutions, with all their monopolies and prejudices, presses heavily on the young science, and not only in some decrepit continental countries, but even in Great Britain, the land of progress and professed liberality. Is there a country in the world, unsaddled with the dead-weight of ancient prejudice in power, where free opinion in science has encouragement to become free action, untampered with by bribes and unchecked by bigoted corporations,—where the standard of value is not antiquity, but intrinsic worth and usefulness? Look at America, and you have an example of such a country; and how stands Homœopathy there? In many parts of the United States there are societies and minor institutions for the encouragement of the system; and in Pennsylvania a college was founded in 1848, for the complete education of homœopathic physicians, and the granting of degrees. It opened with fifteen students; in the following year they amounted to fifty-five; and in 1851 their number was seventy. What the progress has been since, or what other States have followed the example of Pennsylvania, and founded colleges for the encouragement of Homœopathy, I have not learnt; but I have the high authority of Mrs. Beecher Stowe for the fact, that Homœopathy is very widely extended over the Union; and the graduation list of the Pennsylvanian College for 1851, shows that her information is correct, and not the mere conjecture of a zealous disciple. The list referred to contains the names of twenty-nine graduates,* being exactly the number that graduated in Glasgow, one of our most ancient and popular universities, in 1850; and more than half the average number that have annually graduated in Edinburgh during the last six years!

In Britain, which comes next to America in the general liberality of her institutions, and in the spirit of freedom among her people,† no one, not even Dr. Simpson, denies that Homœopathy is on the increase. The fact is too palpable to be concealed. It is *professedly* accounted for by the gullibility of the English, and no one can deny their gullibility, —very far from it. Without an extraordinary amount of that weakness, how could they allow themselves to be so long the martyrs to a drug-system, acknowledged even by the wisest allopathic physicians to be monstrous and mischievous. Their eyes are opening, however, and they will, by and by, open very wide with amazement at the quantity of doctors' stuffs they have swallowed to no good purpose.

*I have just noticed that for 1852-53 the number was *fifty-five*.

† This statement must be qualified by exempting the medical profession and its dependents from the charge of possessing such a spirit. Their exhibition of a very different spirit has exposed them to the contempt of their continental brethren, so much less favourably situated for the growth of liberal principles. An *allopathic* Berlin journal contains the following humiliating paragraph:—Under the head of "London," it says, "The agitation against Homœopathy has given rise to excesses which are more than laughable, they are contemptible. At the instigation of some fanatic medical men, a large publishing house there, (Highly and Son,) have announced, that henceforward they will neither publish nor sell any homœopathic works, and it is expected that other publishers will follow their example. This mode of attempting to stop the child's mouth is absolutely revolting, and all the more barbarous as occurring in a land where the right to give expression to opinion is considered sacred."—Brit. Journal of Homœopathy. 1853.

At Leipsic, as we learn from a correspondent in the "Tenets," there are only "six or seven" homœopathic physicians. When so many are admitted to exist there, by a person who writes in the most ludicrous ignorance and manifestly bad spirit against Homœopathy, we may rest assured that there are "six or seven" *at least;* and shall probably be nearer the mark if we double the number, on the principle that half the truth is a large allowance with which to credit a bitter and not very scrupulous opponent. It is remarkable, however, that there should be seven to a population of only 50,000; and particularly remarkable when it is remembered, that Leipsic about thirty years ago banished, at the instance of the allopathic practitioners, the illustrious Hahnemann himself on account of his homœopathic principles. A great change must have come over the spirit of Leipsic and its laws since that curious passage in their history, and the circumstance calls loudly for congratulation on their relief from the thraldom of the druggists. Leipsic is remarkable, too, as having been the source of Dr. Fickel's publication on the "Nothingness of Homœopathy;" a work which must have told very sadly against the new practice as long as its author remained out of the lock-up; in which, as I have mentioned in the Preface, he was requested to reside under peculiar circumstances. Dr. Oscar Prieger, who endeavours to make an honest living out of the "many English invalids who have of late years visited the Continent,"* has, it seems, "in the strongest manner," and from the most disinterested motives, authorized Dr. Simpson to impress upon the English invalids who visited the Continent, that Homœopathy is in a state of "rapid decline, or indeed total extinction," "in all that part of Germany with which he is acquainted," and where he endeavours to subsist, so that they may ask at once for him, and save themselves the trouble of searching for a homœopathic

* Tenets, p. 35.

doctor: he (Dr. O. P.) will do their business on terms decidedly low,* Did Dr. Simpson really believe when he demeaned himself by admitting the paltry and sinister nonsense of Drs. Prieger and Gerson into his book, that any human being, who knew anything of mankind in general, and of doctors in particular, would believe one word of such interested evidence? I can hardly suppose it. But there are many who don't know mankind in general, or doctors in particular, and they may swallow these allopathic absurdities as they do other allopathic stuff, which has an equal title to their confidence. I wonder what Homœopathy is, after all; for ever since I heard of it, it has been "rapidly declining," or has been sunk in "total extinction." I wish I could believe this assertion: if true, it would save me a world of trouble, and leave me alternately to the peaceful occupations of retirement, and the pleasures of academical duty, instead of worrying myself with combating the follies and improprieties of allopathic controversialists.

But the Leipsic hospital *is* defunct. Dr. Gerson is right for once, and it is "curious, and well worthy of attention," as Hoffmann says of what happened to the musk, *in latrina*, that when an odour of decay is being pretended as traceable to Homœopathy, the minutest particulars, real or imaginary, are all well known to our allopathic contemporaries; while every thing that argues vigour, growth, and prosperity, is carefully debarred all entrance into their supercilious nostrils. Well, if such odours would only make them as sweet as Hoffmann's renovated musk-bags, they would be heartily welcome to the olfactory entertainment; but the misery is, that the more rapidly Homœopathy "decays," the more they

* Dr. O. P. overdoes his part in the most amusing manner. "In fact, he had *heard the word* (Homœopathy) only in England or from English patients, *during the last five or six years*." An excellent example of the credibility of his whole story.

fume and fret, write big books, denounce, and persecute. The Leipsic hospital, however, is defunct, and yields a very strong odour of decay, and so is an acceptable event. But it should be added that the hospital was set agoing by private subscription, (in a country where hospitals are commonly maintained at the public expense,) and *for a definite number of years only*, to afford scope for homœopathic experiment; and that, after the intended period of its existence was over, it was closed, according to the original purpose. Dr. Gerson perhaps knew that too, but it would not do to tell.

As to the small attendance of students at Gumpendorf and Kremsier, places in the suburbs of Vienna, where homœopathic hospitals, for merely charitable purposes, have been erected,—the following reflections may be considered sufficient. In the first place, it is to us a subject of gratulation that Dr. Simpson has been compelled to adopt so pitiful a line of argument against Homœopathy. It proves that he must be painfully conscious of the absence of legitimate objections to the new system, for it is incredible that any man with the smallest modicum of common sense would employ such an argument as this, if he felt that he had any others that were sounder. The Vienna homœopathic hospitals are not *educational* institutions; the attending physicians take no trouble with students, tell them little, and teach them nothing; it is none of their business to do so. Medical students, with comparatively few exceptions, attend hospitals only for such a time as is required to complete the curriculum for graduation, and only such hospitals as can furnish them the necessary qualification for that great aim of their ambition. Suppose that two small allopathic hospitals were opened in the suburbs of Edinburgh, as the homœopathic hospitals are in the suburbs of Vienna,—one at Newington, and another at Morningside, how many medical students would be found to attend them? Medical students, when they attend hospitals, not merely in compliance with academic regulations, do so for the purpose of acquiring an acquaintance with the phenomena of diseases, and with morbid anatomy, *very much more* than with the desire or expectation of being initiated into the mysteries of prescribing drugs; and hospital physicians, as I know from experience, who lecture to students on their hospital cases, confine themselves, for the most part, to the former subjects, and have very little to say regarding remedies and their actions. These latter themes may do very well for a book expressly devoted to drugs, and the theories of their operation, where something must be said in order to fill the pages, and give a finished air to the productions; but they don't do well for the clinical lecture-room,—few would care to dwell upon them, and still fewer would care to listen. I was once a clinical professor, and such were my feelings and experience. In the homœopathic hospitals at Vienna, owing to the smaller size, and smaller mortality, there are no attractions for the student of morbid anatomy for a moment to be compared with the extraordinary opportunities for the study presented in the large allopathic hospitals; and there is no one to instruct the student of disease in the meaning of symptoms and the art of diagnosis. But the *homœopathic* treatment, it may be said, is to be witnessed in them, and in no other hospitals. True; yet who is the wiser of seeing homœopathic treatment conducted by another, who, if he mentions the name of the disease, and the name of the medicine he gives, says nothing of the special grounds of his selection, and takes no concern to interest the understanding or engage the attention of young persons, to whom, therefore, all that they witness is strange, unintelligible, and consequently indifferent. If a young man is left to teach himself the practice of Homœopathy, he can do it far better, and certainly in a manner much more interesting and satisfactory, *by* himself, among that class of the community which is left, humanely or not I do not say, to the tender mercies of young doctors in all the great cities of Europe and America. And I am sure of one thing, that imperfect as homœopathic practice must be in the hands of a novice, it will be, comparatively, a blessing to those of the class in question, who have the fortune to become the subjects of that experiment, instead of an allopathic one. And this, in fact, is the way in which physicians, young and old, who embrace Homœopathy, actually acquire a practical knowledge of the system. They have no hospitals in which they can be taught to know it when they are students, and they do not want hospitals in which to learn when they have become physicians.

Perhaps the odour of Homœopathic decay, which is felt to be the most grateful and consoling, is that which is said to be exhaled from Hamburg. The friendly Dr. Gerson tells the author of the "Tenets," that the son of a homœopathic physician of that city "has entered the medical profession, but has not adopted the homœopathic principles of his father." Why so? Did he abjure the principles of his respected parent from a deliberate conviction, founded on personal experience, that his father was wrong? If he did, why, *valeat quantum;* let his abjuration be estimated at its true worth; and, in order that it may, let us know what sort of youth he is who thinks himself so much wiser than his sire. If he did not, but acted from a distaste for martyrdom,—the posthumous honours whereof did not, in his estimation, possess half the value of even the slenderest reputation *in esse*;—he may be Homœopathic at heart from filial piety and actual knowledge, and Allopathic from timidity, and in profession only. As I would be tender to the softness of youth, I shall grant that there may be some excuse in this plea for even so grave an offence as appearing under false colours. I can understand, if I cannot, at my time of life, sympathize with that shamefacedness which makes singularity so hateful to raw and inexperienced boyhood. To disdain reproach, to bear contempt with a calm front and unshaken mind, in the service of truth and of a good conscience, are the endowments of veteran soldiers in the warfare of life. Courage, elevation, and endurance, need the discipline of foughten fields, the tempering heat of rough encounters, and the tried trustiness of Him who gives them, before they wax strong enough to brave the temptations and chidings of the world. We must not look for such attributes of manhood in beardless youths, who naturally judge of things by outward glitter, gape in admiration of the vulgar idol, and sigh for popular applause. I have a few of these young idolaters in my eye, who are no strangers to certain truths, which they have not yet the virtue to confess.

As the text which M. Gerson has furnished in this Hamburg incident has a general as well as a special application, I shall dwell upon it for a little longer; and observe, in the third place, that perhaps the homœopathic parent himself placed the youth under the allopathic colours, since a doctor he must be, because he wanted the mettle necessary for a homœopathic physician in these days of rebuke. The senior might hope, at the same time, that with the advantage of some paternal instructions, the junior might prove so little injurious, nay, of such service, to humanity, that he might be pardoned for sending him to enlist under the old standard. He need not always load his blunderbuss, or fire the "great guns," (as I think Dr. Symonds calls venesection and calomel,) when the old word of command is given, and so he will do less execution than another would in his place; while now and then he may put in a pellet from his father's shot-bag, and thus do good by stealth without the risk of blushing when he finds it fame. I myself, who have no small opinion of Homœopathy, and a thorough confidence in its destiny, have dissuaded an allopathic physician from studying it. The gentleman in question is now, I learn, a bitter opponent of Homœopathy, though without knowing anything about it; for he took my advice and remained in his primordial ignorance. The circumstances were briefly these: A patient of the once liberal allopathist was sent to have my opinion of his case,—but not to be submitted to my treatment; and a bad case it was —one, indeed, which I had no particular desire to undertake. As little desire had the late sagacious Dr. Harry Davidson, who shook his long head, and prescribed a few grains of potash. No good having followed, and no good being promised, it was resolved that Homœopathy should have a trial at least. Homœopathy succeeded; and so extraordinary did the success appear to the original proprietor of the case, that nothing would satisfy him but an immediate study of the wonderful system; and I had the honour of being applied to, by the zealous inquirer after medical wisdom, for guidance in his studies. But I knew that he was not made of the right material for withstanding the gibes of the scorner, the cold eye of former friendship, and the fiery face of professional hatred; that he would sink under the fear of alienated patients, and make a very equivocal martyr even in so good a cause. He was accordingly dissuaded from the nobler career, and, as gently as might be, for the very reasons I have given. He knew himself nearly as well as I did, and concurred; while I hope he took the additional advice—to do as little harm as he honestly could with his lancet and his old drugs.

I have a "fourthly" upon Dr. Gerson's text; but perhaps it had better be put after the Socratic fashion. Are there no obstacle in some parts of Germany to the graduation of sons of homœopathic fathers? Where in "broad Scotland" could any son of mine graduate in medicine? I have no intention of putting the question to the proof; but I cannot hide altogether feelings of shame and indignation—shame for the sake of my country, and indignation for the sake of our common humanity—that it can be a question.

To the tenth charge Dr. Simpson devotes a whole chapter of his veracious chronicle. It consists of no less an accusation than that of witchcraft; for Hahnemann says, that by his method of preparing medicines, by hours of trituration in a mortar, &c., "the *spiritual* medicinal powers of the crude substances" are developed to a remarkable degree. If I could suppose the author of the "Tenets" capable of a jest, I would smile with him at his construction of this passage; but I fear that his dissertation on the subject must be put down to sober ignorance, or inebriated ill-will. In either case it is so easily answered that it need not detain us long. Of course every man of ordinary information knows, that medicinal, as well as other substances, possess essential or peculiar properties, different from the physical properties which are common to all kinds of matter. The essence of some substances was recognised as of a material and tangible description, capable of being extricated from its intermixture with other substances in crude compounds. When so extricated it was, and still is, termed *spirit*,—as the *spirit* of wine, the *spirit* of turpentine, the *spirit* of salts, and so on. In other instances the quintessence (quinta essentia) of material bodies is, or rather was, regarded as an imponderable, immaterial something, on which the specific peculiarities of each body depended, and by which it was distinguishable from all other bodies, when its peculiar endowment was called into play. Scientific men know this quintessence now by the term *force*, which is defined as an *unknown cause of change*, because the *force* of one body is capable of producing effects, phenomena, or changes, in the states of other bodies, and because its inmate nature is unknown. The Greek word (δυναμις) for power or force gives us two nouns, one expressive of the science to which such causes of phenomena belong, viz., dynamics, and another expressive of the communication of such force or power, either of new, or in a higher degree than was previously possessed, viz., dynamization. The term *spirit* has been frequently employed to denominate what, while it was believed to be an entity, or existent something, was yet not regarded as of the nature of matter, as that is perceivable by the senses. It was, then, the name for that essential something in matter on which its power to produce phenomena depended, and was thus used with exactly the same meaning as now is attached to the term force. The *spiritual* powers of medicines are, therefore, their dynamic endowments or forces, and "spiritualization" of a medicine is synonymous with its dynamization, or the development of its force, or spirit, or *essential* property. Some "spirits," or forces, are common to material bodies, such as heat and electricity; and are capable of being excited or augmented in many of them by friction. Hahnemann supposed that the spiritual or dynamic powers of medicines were susceptible of a similar increase of energy, by similar means. This, then, is the plain and simple truth on which Dr. Simpson has built his contemptible charge of superstition against Hahnemann and his followers; and I am surely entitled to say that, if he did not know all that I have now explained, he is ignorant to a most discreditable extent; and that, if he *did* know it, and yet deliberately misled his readers in the matter, he has shown a state of mind compared to which "ignorance is bliss."

But I am not yet done with the subject of spirits. In these days of "table-turning," I shall try my hand at the curious experiment. I find a "table" in the twentieth number of the British and Foreign Medico-Chirurgical Review, which I am sure will answer the purpose; and I request the reader to sit down with me beside that part of it which is entitled "The Relations between Mind and Matter." In order to make the experiment plain and intelligible, I must commence with a short introduction. Professor Grove of London published, in 1846, the substance of some lectures on what he terms the correlation, or reciprocal convertibility of the ordinary physical forces; in the course of which he sought to show "that the various imponderable agencies, or the affections of matter, which constitute the main objects of experimental physics, viz., heat, light, electricity, magnetism, chemical affinity, and motion, are all correlative, or have a reciprocal dependence," each being "convertible into the other." According to his view no force is annihilated, but when it seems to be so is merely converted into another form of force; and the doctrine is illustrated throughout his work with great ingenuity and felicity. Having done with the physical forces, Mr. Grove throws out the hint that the same correlation, of convertibility, may be found to exist among the forces of organic nature; that muscular force, animal and vegetable heat, &c., are reciprocally convertible forces. Profiting by this hint, the well-known Dr. Carpenter wrote an essay on the correlation of vital and physical forces, in which he attempts to show that the forces of these two kingdoms of nature are *reciprocally* convertible, like the physical forces themselves. All this too, is ingenious, and possibly true. But a step farther remained to be taken by some not over-squeamish speculator; and that step soon followed in the article of the great allopathic review to which I have referred, and, I believe, from the pen of Dr. Carpenter. It is there plainly laid down that MIND, which is called "the manifestation of the dynamic activity of the cerebrum," is, in all "those active states known as Passions, Emotions, Moral Feelings, Sentiments," &c., correlative with, or *convertible* into, the vital forces of the body, (nerve force, muscular force, &c.,) which in the previous essay were shown to be *convertible* into the ordinary physical forces of inanimate nature! "Mind," says the writer, "is *one* of the dynamicala agencies which is capable of acting on matter; and in what we know of the physiological conditions under which Mind produces Motion, we have evidence that certain forms of vital force constitute the connecting link between the two; so that it is difficult to see that the dynamical agency we term Will is more removed from nerve-force on the one hand, than nerve-force is itself from muscular force. Each, on giving origin to the next, is itself expended, or ceases to exist as such." (P. 513.) The Will, in producing motion of the body, is held to be *converted* into the organic force of the nerves, that into muscular force; and so on with all the "dynamical" activities of the brain, including the *Moral Feelings;* each is *convertible* into nerve force, that into muscular force, that again into motion, that possibly into heat, magnetism, electricity, and chemical affinity. In illustration of this original doctrine, it is remarked, "Thus, it may be commonly noticed that those who are termed *demonstrative* persons are less firm and deep in their attachments than those who manifest their feelings less.". . . "So again, persons who are 'quick-tempered,' manifesting great irascibility upon small provocations, are usually soon appeased . . . . There is an instinctive restlessness, or tendency to general bodily movement, in some individuals, when they are suffering under emotional excitement, the indulgence of which appears to be a sort of safety-valve for the excess of nerve-force," into which, as we have seen, moral feelings and passions are liable to be *converted*, and thus to escape by the safety-valve when the pressure is high. "Thus many irascible persons find great relief in a hearty explosion of oaths, others by a violent slamming of the door, and others in a prolonged fit of grumbling. It is well known, again, that the depressing emotions are often *worked off* by a good fit of crying and sobbing." . . . . (P. 515.) In further illustration, we have the following:—"A half-idiotic youth in the Lunatic Asylum of Boston was the subject (like many of his condition) of frequent and violent paroxysms of anger; and, with the view of moderating these, it was suggested that he should be kept for some time every day in rather fatiguing exercise. Accordingly, he was employed for two or three hours daily in sawing wood, to which task he made no objection, and the paroxysms of rage never displayed themselves except on Sundays, when his employment was intermitted." The passion worked itself off through the safety-valve by being converted into nervous force, muscular force, motion, down into spiritual saw-dust. And, as the whole doctrine of correlation holds that it is reciprocal, that the downward process may be reversed, so the spiritual saw-dust, if swallowed and digested by some dreamy youth, may get up by the nerve force, and into the brain, to expend itself, as Tennyson phrases it, in "fiery" frenzies for the poetic page. This is a sort of spiritualism which recognises no *essential* difference between the boiling of a tea-kettle and the boiling of human passion,—between the working of the moral feelings and the working of a beer-barrel,—between "thoughts that breathe," and the asthmatic gaspings of an old bellows,—between the immortal spirit of a man, and a spark in candle-snuff. The "practical bearings" of the doctrine are meekly said to be "most important," and no doubt they are. The man who wishes to "come out strong" in any branch of sentiment or morals, has only to bottle up for a week or two in the dark, and feed on correlative impregnations pounded down,—through somebody's "safety-valve," who happens to have his cerebral spirits in excess,—into a mortar-full of sugar-of-milk, in order to excel all Roman and all Grecian fame. By and by congenial spirits for great occasions may be raised (like queen-bees from royal hive-bread) from patent "force"-meats, and spiritual dynamization cakes. While, on the other hand, exuberances of fancy, of sad emotions, of moral or immoral feelings, may be *worked off* by lachrymal snuffs, the saw-pit the mortar, or the tread-mill. "Vir sapit," says the old proverb, "qui pauca loquitur;" "not so," says the modern allopathic philosophy, "grumble, slam the door, explode in oaths, and you'll '*find great relief*,' on every painful occasion." No man need want any sort of cerebral dynamics long, all may soon be had in some great correlative spiritual Exchange, from a scruple of suavity in dynamized milk-sugar, to pounds of "wise saw"-dust, and bushels of conceit in triturated starch.

The eleventh and last charge against us is, that Hahnemann was fond of money, took his fees as if he was entitled to them, and advised his followers to do the same. I think his advice a very good one in the general, for I have observed that medical services which are not paid are commonly not worth paying for. It may be scarcely worth while to say, that the charge of fondness for money, made against Hahnemann, has not a shadow of foundation to rest upon. At the age of eighty the physician who, for some thirty years, had a professional fame which attracted patients to him from all parts of Europe, and from some parts of America; who lived the unexpensive life of a student in a small town; when he divided his accumulated gains among his children, previously to his second marriage, had no more to present to them, as the fruit of all his labour and celebrity, than the value of ten thousand pounds sterling. He must, then, have saved money at the unprecedented rate of £333, 6s. 8d. per annum!

But even though he had been avaricious, is the value of a man's doctrines in science inversely as *his* value for money? If so, what is to become of the Baconian system, considering that his lordship had an itching palm? Or what is to become of the nervous system, and the foundations of modern pathology, seeing that immortal Hoffmann, with the "capacious mind" had capacious pockets too? Haller asserts of him, that he acquired great wealth *by the sale of various nostrums*,

—certainly not a very creditable practice to be followed by a physician to the King of Prussia, and a professor in the University of Halle. Poor Hahnemann has been mercilessly abused for trying to get a scanty subsistence for his family, when he was oppressed with poverty, by once or twice offering a chemical or a medicine for sale; but not a word do we hear against Hoffmann for becoming rich by the systematic vending of his nostrums. Possibly success or failure makes the whole difference between an honourable and a sordid action in the estimation of our discriminating opponents.

The truth of Haller's story about Hoffmann's avarice appears to be attested by some very curious advices regarding fees, which we have direct from the illustrious founder of modern pathology himself. His first rule on the subject, for the benefit of the "prudent physician," runs thus:—"*Take your fee while the patient is in pain, for, when the disease is over the doctor becomes offensive.*"* Upon which precious text he delivers the following observations for the edification of his allopathic brethren. "This is a general rule, to be properly observed, that the physician may know how to make a use of suffering, and then he will not refuse the offered money, for such promptitude in paying does not always occur, but, for the most part, vanishes with the pain. Sometimes the most trifling anxiety brings much gain to the prudent doctor. Patients seized with the severer sufferings, persuaded that they are the forerunners of death, offer large fees; when the pain ceases, however, the fear of death ceases too, and the doctor may look out for smaller donations, especially from the Jews, who often select the best physician in the town, and too often forget the fee." The fourth rule of the same chapter has a very knowing bit of advice, which is too good to be kept from the simple-minded public. "We dispense

* Medicus Politicus, cap. x.

medicines without affixing the price, and thus receive for them very often double their value and more; for the sick are not in the habit of asking attendance for nothing, and spontaneous payments are larger than there was any necessity for giving!" Is the nervous system "declining rapidly, or indeed totally extinct?"

CHAPTER V.

The Homœopathic law, provings, and doses—Dr. Simpson's four "instances" against Homœopathy proved to be in its favour—The use of cinchona, vaccination, lemon-juice, and iodine, not due to allopathic *science*, but to chance or popular opinion—Allopathic specifics shown to be properly Homœopathic—Dr. Simpson's errors and mis-statements regarding the provings—Homœopathic doses justified by experience—Andral's experiments conducted in ignorance and bad faith.

Dr. Simpson's attack on the homœopathic law is not so much upon it as *a* law of therapeutics, as against its supposed claim to be regarded as the *universal* and *only* law; for, while he disputes that claim, he thinks it only "*doubtful* if it is *one* of the general laws of therapeutics." He has, however, advanced no argument, or fact, that affords the smallest evidence of the reasonableness of his doubt regarding the existence of such a law; and the four "instances" which form the groundwork of his contest with it bear only upon the question of its being the *universal and only* law of therapeutics. In attacking such a proposition as this he has thrown away his time, for I maintain that no one, not even Hahnemann, ever asserted, in the unqualified sense represented by Dr. Simpson, that no benefit can accrue from the employment of drugs, unless they be administered according to the homœopathic law. In the following passages Hahnemann admits that other than homœopathic remedies are *sometimes* of service: "In far the greatest number of cases of disease, however, I mean those of a chronic nature, these stormy, debilitating, indirect modes of treatment of the old school are *scarcely* ever of the slightest use."—*Intr. to Organon*, p. 32. In another work, referring to emetics and purgatives, he observes, "When substances of a completely indigestible, or foreign and very poisonous nature, oppress the stomach and bowels," "it is permitted in some few cases to effect their expulsion by such evacuant medicines."—*Lesser Writings*, p. 530. And in another, still, of his works, he observes, "In the most urgent cases, where danger to life and imminent death allow no time for the action of a homœopathic remedy—not hours, sometimes even not quarter-hours, and scarcely minutes—in sudden accidents occurring to previously healthy individuals, for example, in asphyxia and suspended animation from lightning, from suffocation, freezing, drowning, &c.—it is admissible and judicious as a preliminary measure, to stimulate the irritability and sensibility (the physical life) with a palliative, as, for instance, with mild electric shocks, with *enemata* of strong coffee, with a stimulating odour, gradual application of heat, &c. . . . . To this category belong various antidotes to sudden poisonings: alkalies for mineral acids, hepar sulphuris for metallic poisons, coffee and camphor, and ipecacuanha, for poisoning by opium," &c. Again, "In the ordinary school of medicine, the efforts made by nature for the relief of the organism in diseases where no medicine was given, were regarded as models of treatment worthy of imitation. But this was a great error. . . . These self-aiding operations of the vital force for the removal of an acute disease, performed only in obedience to the laws of organic life, and not guided by the reflection of an intellect, are at the most but a species of Allopathy;" the "vomitings, purgings, diuresis, diaphoresis, abscesses, &c.," constituting "a sort of derivation from the primarily diseased parts," which he admits to lead sometimes to "spontaneous cures," but which at the same time he affirms, to display to the observer "nothing that he could or ought to imitate if he wishes to cure disease in a truly artistic manner."—*Intr. to Organ.*, pp. 27-29. Besides, many examples occur throughout his works, in which Hahnemann notices the recoveries effected by other than Homœopathic methods as "circuitous" and "indirect," and therefore unworthy of "the honourable name of *cure*," which is a term he restricts to recoveries under the homœopathic treatment, as the "only proper one, because of the three possible modes of applying medicines in diseases, it is the only *direct* way to a mild, sure, permanent cure, without injury to another part, and without weakening the patient."—*Organ.*, p. 156. The circuitous and indirect treatment, he condemns as too commonly injurious in many more particulars than it is beneficial, and as, at the best, or when not positively injurious, seldom more than palliative, that is, productive of temporary relief only. He does not overlook the fact that even acute diseases may *recover* under the indirect treatment, as the following passage very plainly testifies:—"The disease, if it be acute, and consequently naturally but of short duration, may certainly disappear, even during those heterogeneous attacks on distant and dissimilar parts—but *cured* it was not. There is nothing that can merit the honourable name of *cure* in this revolutionary treatment, which has no direct, immediate, pathological relation to the tissues primarily affected. Often, indeed, without these serious attacks on the rest of the organism, would the acute disease have ceased of itself, sooner, most likely, with fewer secondary sufferings, and less sacrifice of strength. But neither the mode of operation of the crude natural forces, nor the allopathic copy of that can for a moment be compared to the dynamic (homœopathic) treatment, which sustains the strength, while it extinguishes the disease in a direct and rapid manner."—*Organ.*, p. 32.

These extracts from the writings of Hahnemann amply

justify me in saying that he employed the terms "universal," "infallible," "unerring," and "great sole" therapeutic law, to Homœopathy, not with the purpose of asserting that there was no other therapeutic principle whatever, or that was in any case capable of benefiting the sick, but that there was no other law in medicine that pointed to the means of *curing* diseases *directly*, by operating *immediately*, and in a *purely remedial* manner, on the individual tissues or organs that were diseased, and on them only. His law is *infallible* in the sense that it *cannot fail*, if all the conditions necessary for its action be scrupulously sought out and complied with; it is *universal* in the sense in which any other law in a science of observation and induction is universal, that it is found to have no exceptions in so far as experience of it has gone, in compliance with the conditions which are held to be necessary for its success; it is the "sole" therapeutic law, in the sense of being the only known direct, immediate, and purely remedial law for the extinguishing of *diseased action*. In order that it may deserve all these designations it is not necessary that it should enable us to cure all diseases, nor does Hahnemann maintain that it does so. He admits that some diseases are incurable, as in this passage: "There is in the interior of man nothing morbid that is *curable*, . . . which does not make itself known," &c.—*Organ.*, p. 117; and he professes, by an implication which all candid medical men will readily understand, to furnish by his homœopathic law a rule of curative treatment for diseases which are not organic and incurable, as when he says, "all medicines cure those diseases whose symptoms most nearly resemble their own," which excludes, at least as yet, organic diseases in general, or all of them, excepting the simpler and more elementary forms, which latter *may* be produced in the *provings* of medicine on previously healthy persons, and may thus become in some sense *symptoms* (because *effects*) of particular drugs. At the same time, it must be freely admitted, that Hahnemann adverts with too much reserve to incurable organic diseases, whether in consequence of the little progress of morbid anatomy at the time his works were composed, or from a lurking hope that even serious organic diseases might be eventually combated with some measure of success, when the system he launched into the world should, in the course of ages, have reached the highest development of which it was capable.

The preceding observations are, I conceive, quite an adequate and satisfactory reply to all that Dr. Simpson has said in condemnation of Hahnemann's high estimate of his therapeutic law. But if it were not possible to explain Hahnemann's opinions on that point, in a way calculated to justify the language he employs, that impossibility could be of no real consequence to the homœopathic system. It would be enough, in vindication of its claims, if we, who are the followers of Hahnemann, could only prove his law to be a *general* one. We might meet the opponent who should taunt us with the indefensible assertions of our master, with the remark of Thomas Reid, that "it is natural and almost unavoidable, to one who hath made an important discovery in philosophy, to carry it a little beyond its sphere, and to apply it to the resolution of phenomena which do not fall within its province." And in reference to all the opinions and doctrines of Hahnemann, it can scarcely be necessary for me to say more than this, that we embrace or reject them only after inquiry, when our own judgment and experience appear to qualify and entitle us to form an opinion concerning them; neither slavishly acquiescing in his maxims when they appear to us erroneous, nor afraid to avow our conviction of their truth when they harmonize with the conclusions of our understanding and the evidence of our senses. We do not recognise in Hahnemann an infallible teacher, though we revere him for his matchless sagacity, and wonder at his patience under trials, his perseverance amidst difficulties, and his courage among dangers, at the vast amount of his labours, at his diligence, and his erudition. To the four instances on which Dr. Simpson has lighted, and which he has adopted as the media of his attack on the homœopathic law, I have no disposition to object; and if I shall succeed in showing that his reasonings, allegations, and conclusions in connexion with them, are all absolutely and alike fallacious, I shall be entitled to claim the palm for Homœopathy; for although he professes to have fixed on them almost by accident, it will not be doubted that he would have selected others if he only knew any that were more to the purpose.

First Instance.—Cure of Ague by Quinine, or Cinchona Bark. In reference to the relation between cinchona (Peruvian bark) and the discovery of the homœopathic law, Dr. Simpson commits the same mistake as others had done before him, of asserting that its alleged production of symptoms of ague, (for the cure of which disease it is the ordinary remedy,) constitutes the *foundation* of the homœopathic doctrine. This error he appears plainly to patronise by quoting with approbation these expressions of a Dr. Balfour in reference to the subject, "What are we to think of a system whose very foundation is so unstable?" The error is inexcusable, because it has been fully exposed on many occasions. What would be thought of the opponent of Newton's discovery of the law of gravitation, or mutual attraction among the heavenly bodies, who should object to it that it was *based* on the accidental witnessing, by the great philospher, of an apple falling to the ground? yet the relation between the observed effects of cinchona by Hahnemann, and its curative virtues, bears a less important part, in the discovery or the proof of the homœopathic law than did the fall of the apple in the discovery or the proof of the universal law of gravitation. To Hahnemann the symptoms he observed in sensitive persons from large doses of cinchona, appeared merely to strengthen his idea of homœopathicity between drugs and the diseases they specifically cured, being the reason of their curative effects. Even if the instances which were the first proofs of that notion were fallacious, that circumstance would be of no consequence whatever to the homœopathic doctrine; the remedial virtues of cinchona would then stand merely as an exception to the law, or as an instance of the operation of some other law. In regard to Homœopathy we should, in either event, be entitled to say that cinchona, when tested by Hahnemann, *appeared* to illustrate the homœopathic law; while the provings, and employment in disease of hundreds of other remedies would still remain as incontestable evidences of the reality of a homœopathic law of cure.

But are these "so-called provings" and the curative use of cinchona actually exceptions to Homœopathy? Most assuredly they are not. Dr. Simpson falls again into gross error on both of these points. He assumes that cinchona, and, by implication, that every other alleged homœopathic remedy, when taken in considerable quantities, ought invariably to produce all the symptoms or diseases similar to those which they cure, if Homœopathy be true. Hahnemann expressly denies this. He knew, from a vast amount of experiment, that the susceptibility of human beings to suffer the pathogenetic, or, in ordinary language, the poisonous effects of medicines, differed so as to present "a vast variety on this point," while still the production of such effects in *some* he thought should be regarded as enough to show, that the *human constitution* was liable to be so affected by such medicines, and that consequently, (in accordance with the homœopathic law,) those medicines would cure such diseases, (when they arose from any other causes,) because in disease susceptibility to the action of medicines was very greatly increased, if the disease and the medicines held the homœopathic relation to one another. His words are, "all the symptoms peculiar to a medicine do not appear in one person,"—*Organon*, p. 221; and "although, as has been said, a medicine, on being proved on healthy subjects, cannot develop in one person all the alterations of health it is capable of causing, but can only do this when given to many different individuals, varying in their corporeal and mental constitution, yet the disposition (tendency) to excite all these symptoms in every human being exists in it according to an eternal and immutable law of nature, agreeably to which all its actions, even those that are but rarely developed in the healthy person, are brought into operation in the case of every individual, if administered to him when he is in a morbid state presenting similar symptoms; it then, even in the smallest dose, if homœopathically selected, silently produces in the patient an artificial state closely resembling the natural disease, which rapidly and permanently (homœopathically) frees and cures him of his original malady."—*Org.*, p. 222. All this is not in the least degree contradicted by the quotation partially given by Dr. Simpson from the same work, in which Hahnemann says, that "every real medicine acts at *all* times, and under *all* circumstances, on every living human being, and produces in him the symptoms peculiar to it, (directly perceptible if the dose be *large* enough,) so that, evidently, every living human organism is liable to be affected, and, as it were, inoculated with the medicinal disease at any time, and absolutely, (*unconditionally*,) which, as before said, is by no means the case with the natural diseases."—*Org.*, p. 132. By omitting the last clause, in quoting this passage, Dr. Simpson has left what precedes it open to an unfair construction; he has, in fact, concealed the key to the meaning of the whole of what he did quote. Hahnemann, with his wonted sagacity, was contrasting the certainty with which medicines will produce some of their peculiar effects on human beings, with the uncertainty and want of uniformity in the noxious agents of disease in *their* power to affect us, so that while the former will act upon us at all times if we take enough of them, the latter "do not produce disease in every one, nor at all times," however free his exposure to them may be. He obviously never means to say that medicines will produce *all* their peculiar effects at *all* times and under *all* circumstances, but simply *some* peculiar effects, and that *that* is more than the causes of natural disease can do.

That cinchona *does* produce symptoms of fever in man (though not in all) when taken largely in health, is attested by the experience of some dozen of persons on whom Hahnemann proved the drug; producing some symptoms in one or two, some in others. Nor is the fact doubted even by allopathic physicians of eminence, imperfect as their acquaintance is with the action of medicines on healthy persons. In his work on Materia Medica, Dr. Pereira says of cinchona, that by large doses "a febrile state is set up, (manifested by the excitement of the vascular system and dry tongue,") (p. 1404;) and Guersant observes of sulphate of quinine, a preparation of its chief therapeutic principle, that it "excites a true febrile movement of more or less duration;" and of the bark itself he says, "the reaction which it manifests many hours after its reception is, in general, much more marked (than of the sulphate;) it manifests itself by heat of skin, by more vivacity and energy in the motions, &c., although the *febrile condition* is not long continued."—*Dict. de Méd.* Again, in regard to the sulphate, the same author says, that in some it produces "great anxiety, accompanied with *shiverings*, faintness, *cold sweats*, and agitation." And Dr. Christison says of cinchona, "it is apt to excite nausea, pain in the stomach, and *febrile symptoms*."—P. 772. These are meager details compared to those of Hahnemann, but they are, in so far as they go, all directly corroborative of the accuracy of his provings; and they, altogether, form a sufficient answer to Dr. Simpson's extraordinary statement, that "observation roundly and entirely contradicts the allegation of Hahnemann, that its use can also produce ague." An ague, when its complement of leading symptoms is complete, consists, of *shiverings*, of *febrile heat*, of *sweatings*, all of which symptoms, and many more that resemble those of *particular cases* of ague, can be produced by cinchona.

As to the occasional failure of Homœopathy to cure agues by cinchona in minute doses, the fact proves nothing against its homœopathic relation to ague. Its homœopathicity being *proved* in the manner cited above, it ought to be given in *such quantities as suffice* to produce its curative results, if it be regarded as a proper and safe remedy in large doses. In this last particular Hahnemann is at variance with most other physicians. He held, as Ramazzini had done long before him, that while large doses of cinchona would indeed, often remove or repress the fever, it was dangerous to employ it in large quantities for such a purpose, because, as he thought, it was apt then to produce serious, and even ultimately fatal diseases of internal organs. His fears upon that subject were probably carried too far; but that they were not entirely unfounded appears from the statements of MM. Itard and Piorry, (Allopaths,) that they have known permanent and complete deafness follow the use of quinine for the cure of agues. Hahnemann's excessive caution was at least an error on the safe side, provided he could point out other remedies capable of removing the fever without any bad consequences. Such other remedies he *does* point out; and on the whole subject of agues he recommends that the remedy should be varied according to the particular symptoms of each case, in which event, that is, when the remedy selected is homœopathically suited to the peculiarities of *each separate case* of ague, small doses of cinchona will cure some, small doses of other medicines will cure others, and without any risk of evil consequences. In point of fact it is found, by even allopathic physicians, that agues often do not yield in any degree to any preparation of cinchona, while other medicines prove effectual; for cinchona is far from being the panacea for agues that Dr. Simpson seems to suppose. Not to multiply examples of an experience of which every intelligent physician knows something, I content myself with the testimony of a single unquestionable authority—that of M. Boudin, an allopathic physician high in the medical service of the French army. Treating of agues as they occurred among the French troops in Algeria, and of the comparative merits of cinchona and arsenic as remedies, he observes,—"I have just said that cinchona sometimes succeeded, in cases in which arsenic had failed, it must, however, be confessed, that such results, to the credit of the former, constitute the exception, whilst nothing is more frequent than the success of the arsenic in curing agues rebellious to quinine. I have succeeded in a great number of cases, and that by very feeble doses of arsenic, in putting an end, in a short time, to quotidian, tertian, and quartan agues, contracted in latitudes the most various, often complicated with chronic engorgements of the abdominal viscera, and which for a long time had resisted the sulphate of quinine."* Boudin is an allopathic physician, yet he tells us that the dose he latterly employed did not exceed the *hundredth* of a grain of arsenic. I shall let him tell his own tale:—"I have often obtained by a *single* dose of the hundredth of a grain of this medicine the radical cure of fevers contracted either in Algeria or in Senegal, and which had resisted means of various kinds, including sulphate of quinine and change of climate." —P. 277. Now arsenic, according to Hahnemann, (and Dr. Christison, in his work on poisons, quotes his account of the

* *Traité des Fièvres Intermit, p.* 280.

poisonous effects of this substance, which is no small proof of Hahnemann's accuracy,) produces many of the symptoms noticed in agues, and must therefore be homœopathic to *some* agues; and M. Boudin, an enemy to Homœopathy, informs us that a patient of his own, labouring under a skin disease, and otherwise in good health, at a time when no agues existed in the city, became affected with a quotidian ague after having taken in divided doses, a quarter of a grain of arsenic, and, as he believed, in *consequence* of his having taken the drug. Biet, again, another allopathic physician of eminence, affirms that he has remarked the effects of arsenic to observe a certain *periodicity* in their occurrence, an important remark when it is considered that the medicine in question has been so much employed, and with success, too, in ague, neuralgia, and other diseases of an intermittent nature.*

* Africa is not the only quarter of the globe in which intermittents are found which pay little heed to quinine, as the following serio-comic narrative by Guersant abundantly proves. He is writing of a physician in France who believed that quinine failed only because not given in sufficiently large doses. "Such was the state of mind of our colleague, when his wife was attacked with a paroxysm of ague, which he thought grave enough to need energetic treatment. Consequently he gave her 16 grammes of sulphate of quinine in a very short space of time. The patient soon fell into a state of stupor, with weight in the head, dazzling, and then blindness, deafness, &c. M. Bazire, conceiving that these new symptoms were due to the approach of a new paroxysm of pernicious ague, gave his wife 25 grammes more of the drug. After the reception of this considerable dose, the symptoms increased with frightful rapidity; the patient became completely deaf and blind, her respiration embarrassed, pulse miserable, skin cold. . . . . . . Whilst this deplorable scene passed, our unhappy colleague was a prey to many fatigues, on account of the great number of bad agues which abounded in the province; the reverses which he experienced had thrown despair into his imagination already exalted; he saw with dismay the malady triumphant, and the power of his remedy, which he believed infallible, too often useless. However, by a singular fatality, his very want of success only increased his blind devotion to the sulphate of quinine." Happily for his wife, it is added, he took the disease himself, and dosed himself so effectually with his infallible specific as soon to put an end to the disease and his own life together.—*Dict. de Méd.*

Second Instance.—Vaccination and its Effects upon Small-pox.—I cannot avoid expressing my surprise at the want of information, as well as of reasoning power, displayed by the Professor of Midwifery in connexion with this subject, especially considering that it lies within his own province—the diseases of children. I was not so unprepared for the *unfairness* of shifting the argument from vaccination to artificial inoculation with small-pox, an evasion which I think it unnecessary to follow and to expose in detail, but merely remark on the subject, that Hahnemann and his followers hold exactly the same opinions on the relation between inoculated and ordinary small-pox as other physicians do. Confining attention to vaccination and *its* relation to small-pox, I can prove that Hahnemann's view of the subject is the *only* view that is consistent with sound logic and actual experience. His opinions are contained in the following passage from his Organon:—"The cow-pox would even destroy the small-pox on its first appearance; that is to say, it would cure this malady when already present, if the small-pox were not stronger than it. To produce this effect, then, it only wants that excess of power, which, according to the law of nature, ought to accompany the homœopathic resemblance in order to effect a cure. Vaccination, considered as a homœopathic remedy, cannot therefore prove efficacious, except when employed previous to the appearance of the small-pox, which is the stronger of the two. When so employed it excites a disease very analogous (and consequently homœopathic) to the small-pox, after whose course the human body, which, as usual, can only be attacked once with a disease of this nature, is henceforward protected against a similar contagion." P. 83. Now, the whole question turns upon this, are the vaccine disease and small-pox *identical?* If they are, then vaccination does *not* prevent small-pox by homœopathic *anticessum*, as Hahnemann calls it, but by being the *same* as small-pox, which, by *once* occurring, even in this mild form, does not usually occur again. If they are *not identical*, however *similar*, then we are entitled to claim vaccination as an instance illustrative of the law relating to *similars*. Dr. Simpson allows that pathologists are not all agreed regarding the identity of the two diseases. He might have mentioned Dr. Gregory of London, physician to the Small-pox Hospital, and therefore likely to have more experience than others on the subject, as *one* who is opposed to the doctrine of their identity. However, we do not care about *authorities*, we appeal to facts. It is no doubt true that inoculating the cow with small-pox virus will produce the vaccine disease; but the question remains,—Is the virus of this vaccine disease the same in all respects excepting *strength* as the small-pox virus, or is it modified in *nature* too? If modified in *nature* as well as strength, it is no longer *identical* with small-pox virus, however closely it may resemble it. That it *is* changed in its *nature*, appears plainly the only rational conclusion, from the following considerations:—

1. The mildest case of modified small-pox, where only half-a-dozen pocks occur, will still produce by inoculation or contagion only small-pox, and *may* produce severe and even fatal small-pox, in others. Vaccinia may be said, however, to be still milder than the mildest *small-pox;* well,—

2. Dilute small-pox virus with *water*, and thus *weaken* it to the lowest potency still capable of acting by inoculation, and it will *still produce small-pox*, not the solitary vaccine vesicle.

3. Dilute small-pox virus with *cow's milk*, and, according to the experience of Dr. Basil Thiele in 3000 cases, inoculation with the mixture *will produce the vaccine vesicle*, and *not the small-pox* eruption.

Am I not then amply entitled to say, that the two diseases are *not identical?* If only *similar*, *very* similar it may be, the just conclusion manifestly is, that vaccination by producing a disease *similar* to small-pox, and which can occur only once, in general, prevents the occurrence of small-pox; that, in a word, vaccination acts *homœopathically*, or according to one rule of the law of *similars*. I might adduce other reasons for the opinion that the vaccine virus and that of small-pox are not identical; in particular, the pretty certain, and very interesting circumstance, that *vaccination* is a surer preventive of future small-pox, than even an attack of small-pox itself is; but I believe I have said enough to establish our claims to vaccination.

Third Instance.—Prevention and Cure of Sea-scurvy by Lemon-juice.—I must reiterate here my astonishment at Dr. Simpson's want of information, and express also my surprise that he should have adduced scurvy as a case for drugs at all.

He says, "I am aware, that on theoretical grounds, Dr. Stevens supposes that the use of lemon-juice should produce scurvy; but I believe that neither he nor any one else ever observed that disease to result *from* the use of lemon-juice. Dr. Stevens, I venture to say makes no theoretical assertions on the subject, at least I have never been able to find them, but *he does give an instance in which the citric acid* (the acid of lemon juice) *produced scurvy*! His words are,—the scurvy "was decidedly brought on by the excessive use of citric acid, which an American gentleman had been recommended to use as a preventive against the yellow fever. His own conviction, as well as mine, was, that the scorbutic symptoms had been brought on by the acid." *—(*On the Blood*, p. 451.)

* Dr. Simpson's ignorance on this subject having been exposed in my former reply, he adds a note, in his republication of this "Third Instance," with the hope of regaining his credit. He there argues that when men take scurvy who are living upon insufficient diet, and are also taking bad or too little lemon-juice, the scurvy is to be ascribed to the diet and not to the lemon-juice! This is a great discovery: as also is the admission that Stevens "fancied" he

Here I might close the case for Homœopathy, for, in order to be homœopathic to a disease, the remedy need not be as Dr. Simpson erroneously supposes, "often and constantly" the cause of similar symptoms.

But I prefer disposing of this "Third Instance" on entirely different grounds. Scurvy is a disease acknowledged on all hands, to be essentially due to *unsuitable diet*,—especially, if not indeed solely, to the loss or deficiency of some customary article of food. It is *cured*, therefore, by restoring to the diet the deficient ingredient, or something that will answer instead. The former is by far the more reasonable and effectual procedure; and, accordingly, a mess of potatoes, or a ration of milk, will answer as well as, or better than, the substitutes given by physicians, either to prevent or to cure scurvy. If one man gives a salt of potash, it is still not as a *drug* but as *food* to supply the unhealthful deficiency of such salt in the blood and in the food; if another recommends sulphur, phosphorus, &c., it is for the same reason, to supply the deficiency he supposes of these elements in the altered dietary of the scorbutic; and if a third recommends cheese, milk, or beef, it is because he presumes the patient to be suffering from want of the due supply of nitrogenous elements in his food. Lemon-juice itself is said by some to act merely dietetically, supplying to the food, and consequently to the body, the potash salts which are believed to be defective. Even pure citric acid has been regarded in the same light, as furnishing elements suitable for the respiratory process, in the absence of the necessary quantity of combustible matter in the food. It is absolutely grotesque, therefore, to adduce scurvy as an instance opposed to Homœopathy. The ingenious Professor of Midwifery might as well have brought against us

had seen lemon-juice cause scurvy,—an admission made since I exposed his ignorance of Stevens' experience on the subject.

a case of starvation, with all its sufferings, and argued, that because we could not cure it by an additional dose of abstinence, or something *similar*, while *he* could by wholesome nutriment, therefore Homœopathy was unsound!

Fourth Instance.—Cure of Goître by the exhibition of Iodine.—Under this head I shall first correct a mis-statement. Dr. Simpson says, at p. 55, "The homœopathists, in order to keep up this alleged universality of their immutable law of 'similia similibus,' are obliged, in contradiction to every rule in logic and philosophy, to enter in their Materia Medica, this (curative) action of iodine as one of the symptoms produced by iodine, though goître was never, I believe, observed as a symptom of the use of iodine," &c. Now, the reply is, that homœopathists do nothing of the kind. They prefix to the notice of such curative action of iodine a mark (o) indicating the very opposite of all this, or, that iodine has been *hitherto known not to produce goître, but to cure it!* But why do they put this curative action into their books at all? Just because they believe, and have no doubt that experience will ultimately *prove*, that this curative action depends on the capacity of iodine to produce the disease,* though the circumstances necessary for such a pathogenetic effect have not yet been discovered. If iodine be not homœopathic in its action, what is it? no one can tell, or at least *prove*, anything on the subject.

I need not repeat at length what I have said regarding the rarity, sometimes, of certain effects in the proving of drugs. To be characteristic, they need not be *constantly* pro-

* This expectation, expressed in my former publication of the above, in reply to Dr. Simpson's second edition, has been fulfilled. A man taking five grains of hydriodate of potass twice a-day, after eight days became affected with a "rapidly growing swelling of the thyroid gland." See Brit. Journ. of Hom., No. xliv.

duced, or even at all in many persons. Some approach to the pathogenetic effect in question,—in addition to the instance mentioned in the note I have just given, of thyroid enlargement, produced by the action of hydriodate of potass,—has been made in the provings of iodine; witness the glandular swellings in the neck and elsewhere that have followed its use. We have also an instance suggestive of its homœopathicity to goître, in the increase or aggravation of the disease noticed at the commencement of the treatment.—*See Jahr's Manual, Iodine. American Edition.*

Dr. Simpson, in the four instances he has selected for the double purpose of magnifying allopathic science and opposing the claims of Homœopathy, has been peculiarly unfortunate in his choice. He takes them from Sir John Herschel's "Preliminary Discourse," &c., as furnishing examples of disease "for which the *advancement of science of late years* has devised more or less certain means of removal and cure." (P. 241.) Science! Does Dr. Simpson actually not know *how* the virtues of cinchona, vaccination, lemon-juice, and iodine were discovered? Fine instances they certainly present of the appropriating capacity of allopathic science. The discoveries being made somehow, Allopathy lays hold of them as hers, though she had in reality no more title to them than the man in the moon. Sir John Herschel's ignorance may be excused, if he was so ill informed as to suppose the four "instances" to be four instances of the triumph of medical science; his walk is too much in the "milky way" of real science to allow of his knowing much of the dark and crooked ways of physic; but those who know a little more of these may be permitted to supply his deficiencies. The literal fact then is, that every one of these discoveries, so much vaunted as the trophies of modern science, was (with one apparent exception which shall be explained) made without the very smallest assistance from any science under the sun. Cinchona bark was introduced into notice as a cure for agues more than two hundred years ago, and a knowledge of its virtues is supposed to have been originally derived from the wild Indian *aborigines* of South America. "This heroic remedy," says Dr. Paris, (an Allopath,) "was first brought to Spain in the year 1632; and we learn from Villerobel, that it remained for seven years in that country before any trial was made of its powers: a certain ecclesiastic of Alcala being the first person in Spain to whom it was administered in the year 1639. But even at this period its use was limited, and it would have sunk into oblivion but for the supreme power of the Roman Church, by whose auspices it was enabled to gain a temporary triumph over the *passions and prejudices which opposed* its introduction." (*Pharm.*, t. i. p. 56.) So much for modern allopathic science, and its claims to the discovery of cinchona as a cure for ague. This, in fact, was one of the instances expressly referred to by Hahnemann, in which some accident led to the detection of a remedy, as has been the usual way in which remedies actually *homœopathic* have got into common use.

Vaccination belongs, in the strictest manner, to the same category. I am sorry, in discussing this point, to have even the appearance of detracting from the merits of Dr. Jenner, but the truth must be told, whosoever may seem to suffer a little from the tale. In Gloucestershire, where Jenner was born, it was *notorious*, time out of mind, among the cow-milkers, that those who happened to contract sores upon the hands from disease on the udders of the cows were protected from the small-pox! Jenner heard of this popular doctrine thirty years before he made any experiment on the subject, ay, even before he began his medical studies. The discovery of the protective power of vaccinia against small-pox was, therefore, not due to medical science, but, *as usual*, to accident. Jenner had, notwithstanding, the very high distinction of sifting the popular experience on the subject, determining what stage of the disease in the cow it was which produced the protecting sores in man, and of proposing that so important an effect should no longer be left to accident, but should be artificially and purposely produced. Allopathic science, however, had nothing to do with the discovery.

Lemon-juice, again, as a dietetic remedy for scurvy, was also, and *of course* discovered by accident, as the following allopathic authority admits:—"The earliest notice we can find in reference to this point is in the 3d epistle of Rousseus, dated 1564, wherein it appears that some Dutch sailors who were suffering from scurvy, and the cargo of whose ship on their return from Spain, consisted of lemons and oranges, *accidentally* discovered that their use was the means by which they recovered their health." (Cycl. of Pract. Med., vol. iii. p. 695.) Lastly, iodine as a remedy for bronchocele is just thus much indebted to science, (but only to *chemical* science,) that chemistry discovered it in sponges, which as *burnt sponge* had long previously been popularly employed in that disease. "For centuries," says Dr. Manson, writing in 1825, "burnt-sponge was the chief remedial agent in the cure of bronchocele." (Med. Researches, &c., p. 8.) Iodine being discovered in sponges, it was easy to conclude that it was probably the source of their medicinal virtue, and it needed no scientific wisdom to try if the conclusion was just.

I might go over every specific employed by ordinary physicians, and show that in *not a single instance* can the discovery of their medicinal properties be traced to *science*, as the guide by whose instrumentality it was made. Tradition, descending from periods when no medical *science* can be said to have existed,—accident,—fanciful hypotheses and theories,—mere hap-hazard experiments,—resemblances between a new substance and one long in use; these have been the modes by which Allopathy has stumbled on *homœopathic* remedies, when she has not silently helped herself from the homœopathic *materia medica.* I say *homœopathic* remedies, because specifies, that is, substances which produce their curative effects without derivations and evacuations, by acting quietly and secretly on the immediate seat of the disease, and on no other part, are most certainly homœopathic, and nothing else.* Cinchona and iodine are so, as has just been shown, in the cure of ague, and bronchocele; mercury plainly is so in the cure of dysentery, hepatitis, and many other diseases in which it is commonly employed by allopathic as well as homœopathic practitioners; arsenic, too, as has been shown already, is homœopathic to certain agues, and to other intermittent diseases, as well as to some scaly affections of the skin, for the cure of which it is given by allopathic practitioners, while they admit that it *produces* a scaly state of the skin; and so on with a great many other medicines, which are classed by allopathic writers under the name of tonics, astringents, alteratives, and so forth, from hypothetical notions of the manner in which they operate as remedies. All this being as I have now represented, and the homœopathic relation between some medicines and the diseases they cure being admitted by the best informed physicians, the non-medical reader may ask what it is we are quarrelling about with so much elaborate vehemence on (I admit) both sides. In answer to the inquiry, I have to say, that the quarrel is partly about the use of the law, partly about the provings, and partly about the

* As a counterpoise to Dr. Simpson's denial of a general homœopathic law, I may mention that the present Professor of Materia Medica objected, some twelve years ago, to Dr. Black's admission into the College of Physicians, partly on the ground that homœopathists arrogated that title to themselves, while they had no right to do so, as the homœopathic relation between diseases and medicines was recognised in the ordinary school.

dose. The nonsense and misrepresentation which Dr. Simpson has so foolishly allowed himself to indulge in against the adherents of Homœopathy,—the witchcraft and other silly charges invented against them, as well as the occasional traces of human imperfection so absurdly proclaimed to their disparagement, as if they alone were subject to errors and weaknesses, are all beside the question, and are of no conceivable consequence to the vital points involved in the present controversy. Even the question of our provings of medicines is not an essential one. It is at the utmost a question of *degree;* for men on both sides concur in the opinion that medicines do produce effects, or medicinal symptoms, when taken by healthy persons, and the only difference between us regarding them is as to what are to be admitted as really due to the medicines so taken,—whether some of them may not be traceable to the imagination of the prover, or are not too insignificant and ordinary to be properly enrolled among the effects of the medicines at all. Of course the objections made against some of the provings may be just enough,—no homœopathist contends for their accuracy in every particular; on the contrary, we are fully aware, indeed a great deal more than our opponents are, of the many difficulties and sources of fallacy that beset the attempt to acquire a full knowledge of the effects which even one medicine is capable of causing, and are, therefore, not so sanguine as to believe that we know all the possible symptoms that any one medicine can produce, or that every phenomenon which follows the taking of medicines by a prover is necessarily due to the substances which were taken. Of this, and other points connected with the provings, more immediately.

The principal, if not the only, dispute between us and the more intelligent of our opponents, in so far as the *law* is concerned, is simply this,—that we, with the help of our provings, make the homœopathic law the *rule* by which we select the medicines we prescribe, giving such medicines only as we know from the provings to be capable of *producing* symptoms and morbid conditions similar to those existing in the diseases which we are called upon to treat; while they (our opponents) do not *act upon* the homœopathic law as a rule in the prescribing of drugs, though they *admit the fact* of a homœopathic relation subsisting between certain diseases and the operations of the medicines which cure them. Our procedure gives us an immense advantage over our opponents, even in the employment of the very medicines which both of us use in diseases which to appearance are the same. For instance, they use ipecacuan, and also mercury in dysentery; we do so likewise, but with this great superiority over them, that our *rule* directs us to the employment of ipecacuan, where ipecacuan is likely to be the most suitable and successful remedy, and of mercury where it is more likely to succeed; for all cases of dysentery are neither exactly similar in every respect, nor curable by the same remedy. Our opponents cannot adapt either of these medicines with any degree of precision or certainty to the different cases for which they are respectively suitable; and when they do give the right remedy in the right case it is simply and solely by *chance*,—for, what they call the *indications* which seem to make it advisable that one of the medicines should be given in preference to the other, are mere matters of opinion, or hypotheses, on which there is no general agreement, and for which no valid reason can be adduced. The illustration I have just adverted to is, perhaps, the most favourable to the allopathic party that can be given, when there is any room for doubt as to what medicine is proper for a particular case of disease. In most of the instances in which, speaking in a general way, we employ the same remedies, their difficulties in fixing upon the right medicine for the right case are vastly increased by the choice lying among several or many.

They have no *rule* to guide them, with the exception of that mis-named experience which proceeds on the resemblance, in some of its chief characters, of the case under treatment, to one which had formerly been treated with success by a certain remedy. This rule is loose and uncertain as a guide to practice, because it never can descend sufficiently to particulars,—because two cases of the same disease, which agree in a few prominent features, may, and very often do, differ materially in their special characters, and in what they want in order to be successfully treated. On this subject Dr. Abercrombie makes the following judicious reflections, and I suppose his authority will hardly be rejected:—"When, in the practice of medicine, we apply to new cases the knowledge acquired from others which we believe to have been of the same nature, the difficulties are so great, that it is doubtful whether in any case we can properly be said to act upon experience, as we do in other departments of science. For we have not the means of determining with certainty that the condition of the disease, the habit of the patient, and all the circumstances which enter into the character of the affection, are in any two cases precisely the same; and if they differ in any one particular, we cannot be said to act from experience, but only from analogy. The difficulties and sources of uncertainty which meet us at every stage of such investigations are, in fact, so great and so numerous, that those who have had the most extensive opportunities of observation will be the first to acknowledge that our pretended experience must, in general, sink into analogy, and even our analogy too often into conjecture."* Homœopathy saves its disciples from most of the doubts and difficulties which perplex the *allopathic* physician, (I use the term merely for the sake of distinction, for when employing specifics he is not an

* Intellectual Powers, p. 395.

allopath, whatever he may think himself to be;) they have provings of so many medicines, so minutely and carefully detailed, that they have usually no difficulty in fixing upon the medicine which, of all that are known, is the most suitable to each particular case of disease. Difficulties, however, even homœopathists sometimes have in selecting a remedy for some peculiar case; for many medicines are yet but imperfectly *proved*, and many more, doubtless, exist in nature which have not hitherto been proved at all, and among which, it may be, the most appropriate homœopathic remedy for such peculiar case exists, though as yet unavailable because unproved. Two instances occur to me which illustrate both this observation and the practical advantages of the homœopathic rule. In the August number of the Monthly Journal of Medical Science for 1852, Dr. Simpson published a case of headache in a female, which, after having been unsuccessfully treated by many physicians, homœopathic and allopathic, yielded to the sulphate of nickel, with which Dr. Simpson was making experiments at the time. Supposing,—as may possibly have been the case, though one instance is not by any means a proof that it was so,—that the headache ceased in consequence of the employment of the sulphate of nickel, we have here an illustration of the *specific* operation of a remedy, and consequently of its *homœopathic* operation, for we have no evidence that any specific remedy is other than homœopathic, and a great mass of evidence that the so-called specifics are in reality homœopathic remedies. There is as yet no homœopathic *proving* of the sulphate of nickel, though there is of the carbonate, but not of a very full and detailed description. Now, if the sulphate of nickel was the proper homœopathic remedy for this case, no homœopathic physician could cure it; he had no proving to guide him, and he has no other guide that he can trust to in selecting a remedy in such a case. How, then, did Dr. Simpson hit upon the sulphate of nickel as the remedy for this headache? What rule or principle had he to guide him? How will he proceed in employing the sulphate in other cases of headache? Sulphate of nickel, he says, is "a gentle tonic," but there are scores of "gentle tonics;" next, it "corresponds with the therapeutic action of the salts of iron," but "they also specifically differ from each other in some respects," and the case of headache under consideration "defied iron in many different forms." On what special ground, then, was the sulphate of nickel used in this case? It may be safely answered, on none whatever of a higher or more scientific description than this, in Dr. Simpson's words, "I began making various experiments upon myself and others with different metals," and because "it seems, *a priori*, highly probable that some of the new, like some of the old metals, will *turn out* to have decided, and it *may be* important therapeutic properties." Without any clear notion of the actual therapeutic powers of these metals, at best with the expectation that they would be found to resemble in their actions other metals which had been accidentally ascertained or theoretically imagined to possess certain medicinal properties, Dr. Simpson experimented at random on one case after another until *accidentally* an instance of headache fell in his way that yielded to the specific virtues of the sulphate of nickel! There was obviously no rational scientific principle to direct the experiments; and, even now, after a case has been happily fallen in with which was cured by the drug, neither Dr. Simpson nor any of his party can give the smallest inkling of a reason why the medicine succeeded, or the slightest appearance of a *rule* for its future successful employment. *Try* iron, or cadmium, or iridium, or tellurium, or zinc, or quinine, or nickel, or any thing, in headaches, and now and then a case will cast up which one of these drugs will cure. No one denies this, and no one will deny that a standing clock will tell the exact time twice in a day, for every hour of the day glides twice past the face of the motionless machine. The medical system which accidentally succeeds in its unregulated career, is just as worthy of confidence as the stirless timepiece; and its instance or two of occasional cures of the kind under consideration are no more entitled to be regarded as proofs of its scientific efficiency, than the perfect exactness with which the stock-still hands of the clock, set at the figure 12, will daily coincide with the solar noon, is entitled to be regarded as a proof of the mechanical excellence of the timepiece.

A timepiece which sadly needs cleaning and regulating is not a bad illustration of the common practice of medicine. The proper machinery is present in both, for we do not deny that Allopathy has many materials for efficiently combating diseases; we condemn her for suffering herself to be clogged with the dust and cobwebs of a pragmatical ancestry, and for trying to work by a regulator (if it deserves the name) which has not been touched since the days of Hippocrates, and which was manufactured and adjusted at a time when craftsmen had neither the skill nor the materials wherewith to construct a satisfactory instrument. She either won't go at all, or she goes wrong; yet she won't suffer her regulator to be changed, or her dirt to be removed. And what is the consequence? We have seen the going wrong astoundingly exemplified in the treatment of pneumonia and of other acute inflammations; we see the not going at all (and it is the better of the two) in the presenting of specifics at the array of headaches, &c., as they pass,—like the hours around the dial-plate of the illustrative clock,—and the happy *coincidence* which now and then chances to occur between a drug and a malady in search of a cure: for as matters are managed among our allopathic friends, it is the malady that is on the move from the drug of one standing doctor to that of another, and it must sometimes stumble on the thing it wants. Dr. Simpson has told us of an instance in which one rambling headache fell in with the sulphate of nickel and got well, but he has not told us of the scores which took the same path, and went away as they came. I can tell of one, and as it exemplifies the superiority of the new instrument with the modern regulator, I shall briefly relate its history. In the course of last year a lady had recourse to Homœopathy under the following circumstances:—She had been subject to a particular form of daily headache for fifteen months, when she applied to Dr. Simpson, and got the following prescription,—

Sulph. nickel, gr. xxiv.
Aquæ distil., . ℥xii.
A tablespoonful twice a day.

She continued the medicine as recommended for three months, without the slightest benefit. By carefully comparing the particulars of her sufferings with the *provings* of several medicines, which seemed more or less to correspond with them, *Calcarea carbonica* was selected as the most suitable to all the symptoms, and prescribed in the twelfth dilution, a dose every second night. Within a week the headaches were reported as decidedly better, for one whole day entirely absent, on the other days three hours later than was their invariable period of invasion before, and less severe: while some of the attendant symptoms had ceased altogether. Within a month, the peculiar periodic headaches had entirely ceased, and only a heaviness in the forehead occasionally occurred. Four doses of sepia, No. 12, had removed the little that the calcarea had left; and from that day to this she has had none of her former sufferings from headache, and for many months past not even the feeling of occasional weight in the forehead. The difference presented by the new system, in its working, as compared with the old, is simply this, that it enables us to tell what medicine is likely to succeed before we try it on the particular case which demands our services. Our provings are now so many and so full, that there are probably few chronic diseases, (and I refer now only to them,) not organic and incurable, for which homœopathy has not a remedy ascertained and described at length in the pages of her *Materia Medica.* Of headaches, for instance, there must be few indeed which have not the counterpart of all their symptoms represented in the proving of some one medicine or another, and *that* representation declares such medicine to be the remedy for the headache which it resembles in its pathogenetic effects.

I observed a few pages back that the cures effected by means of specific remedies in the hands of allopathic physicians are *homœopathic* cures. The reader may object: But don't you differ greatly about the doses? How can their doses of the same drugs cure in the same way as yours which are so much smaller? It is remarkable, very remarkable, that it should ever be so; but yet it is undeniable that it is so. Two observations may be made on this subject: The first is, that much of the excessive doses of specific medicines given by allopathic physicians finds its way or is expelled speedily from the body, and does not remain to do harm; while often a powerful drug given in large doses is prevented from injuring, in consequence of chemical changes effected upon part of it in the stomach. In illustration of the former statement, I may mention that the secretion from the kidneys was found by Professor Porta to present distinct traces of iodine in from six to twelve minutes after the fumes of it had been inhaled from a bladder. Every medical man knows that chemistry is rendering it daily more certain that the rule is a very general, if not a universal one, that medicinal substances taken into the body are very speedily expelled by one channel or another, and in more or less abundance; and that the rapidity and the amount of the excretion depend very much on the amount of the dose. The amount which remains behind to act as a remedy is therefore but a proportion, it is likely a very small proportion, of the quantity received. This is one proof of the unnecessary magnitude of allopathic doses, and of how much mankind is indebted for protection from incalculable injuries even from well-meaning persons, by the wise and beneficent provisions of Nature. It was remarked above that the allopathic doses of some substances are also reduced by chemical changes, which make them sometimes in a great measure insoluble, and incapable of being received into the blood, at least in their original and intended quantity. It is thus, for instance, with corrosive sublimate, which, given in doses of one-twelfth of a grain, forms partly an insoluble compound with the albumen of the gastric mucus, and cannot therefore be absorbed, so as to produce its therapeutic effects, but in exceedingly minute, often no doubt "infinitesimal" quantities. Many other metallic salts and also metallic oxides are unquestionably detained, by substances which render them insoluble, in the digestive canal, and very little of them is left free to be absorbed. Altogether, then, the difference between the two systems, in respect to doses, (meaning by the term the quantities of medicines which are received into the circulation, and are at liberty to act as remedies,) is not nearly so great as at first sight it appears to be, of those substances at least which act as specifics. Often it may be—and we know nothing with certainty to the contrary—the allopathic doses of specifics may amount in reality to *working* doses no larger than the ordinary homœopathic ones. The latter, while much smaller as first taken into the body, do not necessarily become lessened by chemical changes and by excretion in the same proportion as the others do, for there is both less matter in them to come into contact with chemical interruptions, and less also to be laid hold of and extracted by the excreting organs from the mass of the blood.

But, in the second place, allopathic doses of specifics, which are truly homœopathic in their action, while they may succeed in curing the disease for which they are given, are liable to do so (and but for the reasons noticed would always do so) at the expense of more or less serious injury to the general health, or to parts of the body. How many are there who, though relieved of their original malady by mercury, in allopathic doses, continue throughout their lives to suffer from the constitutional effects of the poisonous quantities they have received? And when the evils of excessive drugging do not endure so long, or sink so deeply into the system, how often do they add temporary, it may be severe sufferings, to those of the original disease, which by smaller quantities of the same medicine, might have been removed without any medicinal disorders occurring. As an instance of this disadvantage of allopathic doses, compared with the homœopathic, the following case,—quite an ordinary example,—may possess some interest:—A gentleman, in May 1852, became affected with inflammation of one eye, and hastened to place himself under the care of an eminent oculist in Glasgow. The disease was declared to be rheumatic iritis; and for the cure of it venesection was practised, and calomel and opium prescribed. The eye got gradually well, but the improvement became associated with mercurial inflammation of the mouth and tongue, which confined him to the house for a month, and part of that time to his bed. He had, within a few months after, several relapses, though not severe. During the winter he continued well, but in March 1853 he was seized with an attack of iritis as severe as that of the previous May. The sclerotic, around the cornea, was closely and intensely injected with straight vessels, and so deeply coloured as to present almost the appearance of ecchymosis. An aching pain affected the eyeball, the iris was duller coloured than the other, and the pupil regular though somewhat dilated. The disease lasted four days, when the second homœopathic dilution of corrosive sublimate was prescribed, in doses of a drop every four hours. Each dose consisted, therefore, of only the ten-thousandth of a grain of the medicine. In four days the eye was nearly well, and on the eighth day of the treatment, the patient was at his usual business occupations in perfect health. He had taken only five doses a day of the medicine, as one of the nocturnal periods for a dose was passed over. A slight relapse took place in a few weeks, and was quickly removed by the same remedy, without confining him to the house. No mercurial *disease* accompanied this mercurial treatment. Homœopathic experience abounds with similar cases.

Those who object to the homœopathic doses constantly forget that Homœopathists have no other reason for their preference for minute quantities of medicines than simply and solely their *sufficiency* for curing diseases, without the danger of aggravating them, or of causing other diseases. If drachm or scruple doses were the safest and most effectual, there is nothing in the world to prevent us from employing them. Hahnemann employed them till he found that they were often too large, and liable to produce bad effects, as has been shown to be the case by the instance I have adduced above. And though it is not likely that Hahnemann was led, throughout his discovery of the necessity for extreme attenuations of the medicines which are to be used homœopathically with the most success, by *mere* experiment, and step by step from dilution to dilution on to the highest of his potencies, it is so manifest that medicines which are homœopathic to a diseased condition ought to be given in much reduced doses, that it would be a waste of time to reason on the subject. Let the following admission by a high allopathic authority suffice: "Medicines operate most powerfully upon the sick when the symptoms correspond with those of the disease.

A very small quantity of medicinal arnica will produce a violent effect upon persons who have an irritable state of the œsophagus and stomach, [that state being *producible* by arnica,—W. H.] Mercurial preparations have, in very small doses, given rise to pains and loose stools when administered in an inflammatory state of the intestines, [mercurials produce in healthy persons inflammation of the intestines,—W. H.] . . . Yet why should I occupy time in adducing more examples of a similar operation of medicines, since it is in the very nature of the thing that a medicine must produce a greater effect when it is applied to a body already suffering under an affection similar to that which the medicine itself is capable of producing."* Hahnemann, no doubt, went far beyond what is granted in this general admission regarding the relation between diseases and the doses of medicines which are homœopathic to them, and he did so partly, it is probable enough, by anticipation or inference from the reason of the thing, the earlier facts of his first steps in attenuating medicines having suggested a leap at once to the more extreme parts of his scale of potencies. Having found, by experiment, that even these extraordinary exiguities were often efficient as remedies, it may safely be supposed that the incomprehensible minuteness of the still active doses gave rise in his mind to the notion that possibly the means employed for subdividing the medicines produced at the same time a developement of medicinal force or energy. This idea of *dynamization* by friction and shaking is a mere hypothesis, is of no consequence whatever to the theory or practice of Homœopathy, and has no kind or measure of likelihood in its favour, as most Homœopathists believe. Minute doses must be contented to pass for no more than they are—just minute doses, with their own proper contin-

* Professor Jorg in Materialien zu einer künftigen Heilmittellehre, p. 9. 1825.

gent of medicinal force, and nothing beyond that. It is not a necessary or even a general tenet of Homœopathy, that small quantities of matter are more potent than larger are; and Homœopathy does not, as is ignorantly supposed, demand that for her efficiency the "ordinary laws of matter should be reversed." And yet there are circumstances in which the paradox, that "the smaller the amount of matter the greater the effect," is literally true. This depends partly upon the effect that is to be produced. An ounce of gunpowder will certainly do more by its explosion than a grain can do, and a crowbar an inch thick is a far more effective tool in raising heavy weights than the blade of a penknife. But supposing that one is not intent on blowing up any body, or on raising anything, it may happen that the smaller quantity of matter will prove by far the most effectual. If the object in view is a smooth shave, I believe even allopathic experience is in favour of the edge of a razor as preferable to the back, though the latter comprises a much greater amount of steel. So likewise in physic, if the object be to produce the remedial operation of ipecacuan in bronchitis, a sixth of a grain may effect that end, while a scruple dose will not, because it proves an emetic; and if it be the purpose to get turpentine to act on the kidneys, doses of five or six drops will succeed, while doses of two ounces will totally fail. The relation between medicinal substances and living bodies is very curious, very perplexing, and very little understood; and those gentlemen, whether of the press or of the profession, who fancy their undoubted "common sense" quite competent to resolve all its mysteries, without any special study of the subject, will find themselves eventually very much in the wrong — their laughter at homœopathic therapeutics the laughter of ignorance, their sneer the grimace of folly. Many Homœopathists, I grant, hold that the minuter the dose the greater is the power of the medicine in causing effects similar in kind to those which the larger doses sometimes or in some degree produce. The causes of this belief are twofold,—first, it rests upon Hahnemann's doctrine of *dynamization*, or increase of medicinal power, being produced by the many poundings and shakings which the medicines undergo in the manufacture of the successive attenuations; a doctrine which it is difficult *practically* to disprove, because when different attenuations of the same medicine are successively employed in the same case, if the good effects follow the use of the higher attenuation, (say No. 30,) while the lower, (say No. 3,) previously given, had produced no apparent effect, the physician may conclude that the former was the more powerful, while actually the improvement may have been due to the slow operation of the previous and stronger doses. If, reversing the order, the good effects become first visible under the use of the lower and, as is more generally believed, the stronger attenuations, the physician who is prepossessed with the dogma of Hahnemann may believe that the happy results are really traceable to the higher *potency*, which had been previously administered. The second reason of the difficulty which many feel in deciding that the lower dilutions are the strongest is this: in some diseases, especially the acute, frequently repeated and strong doses, as of Nos. 1, 2, or 3, without very pointedly aggravating the diseases for which they are given, keep them up to the full pitch of their previous intensity, or augment them so gradually that the increased severity of the symptoms may appear to be due to the natural and regular progress of the disease; while, if these stronger dilutions be omitted, and No. 12 or 20 be substituted, and not urgently repeated, after no very long time amendment may commence, and go on rapidly to cure. The physician is liable to be induced by such experience as this to conclude that the lower dilutions were powerless in the case, and the higher dilutions successful because *more* potent, while in reality they were so because *less* potent, and therefore less capable of keeping up the morbid action.

Another reason still for the belief that the smaller doses are more powerful than the larger is, that a number of medicinal substances remain insoluble, and therefore *inactive*, until they have been subdivided, or attenuated, by trituration with some inert powder. A few grains of this attenuation contain, of course, much less medicine than a similar amount of the crude mass itself does, and yet the former will prove an active therapeutic agent, while the latter will be wholly inert. A familiar illustration is furnished by mercury. In its fluid reguline state it may be swallowed in ounces or pounds at a time, without any other consequences than such as are due to its weight; but if a little of it be well triturated and subdivided, as stated above, a few grains are enough to produce violent effects.

From all that has been said on the subject of doses, it appears that minute division of medicines is sometimes necessary in order to bestow activity on otherwise inert substances; sometimes in order to get doses so small as to be sufficient without being too strong. There is nothing more remarkable in nature, or rather in science, which is the knowledge of nature, while there is nothing more unequivocally certain as the result of experience, than the fact that diseases render the body so sensitive to the action of medicines, that quantities of them, minute beyond conception, are liable to produce aggravations of the diseased states to which the medicines employed have a homœopathic relation. It is this liability which renders attenuation of the medicines to so great a degree, absolutely necessary for the safety of homœopathic practice. Cases may not occur very frequently of extreme sensitiveness to medicines, but they do occur from time to time, and sufficiently often to render it imperative that we should have at command, and in reserve, even the highest of Hahnemann's attenuations. From among not a few instances which I might adduce, from a ten years' experience, of extreme sensibility to the action of medicines, I can afford space but for two or three in illustration of the argument.

First Example.—A married woman affected with hematuria to a remarkable degree for four days, was ordered to have one-twelfth of a drop of turpentine for a dose, every four hours. In twenty-four hours the sanguineous appearance was quite gone, but much irritability of the *vesica*, pains in the region of the kidneys, and shootings from that region down the limbs, made their appearance. Several weeks afterwards she had a return of the disease to a considerable amount, owing to indiscretions in diet, and was directed to have one-hundredth of a drop of the turpentine for a dose, every few hours. The effect on the secretion was slower; it took five days entirely to remove the morbid state, but then no painful consequences were produced by the weaker doses.

Second Example.—A middle-aged lady long subject to constipation, applied for a remedy for her ailment, and got the third attenuation of nux vomica, of which she was desired to take half a drop twice a-day. As she lived in the country, she did not present herself for a fortnight afterwards, when her report was, that soon after commencing the medicine, she began to feel extremely weak, sleepy all day, headache all over the forehead, a creeping or trickling feeling in the lower limbs, extremely cold feet, cold sensation in the chest, and extreme exhaustion. Being very desirous of getting rid of her complaint, and not alarmed by the feelings she experienced, she persevered for four days taking the medicine according to directions, when her state became so alarming to her friends that they compelled her to desist, and sent for their ordinary medical attendant, who declared her to be suffering from over doses of strychnia,—one of the active principles of nux vomica. The third homœopathic attenuation contains in every drop only the millionth of a drop of the mother tincture of nux vomica.

Third Example.—An old lady was committed to my care by a homœopathic physician, who remarked to me that she was so extremely sensitive to the action of mercury as to have been salivated by the sixth attenuation. Having had to attend her for a swelling over the nose, I prescribed the soluble mercury in its sixth dilution, every four hours. The consequence was, that in two days the mouth began to be affected, and as well marked an instance of mercurial stomatitis,—with loosening of the teeth, purple margins of the gums, salivation and fœtor,—set in, as I have ever witnessed.

Fourth Example.—A gentleman, seventy-five years old, had for many years (fifteen or sixteen) been affected with a scaly eruption on the legs, on a dark dusky redness of the skin,—it occasionally improved, but never disappeared, and had been for five months in a very bad state, when he was ordered sepia, of the thirtieth attenuation. Having taken one dose, he became affected in the course of the day with so great a sense of exhaustion as to be unfit for any exertion, and so to alarm his family that he had stimulants administered, and the medicine forthwith stopped, never to be resumed. In a week a sensible amendment was observable in the limbs, in a month the redness was gone, and nothing remained of the eruption but a white and furfuraceous desquamation, which gradually disappeared also. When seen and examined four years afterwards, the skin was ascertained to have remained perfectly well. This sense of prostration is often noticed when the medicines are suited to the diseases for which they are prescribed, and nothing surprised me more in my first experiments than the degree to which it sometimes went.

It is unnecessary to multiply examples of what few will appreciate who have not personally experimented on the subject, and what is familiar to every one who has had even a moderate experience of the practice of Homœopathy. Let those who know no better be as incredulous as their ignorance can make them, the facts which are so well known to thousands who are better informed remain the same, and so will the convictions and the practice to which they have given rise. I may remark, however, that the bitter hostility excited among allopathic practitioners by the promulgation of such facts as I have been adverting to, regarding the necessity of minute doses, comes with a very bad grace from them, and that they cannot but see that it does if they will only reflect a little on the subject. What do they know of the quantity of a specific medicine which is actually operative, or needed, in any given case? It is obviously not the whole of the dose which they administer, for some of it is arrested before it reaches the circulation, and some of it is cast out speedily after it has been absorbed into the blood. How much remains? No mortal knows anything whatever on the subject. When these facts are considered in connexion with the circumstance, that even allopathic physicians have witnessed most remarkable effects from exceedingly minute doses, the difference between them and their homœopathic brethren must, to all men of candour and moderation, appear to be inconsiderable indeed. If allopathists were in the habit of prescribing "porridges," as has been well said, of arsenic, and corrosive sublimate, and strychnia, there might be some show of reason in their vehement denunciations of the homœopathic doses; but since they give not grains, or half grains, or even quarter grains, of these substances, and others, even to the largest man, their violence and passion on the subject of doses become in the highest degree absurd and irrational. M. Boudin, as we have seen, cured agues, which had resisted quinine, with a *single* dose of the hundredth of a grain of arsenic;* now the hundredth of a grain is to the weight of a man of fifteen stone, as one is to one hundred and fifty millions. What an infinitesimal quantity of medicine to affect so powerfully so vast and disproportionate a quantity of matter! But Allopathy affords a still more remarkable fact,—a fact, indeed, which deprives her of all right to quarrel with any system on the score of its minute doses. Mr. Hunt, an allopathic physician, apparently of long standing and much experience, published in 1847 an interesting little volume on the treatment of certain intractable chronic skin diseases. At p. 14 of that work he says,—"*A fourth part of a minim* of Fowler's solution, taken thrice a-day, has, in a few weeks, effected the permanent cure of psoriasis guttata, in a female of delicate habit, intolerant alike in a high degree of all mineral substances." Fowler's solution is a solution of arsenite of potass, in which the arsenious acid and the potass are present in about equal quantities. The great allopathic Review,—the British and Foreign,—in 1847, accepts Mr. Hunt's case as genuine and true, and remarks that each of his doses contained only *the four hundred and eightieth part of a grain* of the white arsenic, or arsenious acid. Now, as susceptibility to arsenic, or to any other medicine, does not depend on, and has no connexion with the weight of the individual, there is no reason whatever why our already selected fifteen-stone patient should not be sensitive to the same dose. The 480th part of a grain is to fifteen stone as one is to seven hundred and five millions six hundred thousand; or as a mile to a line that might pass above seven times between the earth and sun; or that might pass twenty-eight thousand two hundred times round the earth! In short, nearly as one pound is to the whole national debt,—or as one man to all the inhabitants of the world. Since doses of

* If he used the arsenite of potass, his dose of *white arsenic* must have been the two hundredth of a grain.

medicine do not require to be increased in proportion to the weight of the person who takes them, and if in the proportion of one to about seven hundred millions they are unquestionably effectual as remedies, why may they not when in proportion of one to seven thousand millions, or seven hundred thousand millions? Mr. Hunt does not tell us that he found smaller doses of arsenic than the four hundred and eightieth of a grain ineffectual. He appears to have tried none more minute. But physicians, in every respect as much entitled to credit, have maintained that doses a very great deal smaller have proved effectual in their experience, and the experience of homœopathic physicians is now so great in all quarters of the globe, that it can no longer be ignored, or explained away. Allopathic controversialists, and others who have a deep personal interest in resisting and endeavouring to quash Homœopathy, may remain as blind as they please by wilfully closing their eyes, but their blindness will not prevent other men from seeing. And no man of calm and ordinary judgment can fail to see, when the question between us and our opponents is not one of ounces or pounds of drugs against fractions of grains, but really and truly one of fractions of grains against fractions of grains, that the dispute lies within a very narrow compass, and that the opposing parties do not differ so very much as some either ignorant or designing persons have endeavoured to make the public believe. Allopathy has committed herself to the infinitesimal doses in the instances I have mentioned. Doses of the hundredth and of the four hundred and eightieth of a grain are as inconceivable as remedies as doses of the millionth or decillionth of a grain. Nothing but experience could render the former doses credible as efficient doses; there is no process of reasoning, no *a priori* probability apart from experience to suggest the expectation that doses so minute could be effectual in curing diseases; and the same experience which is adequate to prove their efficiency is adequate to prove the efficiency of the still more minute doses; in point of fact, there is an experience and a testimony immensely greater on the side of Homœopathy in favour of its usual doses, than there is on the side of Allopathy in favour of the doses I have adduced from its authenticated records. How absurd is the notion that there can be no testimony or experience on the subject of the usual homœopathic doses, but such as are presented by *allopathic* authorities. A pretty mode of settling the dispute indeed! If this original method be introduced into universal practice, and the adherents of any prevalent doctrine are to utter the final judgment that must settle the character of every question that arises in opposition to the common beliefs,—Protestantism is easily proved to be false in Roman Catholic countries; Christianity itself is at once proved to be a delusion among the Chinese, as well as the religion of that ancient people to be a miserable idolatry among the enlightened citizens of Great Britain. And if Homœopathy is thus shown to be visionary by the allopathic Andral, Allopathy is proved to be equally so, or worse, by Hahnemann, backed by thousands of followers, and corroborated by Allopathy itself, as we have seen from the testimony of Dietl, Forbes, and others. Andral's experiments are in the highest degree disgraceful to him as a man of science, or rather they prove him to be utterly undeserving of the name. As great stress has been laid upon them by our allopathic opponents, I have given in an appendix a complete account of them from the pen of a homœopathic physician, remarkable alike for his intelligence and his moderation. Few among us would, I think, have dealt so forbearingly with such a tissue of unfairness and presumptuous ignorance. Dr. Irvine's narrative will also serve to guard the readers of allopathic works against Homœopathy, from attaching undue credit and importance to alleged experimental refutations of it, whether in Russia or in Britain.

If a man formerly so respectable as Andral could be guilty of such "experiments" as he has allowed to be published in his name against Homœopathy, what can be expected from men who have no character to lose?

There must, of course, be some limit to the attenuation of medicines, some degree of dilution at which their power of acting, on even the sensitive human frame, though rendered very much more sensitive by disease than it is in health, ceases altogether. At the same time, there is no human being as yet entitled to say where that power ends, what degree of attenuation of any medicine deprives it utterly of all power to affect any one, however strongly predisposed. Attenuations have been pretty extensively employed which purported to be many times higher than the highest of Hahnemann's scale. These, however, had been secretly manufactured by a now deceased German chemist, and since his death it has been discovered that his "high potencies" were made according to such proportions of the drugs and the menstruum in which they were dissolved, as resulted in their containing for the most part *more* medicine than the nominally much lower potencies of Hahnemann. The physicians who tried them, believing that they were as "high" as was pretended, and who reported them as more energetic than the older potencies, in point of fact bear testimony unwittingly to the greater power of such attenuations as contain the larger quantities of medicine. By other chemists, however, attenuations, actually and not professedly merely, have been made, which ascend several hundred degrees of dilution beyond those of Hahnemann. These also have been tried in practice by a few physicians, among whom some give favourable accounts of their efficiency. That they are effective, is, I think, very unlikely, and no evidence worthy of the name has yet been produced in proof of their asserted powers. Still, as the appeal in all such cases is and must be to experiment, it will be time enough for those who acknowledge the sufficiency of the test to give a decided opinion when the results of experiment are made known. Those who do not acknowledge experiment to be the proper test on the subject, repose their confidence on their own preconceptions, or fanciful hypotheses, and are the representatives of a remote and bygone age, so that with them it were needless to argue.

But a very few words are required in answer to the objections which have been made against the homœopathic provings of medicines. As I have already said, the *provings* of a medicine are the effects which it produces on healthy persons, or the new symptoms it causes to appear in persons who are labouring under disease. Three objections have been started against the homœopathic provings, namely, the great number of the symptoms recorded as due to single medicines, the nature of some of the symptoms, and the means or substances by which the symptoms are alleged to have been produced. I shall notice each objection in its order.

First, as to the *number* of the symptoms said to be due to a single medicine. The author of the "Tenets" adverts to a subject pretty much as Dr. Forbes had done before him, and he is quite aware that it is made an objection to the homœopathic provings on very untenable grounds; for the fallacies which pervade his and Dr. Forbes' statements regarding it were fully exposed, years ago, in reply to the latter. Calcarea *appears* to produce 1090 symptoms, according to the "proving" of Hahnemann; but in reality the number of symptoms, even in Hahnemann's record, is very much less, probably not a fourth or a sixth of that number. Thus, one symptom,—vertigo,—appears to be no less than *nine* symptoms in Hahnemann's work, because every little accompanying peculiarity in the state of different persons in whom the vertigo was produced by the medicine, and every sort of variation, whether great or small, in the circumstances under which the symptom was excited or increased, were separately numbered by Hahnemann. Again, another symptom headache, is split up into what *seem* to be above sixty symptoms; and just because some circumstances of their condition, and some modes of expression used by them in describing their sensations, and some causes of increased suffering, *must* have been different among some of the many persons experimented upon by the prover, from what they were among others. Other symptoms have undergone a similar process of apparent multiplication, and from similar causes. The same explanation applies to all the other provings, and is so perfectly *exculpatory* of them from the charge of numerical extravagance revived by Dr. Simpsom, and is at the same time so well known and so easily discerned, that I cannot but wish that those who have aspired to write against Homœopathy had taken some pains, however little, to learn something of the subject of their condemnation. By neglecting to do so they have made so many misrepresentations as greatly to damage their own characters; for ordinary charity cannot, in so many instances of error, always put them down either to want of information, or to want of the proper "dynamic activity" of the organ of common sense. If it should still be objected by any one that even one hundred or two hundred symptoms are too many to have been the product of one medicine; it may be enough to remind him that they are not said to have been produced by any single medicine on only one or two persons. On the contrary, many, it is probable a great many persons, were experimented on by Hahnemann with every one of the medicines which were proved by him; and the experiments were continued through a series of years. Sometimes persons in ordinary health were the subjects of experiment, sometimes persons that were ill, for Hahnemann, I think justly, regarded the new symptoms which a medicine, taken by a patient, caused to appear, as an effect which that medicine was capable of producing on the human body, although it might require the peculiar, or idiosyncratic conditions of disease to be present before it was able to produce them. For instance, in the proving of turpentine there is no mention of *iritis* as producible by that substance; yet not long ago a gentleman who had taken a quantity of that medicine, in allopathic doses, for the cure of an obstinate rheumatic sciatica, became affected with *iritis*, and, as I think, most likely in *consequence* of his having taken the turpentine. This substance may not be capable of exciting iritis in persons enjoying ordinary health, while it may have that power in those of a rheumatic diathesis. I have since employed turpentine, in minute doses of one-twelfth of a drop, in rheumatic iritis, and with the best effects. It is well known to allopathic physicians as a remedy for that disease, though without their knowing why. Thus it is, then, that a great many symptoms may actually be traceable to a single medicine,—when many persons in health are the subjects of experiment, and many also, in disease, and when at the same time the experiments are continued for many years, and by several or many experimenters. Dr. Simpsom supposes that all the symptoms of all diseases do not exceed a thousand; and, estimating symptoms in the rough, wholesale, allopathic way, he may be right. According to that method, a headache is a headache, and a cough a cough, and nothing more is to be said of either. But Homœopathy recognises many different kinds of headache, and makes a headache brought on by wine a different symptom from one brought on by a sudden emotion, and a cough increased by running a different symptom from a cough increased on lying down, and so on of multitudes of other symptoms. But even though there were in nature only a thousand symptoms of disease, or of medicines, how infinitely varied might their combinations be, considering how many words issue from the twenty-six letters of the alphabet.

Secondly, the *nature* of some of the symptoms is made an objection to the provings. Sometimes the symptoms enumerated among those which are supposed due to a medicine are very insignificant. Hahnemann, more especially, committed atrocities of this kind; but it was an error, *if* error it was, on the safe side. If the unimportant phenomena were *not* due to the medicine, their being among the provings can do no harm, for the cases of disease to which the medicine is homœopathically suited will *not* have these symptoms any more than the medicine, properly speaking, and so they will go for nothing. On the other hand, if these seemingly unimportant symptoms in the provings *are* due to the medicine, they may be of considerable consequence in directing the choice of the physician, when a case occurs to him in which their presence is remarked.

Among the unimportant or absurd effects ascribed to a medicine Dr. Simpson selects "cough excited by playing on the piano," and the instance may be taken as the type of this class of objections. If he is serious in adducing this as an objection to the homœopathic provings, I am afraid I must continue to charge him at the end of my book with the distinguishing characteristic which I have so often had occasion to notice in the beginning and the middle of it,—*ignorance.* Is it so very extraordinary that playing on the piano should excite a cough? I don't know,—but I have certainly heard of as curious consequences following the sound of music. Does Dr. Simpson know what happened to Rousseau whenever he heard the bagpipes? Or does he know what befell the musical phenomenon, young Aspul, whenever he heard a performance that was not to his taste? If he does not, I am sorry I dare not tell him. All I can venture to say is, that a cough was a joke to either of their misfortunes. Why, therefore, may not a medicine produce a condition of the nervous system by which a liability to cough should be occasioned on hearing the sound of music? The objection is obviously ignorant and groundless.

It appears that the Homœopathists are so far lost to every right and decorous feeling, as to allege that some of their medicines will produce "*moral and religious* symptoms and states." (Tenets, p. 30.) And why not? On allopathic principles of mental philosophy especially, why not? Are not the moral feelings, passions, sentiments, &c., &c., all manifestations of the "dynamic activity of the brain?" In other words, are not religious and moral feelings *functions* of the brain, according to the principal allopathic authority? And if so, why may not medicines disturb the mind, or the result of cerebral function, as well as the bile, or the result of the function of the liver? No reason in the world can be given for the exemption of the cerebral function from being affected by a class of influences which disturb all other functions of the body; and if, as Allopathists of note and authority maintain, the mind is the mere manifestation of cerebral function, the mind must be liable to be disordered by medicines, just as the bile is. But without holding this allopathic doctrine of mind, so very equivocal in its moral and religious bearings, it may be safely averred, that such is the relation subsisting between mind and body that there is not a faculty or feeling of the former which is not capable of being excited, exalted, depressed, or misguided by influences which act primarily upon the latter, and through it upon the mind. Taking the most important of the sentiments, the religious, —does not *almost* every medical man and clergyman know and acknowledge that religious feelings of every kind may depend upon merely bodily states? I am almost ashamed to produce the authority of a divine on a point so generally agreed upon; but as Dr. Simpson's unaccountable opinions on the subject may be entertained by a few others also, who have not reflected on it, or are but ill informed regarding it, I may quote one author whose eminence and orthodoxy will satisfy the most timid and scrupulous that *any* kind of religious feelings may depend for the time on conditions of the body. Jonathan Edwards, in his treatise on Religious Affections, referring to the "terrors" which are sometimes experienced of hell, &c., combats the idea that they are to be regarded as necessarily of a "gracious" description, or the fruits of a genuinely awakened conscience, and adds, "the terrors of some persons are very much owing to their particular *constitution* and temper." (P. 65.) In another passage, adverting generally to religious impressions of a seemingly good or of an opposite kind, he says, "And where neither a good nor evil spirit have any immediate hand, persons, *especially such as are of a weak and vapoury habit of body, and the brain easily susceptive of impressions*, may have strange apprehensions and imaginations, and strong affections attending them, unaccountably arising, which are not voluntarily produced by themselves." (P. 51.) But enough of this; I appeal to the experience of medical men in general, whether they have not known examples of every kind of religious feeling, from the lively hopes and joys of one who believes himself safe for time and eternity, to the deep despair and agonizing terrors of him who regards himself lost for both, as due to bodily disease, and often the precursors of insanity. Dr. Simpson's error on the whole subject appears to spring from his misconception of what constitutes the genuinely religious state, from his not apprehending that true religion *never* consists of mere feelings, joys, or terrors,—that such feelings may arise from ordinary causes, bodily as well as mental, in reference to religion and eternity as well as in reference to time and to secular affairs. How much do our despondencies and our hopes, our joys and our sorrows, our good and our bad tempers, depend on the state of our digestion,—possibly on the proportion of acid in our gastric juice. And how, then, can it be a matter of surprise to any man, that medicines capable of disordering the body, the stomach as well as other organs, should also, and for that very reason, be capable of exciting or disordering the feelings of the mind! Does not alcohol do so? Do not opium, belladonna, hyoscyamus, "hachisch," and many more? And what medical man can deny that they do?

One remark more upon the *moral* aspect of the provings, and I quit the ridiculous subject. Dr. Simpson, referring to the "moral symptoms" of the provings, in connexion with carbonate of lime and common salt, says of man in general, who takes these substances with his food and his drink, "would not his mind have been rendered *sinful* by the very substances which his Creator obliges him to use constantly in the course of the common and requisite nourishment of his frame? If Homœopathy were true, would not this arrangement form a strong and incontrovertible argument for skeptics to use, who wished to call in question the bountiful and beneficent arrangements of Providence?" (P. 74.) What a prodigious quantity of salt Dr. Simpson must have taken before he wrote this passage! that is to say, if it is *sinful* to assert what is not the fact, and if salt be a cause of sin. But there is not a single *sin* recorded in the provings as producible by either carbonate of lime or salt! The nearest approach to sinfulness that carbonate of lime produces is *peevishness*, and that is no sin unless it be indulged. Salt, however, goes a step nearer, as Dr. Simpson knows experimentally, for it produces "want of discretion," and "vehemence without any special cause." He must really take less salt with his food, lest he should give a handle to the "skeptics."

But the "arrangements of Providence," whatever opinions reckless and skeptical men may form of His bounty and beneficence, are often such, that what we receive "in the course of the common and requisite nourishment" of our frame, even the air we breathe, contains deadly poisons which daily rob some among us of health, of reason, or of life. The waters of some countries, which the inhabitants are compelled to drink, make many among them loathsome from physical disease, others still more so by the addition of moral insensibility, yea, even to the apparent extinction of the moral sense.

Dr. Simpson objects, further, to *opposite* symptoms being recorded among the provings of the same medicine. And why should they not? The same medicines may, in different persons, occasionally produce different effects, according to the temporary or habitual peculiarities of individuals. This has happened in allopathic experience, as well as in the homœopathic. Professor Balfour, in his Inaugural Dissertation on Strychnia, in 1831, has the following observations:—"Alvus secundum Fouquier saepe adstricta purgantibus movenda est; hunc strychniae effectum ego amicusque meus Dr. Henderson apud nosocomium regium Edinense saepe vidimus, et fere semper evenire putavimus. Nuper vero, a Professore Christison meque ipso aliqui aegrivisi sunt, qui diarrhoea propter strychniae usum solum afficiebantur; idcirco haud dubito, quin hoc remedium minime alvum semper adstringat." (P. 88.) In homœopathic practice we are not guided by *one* symptom in the selection of our remedy, but take them collectively, or in their totality, and select for the total symptoms of a disease the medicine which furnishes symptoms similar to them all, as nearly as possible. And as the constipation of strychnia is attended with different symptoms from those which accompany the same effect of other drugs, some cases of constipation will point to that drug as their proper remedy, and some cases of diarrhœa, for a like reason, will point to it too, as preferable to other drugs; for it is capable of causing sometimes constipation, and sometimes diarrhœa, according to circumstances.

Lastly, objections are made to some of the substances which have been asserted by Hahnemann and others to have produced the symptoms of certain provings. The *pediculus capitis*, calcarea or carbonate of lime, and common salt, are the materials specially objected to. I shall not defend the first of these, for two reasons: because Dr. Mure has not established his authority as a *prover* by other and less questionable instances of his title to be regarded as a safe and sufficient observer; and because he has given in his writings some ground to believe that he is a fanciful and indiscreet personage. I do not accuse him of intentional error; for I have no right to do so, in so far either as he himself is concerned, or as regards the alleged subject of his investigations. Without holding that the animal with which he experimented is incapable of acting as a poison to human beings, when administered internally, I think that the sources of fallacy in such experiments are so considerable, that the professed provings of one whose abilities and caution are not guarantied by his known character and previous performances, should not be accepted as authentic. The *Pediculus* is doubtless a loathsome and vulgar animal, and I cannot admire the taste or hardihood of the man who condescended to meddle with it; but its vulgarity and filthiness are no sufficient reasons for concluding that it is innocuous: and the analogy of other instances from beings as low in the scale of existence, which are known to produce poisonous effects, should prevent any one from asserting dogmatically, that the *pediculus* is incapable of doing so in any degree. The itch insect and the blistering beetle are examples from the humbler walks of life of objects apparently contemptible and unpleasant to the eye being endowed with properties injurious to the well-being of the lords of creation; and, therefore, there is in reality no *a priori* objection to the asserted powers of the *pediculus*. As Lord Bacon says, in science we are not engaged "to build a temple to the glory of man," but to take things as we find them, and not to scorn what is to us mean and impure; but, remembering that "the sun shines alike on the palace and the stye," to accept with becoming docility whatever he reveals to our apprehension. If it be said, in defence of Dr. Mure's "proving," that, being honest, he actually witnessed the phenomena he records, in connexion with the administration of his *pediculus*, it may be replied, that we have no certainty that he selected discreet and staid persons as the subjects on whom to experiment, and that imaginative and nervous persons may fancy a great many troubles both of body and mind when they are made aware that such troubles are expected or desired by their kindly physician. For these reasons, I am decidedly of opinion that the *pediculus* should not have been admitted into any homœopathic *materia medica*.

Hahnemann, however, as a man and a prover, had endowments and known characteristics which eminently entitle his *observations*, if not always his *speculations*, to confidence and respect. His experience in disease, in provings, and in human nature, was immense; and the general accuracy of his provings, in so far as they have been repeated, has been attested by a society of continental provers who have been engaged in *re*-proving some of the medicines originally proved by him. At the same time, it is not maintained that his provings are entirely free from errors. He himself acknowledged the liability of provers to include, in the record of their provings, unimportant phenomena that might not be due to the medicines; but he advocated the propriety of including them when they occurred during the course of a proving, because they *might* be due on that occasion to the medicine which had been taken, and, if they were not, their being recorded, as if they were could do no harm; while, on the other hand, if they were due to the medicine, the neglect of them would be a disadvantage. Hence it is partly that the provings of calcarea and natrum muriaticum, or common salt, appear so redundant of symptoms. But the objection I am now discussing is not against the mere number of the symptoms said to have been produced by these substances, but against their producing symptoms at all, or of any consequence. Dr. Simpson objects to calcarea, specially on the ground, that it "exists in most vegetables, and is contained in greater or less quantity—but in doses larger than the Hahnemannic—in almost every water which man drinks." (P. 72) Now it is true that *some* waters, at least, do contain calcarea; but it is not therefore incredible that calcarea should both produce symptoms, and cure diseases, when given even in minute doses. The waters which man drinks when they contain calcarea, have it dissolved by means of carbonic acid, which, in this capacity of a solvent, is not combined with the lime so as to constitute it a super-carbonate, but is free in the water, and may be expelled, or removed by its chemical affinity for some other base, and then the carbonate of lime, or calcarea, becomes insoluble. Heat is one of the means by which carbonic acid may be expelled from water, and if the heat of the stomach expel it from the water which is taken as drink, the carbonate of lime, no longer held in solution, will fail to be absorbed.* Though present in the water which man drinks, it does not follow, therefore, that it, calcarea, must be taken into the circulation, and must

* The crust which lines tea-kettles and boilers is composed of the carbonate deposited in consequence of the free carbonic acid being expelled by heat.

produce always any medicinal or pathogenetic effect which it may, notwithstanding, be capable of producing when absorbed. The formation of calcareous rocks at the bottom and sides of bodies of water is carried on everywhere by this process of precipitation or deposition of the insoluble carbonate of lime, which had been previously held in solution in the water by carbonic acid. The gaseous acid being extracted by the atmosphere, the carbonate falls in proportionate quantities.

The explanation given above is one of several that may be conceived as competent to make it probable, if not certain, that the calcarea of water consumed as drink does not become absorbed. But as most of the drink taken by man is taken with his meals, or while some digestive process is going on in the stomach, and rarely when the stomach is entirely free from chyme or food undergoing digestion, another reason may be given for the opinion that the carbonate of lime contained in the water we drink is not absorbed into the blood. There is much difference of view among physiologists as to the cause of the acidity of the gastric juice, but most of them, indeed all but one, agree in stating that there is some free acid or other in that secretion, muriatic as several believe, acetic according to others. Well, be the acid what it may, muriatic or acetic, the carbonate of lime taken into the stomach, while one of them is there, forthwith must become muriate or acetate of lime, for the carbonic acid quits its place at the bidding of either. Apart, then, from the former explanation, but a very minute quantity of the *carbonate* of lime can ever get into the blood, for the mere reason that but little water is drunk when the stomach is empty, and because that little contains a very small quantity of the substance. The calcarea, therefore, which is given in the course of a proving, is something over and above the minute quantity taken in the drink, and as it is thus given on an empty stomach dose after dose, and day after day, for weeks together, the whole quantity in the end may be considerably more than the individual who is the subject of the experiment had ever taken before in the same space of time. If we add to these considerations, the probability of the carbonate of the water taken as drink becoming precipitated and insoluble, as already mentioned, it is pretty plain that the proving of calcarea does not find the ground habitually preoccupied to such an extent as to preclude the possibility of its causing pathogenetic effects. Calcarea, when taken in the proving of it, is in a state so finely divided, and in quantities so small as to be soluble of itself in the water in which it is swallowed; and it is taken, too, at times, when there is no gastric juice in the stomach to decompose it. The circumstance that plants taken as food contain carbonate of lime, is obviously no objection to the proving of calcarea, for their proportion of the carbonate must be decomposed, and converted into a muriate or acetate during digestion. Nor is the fact that the blood naturally contains some carbonate of lime at all an objection to the proving, for the carbonate of the blood is not free, but a mere ingredient in the compounds of the blood, and therefore not capable of operating as if it were free. Besides, even were no explanations possible on the subject, were all the *a priori* objections to the proving, and to the medicinal use of calcarea, utterly incapable of being met in any other way, we should be entitled to argue, and to hold the argument to be incontrovertible, that *experience and observation* prove the facts to be as we maintain them to be, and that no *a priori* objections can affect the force of the absolute evidence which we possess as to the facts. This remark cannot but have some weight with those who know, and all the more weight with those who are the most alive to the knowledge, that the processes which take place within living animal bodies are still involved to a very great degree in obscurity.

The last two observations apply equally to the facts recorded regarding the proving of common salt. We have one pledge of their general accuracy in the character and abilities of Hahnemann, a pledge which will be sufficient to satisfy his followers, who have had so much occasion to confide in his observations on other substances. No merely speculative objections made by his enemies can unsettle that confidence. That they are merely speculative appears from this, that not one of the objectors has proved, or attempted to prove, in the way Hahnemann suggests, whether or not salt can do what he says it can. They simply say, that salt is taken in tolerable quantities every day with food, and without producing any bad effects. Do they know, are they quite sure, that it produces, even when taken with food, *no* bad effects of any kind, and in any persons? Are they quite able to trace all the unaccountable ailments that sensitive and delicate people are so often complaining of, to their true, real, and indubitable source? And if not, are they absolutely and rationally certain that they can never in any case be possibly due to a modicum of chloride of sodium—common salt? It is a common substance certainly, and one that is very commonly used; but tea is a very common substance, and very commonly used, yet every now and then a case presents itself in which tea, though formerly an agreeable beverage, can no longer be taken without very unpleasant effects; and a temperature of 40° is a very common temperature in this cold island, and air of that temperature is very commonly breathed, yet how often do we meet with sensitive and delicate people who cannot expose themselves to it without aches and pains, or breathe it without coughing and wheezing! Hahnemann expressly says, over and over again, that all persons are not equally sensitive to a medicine, or at all times, and that all the symptoms of a medicine are not producible in all persons; and he expressly advises provings to be specially tried on those who are peculiarly sensitive, either from morbid or original constitution or idiosyncrasy; so that he is greatly misrepresented when he is said to teach that salt, and carbonate of lime, will produce pathogenetic effects of more or less consequence in all persons, and though given in minute quantities. He has asserted, however, that even these ordinary substances do produce numerous symptoms of disorder in some persons, when taken even in small quantities for a considerable time and at certain periods, and the task of proving experimentally that he is wrong lies with his opponents. It is unnecessary to add, that neither experimentally nor argumentatively have they adduced the smallest reason for their opinion that he is wrong. Salt is taken, in the ordinary way, only with the food; and it is far from improbable that it is appropriated in a great measure, during digestion or assimilation, by these processes in forming certain organic compounds. An eminent French chemist is of opinion, that it combines with the albumen of the food, and is the means of keeping that substance in solution in the blood. If it does enter into such combinations, and is but in small quantity in a free state—a quantity rapidly lessening with every round of the circulation by means of incessant excretion—it cannot be expected to produce symptoms of its presence in persons of ordinary constitution and health. In considerable quantities it is well known that it does.

A single point remains, and I do not know that I have omitted any besides that is deserving of even the slight notice due to this. *Olfaction*, or smelling of medicines, recommended by Hahnemann to be sometimes practised, affords of course an opportunity for derision to his opponents. Yet what is this olfaction in reality but the inspiration of air, and whatever it contains, through the nostrils into the lungs?

Chloroform inhaled through the nostrils will produce its characteristic effects as well as when drawn into the lungs through the mouth; and it is well known that there is no way of giving such medicines as are capable of impregnating the air so effectual as that of inhaling them. That Hahnemann often succeeded in curing diseases by medicines administered thus, there can be no reasonable doubt; that he sometimes was mistaken in supposing the inhaling to have been beneficial, may be just as certain as that Louis, Bouillaud, Grisolle, and many thousands of allopathic physicians, were and are mistaken in supposing that they can cure pneumonia by blood-letting and tartar emetic, while in reality they destroy some thirteen or fourteen per cent. of those who labour under that disease, that might be saved if only left to nature!

APPENDIX.

M. ANDRAL'S HOMŒOPATHIC EXPERIMENTS AT LA PITIE.*

BY DR. F. W. IRVINE.

The adherents of Homœopathy have much reason to complain of the want of interest in the subject displayed by the heads of the profession; it is indeed matter of surprise and regret, that they should persist in a resolution not to examine into the merits of a system whose value is attested on the ground of personal experience, by hundreds of their medical brethren, a system whose claims are set forth in able and accessible works, and whose success—both as exhibited in the tables of public hospitals, and the less imposing but more penetrating results of private practice—is making appeal from the bigoted love of the old, and dislike of the new in medicine, to that candour and love of truth which are looked for in the practitioner of the healing art, and are nowhere more requisite.

But great as is the evil resulting from non-inquiry, it is small compared with that arising from the nugatory results attendant on trials of Homœopathy, ignorantly or disingenuously made by Allopaths of renown; for it cannot be doubted that many, and these perhaps the most candid among the adherents of the dominant school, whom the mere novelty and strangeness of our doctrine might not have prevented from examining into its practical working, have been deterred from so doing by the consideration that it were at once superfluous and presumptuous in them to attempt success in a path which men whom they are wont to look up to have already trodden, and declared to lead to nothing but disappointment. When Homœopathy has thus been put upon its trial, it has been the practice to conduct the proceedings with closed doors, advocates for the accused have been excluded, and the witnesses (*i. e.* the cases treated) have been examined, and the evidence summed up in secret; the damnatory verdict alone has been promulgated, unaccompanied by any recommendation to mercy; and the public have had the general character of the judge for ability and uprightness as sole guarantee for the legality of the proceedings and the justness of the sentence; that sentence being usually no less than perpetual banishment from the domain of science.

---

* British Journal of Homœopathy. 1844.

Such trials are quite beyond our reach, and therefore we shall say nothing further of them; but we propose dwelling at some length on one to which the preceding remarks are but partially applicable, and which has been made amenable to criticism by the publication of the details. We refer to the series of experiments, instituted several years ago, by Professor Andral at the Hôpital de la Pitié at Paris. And it seems of peculiar importance to take up these experiments, first, because none are so frequently and so triumphantly referred to by the opponents of Homœopathy in proof of the inefficiency of the system; and, secondly, because the high standing of M. Andral, both at home and abroad, entitles us to consider this trial as a favourable specimen of the class, the more so as the Academy of Medicine evinced the high value they placed upon it, by making it the main ground of their decision against Homœopathy in the year 1835. We have, therefore, made a careful study of the published account of these experiments, contained in the sixth volume of the Bulletin Général de Thérapeutique, (Sept. 1834,) and would invite such of our candid opponents, as may chance to peruse these pages, to look with us for a little into the details of these vaunted experiments, when we trust we shall be able to show that no argument unfavourable to Homœopathy is deducible from them.

When we are told (p. 319) that a faithful application was made of the "principles and ideas" of Hahnemann; that the diet was such as he prescribes; that the experiments were made on an extensive scale, and continued uninterruptedly for several months; finally, that the cases were noted down with "scrupulous attention," and digested in "immense and well drawn up tables," by M. Andral's "interne," M. Maxime Vernois;* the reader is inclined to suppose that all the conditions requisite to make such a trial conclusive were observed, and when he then learns that out of 54 cases treated, only 8 made permanent recoveries, he is ready to conclude that the trial was most damaging to Homœopathy. Such an inference would, however, be premature, and we think erroneous, and we proceed to adduce our reasons.

---

* "Attention minutieuse;"—"tableaux immenses et fort bien faits." Our readers will be able to judge presently how far these commendations are deserved; meanwhile, it may not be amiss to state that they are self-bestowed, for M. Maxime Vernois has informed us, in a pamphlet subsequently published, (Homœopathie: Analyse de la Matière Médicale, &c.,) that the article from which we quote is his own. We might, however, have left this much unnoticed, for we were not without examples of self-commendatory reviews before M. Vernois; this gentleman, however, has quite overstepped the pale of professional courtesy—at least as it is understood and practised in this country—in introducing anecdotes relating to the private practice of his opponents. One does not know at which to wonder most, the spirit of the essayist, who could pen matter of the sort for the grave pages of a scientific journal, or the taste of the editor who could admit it.

We may first notice the manner in which the "principles and ideas" of Hahnemann with respect to diet were observed. We are told (p. 319) that wine was administered to all the patients who could eat. This is manifestly an infraction of the principle on which the peculiarities of the homœopathic diet all depend, viz., that no substance possessed of any but purely nutritive properties should be given to a person under treatment; for what is not nutritive is medicinal, and thus we should have two medicinal forces in play, whose resultant we have no means of calculating. But we may object also on principles acknowledged by every school, that wine should not have been given to patients suffering from chronic inflammation of the stomach, of whom, as well as of other inflammations to which the same remark applies, several cases were subjected to the homœopathic treatment. To the rest of the diet-table (soup, bouilli, roast-meat, fish, bread, and sugared water) there can be no objection, except that to deprive the patients of salt with their food, as was done, is not sanctioned by any of Hahnemann's writings. Let it not be supposed, however, that we imagine that departures from the rules for diet could have had any material effect in paralyzing the influence of the medicines, had the more important items in the treatment been observed; for we are not disposed to assign so important a part to diet as our opponents are in the habit of claiming for it, when homœopathic cures are to be accounted for; we merely notice it as an illustration of the little care that was taken to observe Hahnemann's principles, of which we shall obtain more proofs as we proceed.

The *moral* circumstances in which the patients submitted to homœopathic treatment were placed, were not favourable to the curative action of the medicines. While they saw around them, in full operation, the multiform and imposing appliances of Allopathy, the lancet, leech, and cupping-glass, the blister, the cautery, the nauseous powder, and the bitter draught, the unfortunate patients who, by ones and twos, were selected for experiment, were made to swallow each a tasteless, inodorous globule of starch, amidst the smiles of physician and pupils, without the smallest expectation by any party of the least benefit accruing. It is impossible to assign the exact amount of influence exerted by moral causes on the curative effects of medicines; perhaps it is not very great, but whatever it may be, it ought, in justice, to have been made to act equally on the two sets of patients, which we have just seen was not the case.

But we proceed to much more weighty objections. They relate to the actual treatment, but we think it right first to lay the cases themselves before our readers, as committed to writing, with "minute attention," by M. Maxime Vernois himself, and made public in the journal referred to. We shall thus at once escape any risk of unconsciously mis-stating the facts, and avoid the charge of intentional perversion of them. We only regret that, for some reason unassigned, 19 of the 54 cases, or more than one-third, those, namely, occurring in the first two months, have been kept back. That there were good and sufficient reasons for so doing, we are willing to believe, but should have been better pleased had such been assigned, for not only is it not consonant with the usual procedure in matters of science to give but a partial view of the facts, but, considering the great importance and the public bearing of the subject in hand, nothing but the most cogent considerations could justify the withholding of any of the data on which the conclusions were based. If the results of these 19 cases were less favourable to Homœopathy than those of the 35 which are given, M. Andral must have felt that, by detailing them, he would have added to the force of his conclusions, and would thereby have been able to deal a more effectual blow at the inefficacious and, therefore, dangerous system; if, on the other hand, they showed Homœopathy in a more favourable light, one would have supposed that candour and impartiality would have secured their publication.*

We proceed to the cases, of which there are 35, which we have numbered for facility of reference.

Aconite, 24th dilution. 1st patient, aged 25. Disease, gastritis. Predominating symptom, intense fever. Effect, the pulse fell 2 beats in 24 hours; next day the eruption of small-pox appeared.

2d patient, Intermittent fever of a quotidian type; predominant symptom, action of the heart. No effect.

3d, Acute angina; predominant symptom, intense fever. Effect, diminution of the sore throat, and falling of the pulse.

4th, Phthisis; predominant symptom, frequency of the pulse. Effect, falling of the pulse.

5th, Acute arthritis; predominant symptom, frequency of the pulse. Effect, a violent headache.

Arnica, 6th dilution. 6th, Pulmonary symptoms; predominant symptom, great giddiness. No effect.

7th, Cerebral congestion; predominant symptom, violent vertigo. Effect, the patient said he experienced immediate relief.

8th, Hydro-pericarditis; predominant symptoms, giddiness and vertigo. No effect.

9th, Dysmenorrhœa, with chronic gastritis; predominant symptom, very violent headache. No immediate effect; improvement on the third day.

Belladonna, 24 dilution. 10th, Hemiplegia; predominant symptom, confusion of sight. No effect.

---

* M. Andral made many more experiments after the publication of this article, but did not publish any account of them; indeed, he probably had not the means of doing so, for so loosely had every thing been managed, that, when giving his evidence on the subject before the Academy, he was unable to state the number of patients he had treated. See Léon Simon, Lettre à M. le Ministre de l'Instruction Publique. Paris, 1835.

11th, Bronchitis; predominant symptom, violent cough. No effect.

12th, Bronchitis; predominant symptom, violent cough. No effect.

13th, Affection of the optic nerve; predominant symptom, considerable confusion of sight. No effect.

14th, Heart disease; predominant symptoms, giddiness, vertigo. No effect.

Bryonia, 30th dilution. 15th, Intermittent fever; predominant symptom, flying pains. No effect.

16th, Hypertrophy of the heart; predominant symptom, acute pain at the epigastrium. No effect.

17th, Acute arthritis; predominant symptom, pain at the shoulder. No effect.

18th, Pleurodynia, with bronchitis; predominant symptom, continual fits of coughing. No effect.

19th, Chronic gastro-enteritis; predominant symptom, violent pain in the left knee and shoulder. No effect.

Colchicum, 15th dilution. 20th, Acute arthritis; predominant symptom, violent pain, with redness and swelling of both wrists. Effect, abatement of the pains.

21st, Lumbago; predominant symptom, violent pain in the loins. No effect. This woman was bled.

22d, Tubercular consumption; predominant symptom, stitch in the left side. Effect, abatement of the pain.

Hyoscyamus, 12th dilution. 23d, Pulmonary consumption; predominant symptom, violent cough. No effect.

24th, Pleurisy, with bronchitis; predominant symptom, violent cough. No effect.

25th, Bronchitis; predominant symptom, violent cough. No effect.

Mercurius solubilis, 6th dilution. 26th, Mercurial trembling of upper and lower limbs. No effect.*

27th, Syphilis, ulcerations on the glans. No effect; the ulceration making progress, destroyed the frenum; the disease was checked with mercurial ointment.

Nux vomica, 24th dilution. 28th, A woman aged 21. Dysmenorrhœa, with chronic gastritis; predominant symptom, very great dyspnœa. No effect.

---

* This case shows how little M. Andral understood the system he undertook to subvert. Homœopathy (as the name, indeed, indicates) cures on the principle of similarity, not identity, and we challenge any one to point out a single passage in all Hahnemann's writings to justify such a practice as was here followed. Indeed, such an idea as is implied in this experiment is refuted by daily experience, for, were it true, the last dose of a drug should neutralize the effects of its predecessors, and there could be no such thing as lasting medicinal disease. This case, then, has no title to the place it occupies in a series of experiments on Homœopathy.

29th, A woman aged 22. Dysmenorrhœa, with chronic gastritis; predominant symptom, dyspnœa. No effect.

30th, Female aged 18. Amenorrhœa; predominant symptom, inclination to vomit. No effect.

Pulsatilla, 24th dilution. 31st, Chronic gastro-enteritis; predominant symptom, diarrhœa. Effect, sensible improvement.

32d, A woman aged 22. Chronic gastritis; predominant symptoms, diarrhœa, with colic. No effect.

Chamomilla, 12th dilution. 33d, Diarrhœa without colic. No effect.

Opium, 6th dilution. 34th, Affection of the uterus and the heart; predominant symptom, obstinate constipation. No effect.

Plumbum metallicum (dilution not stated.*) 35th, Obstinate constipation, which had lasted eight days. No effect. It only yielded to purgatives.

Let us now inquire if there is virtue in these 35, or say 54, experiments to shake our confidence in Homœopathy.

The first condition which must be fulfilled to make experiments on this or any other system of any value is, that the experimenter be thoroughly conversant with the principles of that system. This is so obvious as to need no proof. Now, we maintain, that M. Andral had either never read, or, having read, had forgotten the Organon of Hahnemann when he made the experiments in question. Let any one peruse that part of the Organon which relates to the taking of the case, (par. 84-105,) and then say if every one of the cases we have transcribed does not manifest, on the part of Andral, an utter ignorance or neglect of the fundamental principles of the doctrine. Hahnemann repeatedly and earnestly enforces the maxim, that it is only by attending to the totality of the symptoms that we can obtain such an image of the disease as shall then be serviceable in determining the choice of the remedy. M. Andral, however, instead of drawing a finished picture of the disease, contents himself with indicating a single feature, that, namely, which he conceives to be the most prominent, thus acting with about the same degree of reason as a painter who should confine himself to the delineation of the nose, the mouth, or whatever feature happened to be most marked in each particular instance. Portraits of this sort must be quite irrecog-

---

* Though quite a novice in Homœopathy, M. Andral has contrived to be original—in the matter of the dose. Amidst all the differences of opinion existing among homœopathists on this subject, there is unanimity on one point, viz., that the circumstances to be looked to as determining the dilution to be given, are the acuteness or chronicity of the disease, and the age, sex, constitution, and temperament of the patient; in short, that it depends on the nature of the case, more than on that of the remedy. M. Andral, however, while he gives some medicines at high, and others at low dilutions, gives a particular medicine always of one invariable strength, whatever the disease, and whatever the peculiarities of the patient.

nisable, wholly destitute of character or expression, and for the purposes of comparison, which is the object of drawing them in Homœopathy, utterly useless. In some rare instances, it is true, extreme precision is not requisite, and had M. Andral determined with accuracy the condition of time, position, &c., under which the predominating symptom was aggravated or ameliorated, *some possibility* would have existed of finding its counterpart among artificial (medicinal) diseases, in other words, of discovering what medicine would be most likely to neutralize the diseased action, in virtue of its similarity. M. Andral, however, by uniformly neglecting to determine the conditions affecting this or any other symptom, deprived himself of even this chance of success. As if to make his infringement of Hahnemann's canons complete, the learned professor never takes any notice of the remote cause of the disease, (except in the 26th case, which we showed was not treated homœopathically,) or of the temperament and moral state of the patient, on all of which points the founder of Homœopathy strongly insists as essential to the proper treatment of the case.

M. Andral occasionally displays considerable originality in the selection of the "predominating symptom," on which so much is made to hang. We were not prepared to find him, when prescribing for an affection of the heart and uterus, (case 34,) select the remedy by a reference to the state of the bowels; nor could we have anticipated, that a Professor of Pathology would have considered giddiness so important a circumstance in phthisis, (case 6,) as to make it the therapeutic indication, to the neglect of the pulmonary symptoms.

We object further to the conclusiveness of the experiments of La Pitié on the very serious ground, that M. Andral had not the means of *applying* homœopathic principles to practice. We might grant, for argument's sake, that his conception of the homœopathic law was as accurate as we have seen it to be erroneous, and that the symptoms had been noted down with as much circumstantial detail as they were with inexcusable brevity; still the experiments would be without value, for without facts to work with, where is the use of principles on which to work? M. Andral not having a knowledge of the German language, was unable to consult Hahnemann's Materia Medica in the original; no French translation was extant at the time he undertook these experiments, and an acquaintance with English was as yet equally useless to the student of Homœopathy. A seaman wishing to find his longitude, though thoroughly acquainted with navigation, and though perfectly exact in his observation, is yet quite unable to discover his position without a reference to his Nautical Tables. In like manner, an accurate conception of the homœopathic law, and a scrupulous conformity to the rules for taking the case, are of no avail to one who, as in the instance before us, has not the means of consulting the Materia Medica.

But while these considerations suffice to show that these experiments were performed in such circumstances as deprive them of all pretensions to scientific value; and while, therefore, they cannot be allowed the slightest weight in determining the question at issue, it would still be gratifying, could we award merit to M. Andral in taking the earliest opportunity of testing the practical value of an important truth. Did such a line of conduct proceed from an earnest desire to secure, without delay, for the alleviation of disease, the benefits accruing from each discovery in therapeutics as it arose, while we might be inclined to question the wisdom of attempting the solution of so intricate a problem with means so inadequate as he possessed, we could not but feel respect for, and express approbation of, the motives that led to it. It is, therefore, painful to find that facts will scarcely allow us to put so favourable a construction on the conduct of M. Andral. A French translation of Hahnemann's "Chronic Diseases" was published at Paris in the year 1832, and had therefore been a considerable time before the public when the trial at La Pitié was instituted. This work contained a most minute account of the action of twenty-two remedies, the names of which we subjoin, and which, with scarcely an exception, are of the highest value to the practitioner.* Had M. Andral been anxious to practise the system to the best of his ability, he would have found in these medicines a rich store of materials for the cure of the most obstinate diseases. If, however, our readers will take the trouble to compare the list they have just read, with that of the medicines used in Andral's experiments, they will find that they have not *one* remedy in common; in other words, that *Andral abstained from using the only medicines of which he had the means of making a right application.* Does this look like an anxiety to get at the truth? Again, several years have elapsed since the Materia Medica was published in French; but we hear of no trials of Homœopathy at the Parisian hospitals.

M. Maxime Vernois, while admitting (in the pamphlet already referred to) the incapacity of his professor to perform homœopathic experiments from not knowing the action of the medicines, excuses his ignorance by saying it was unavoidable (ignorance obligée.) What we have just mentioned shows this not to be wholly correct; but from whatever cause his ignorance proceeded, surely the consciousness that he did not possess the means of testing the system, should have prevented him from stating before the Academy that he had given it a fair trial in his wards, and found it wanting.

It is scarcely necessary to prove that M. Andral gave the wrong medicines in the majority of cases above detailed, after showing that by chance only he could be right. In fact, he was reduced, partly by the want of

---

* Graphites, Lycopodium, Magnesia, Magnesiæ murias, Ammonium Carbonicum, Baryta carbonica, Calcarea carbonica, Natrum carbonicum, Acidum nitricum, Petroleum, Phosphorus, Sepia, Silicea, Zincum, Carbo vegetabilis, Carbo animalis, Causticum, Cicuta, Kali carbonicum, Natrum muriaticum, and Sulphur.

the Materia Medica, partly by his wilful neglect of such remedies as had been published, to guessing at the medicine which would be prescribed by Homœopathy; and as he did not avail himself of the assistance of any one better acquainted with the subject than himself, he obtained such results as might have been anticipated. These considerations make a detailed examination of the practice adopted quite superfluous; we will, however, notice one or two of the cases, in order to show into what an inextricable maze of difficulties a man is thrown, when deprived of the clue, the knowledge of the pure effects of the medicines.

Let us take as examples the four cases treated with arnica. As the symptoms, with a single exception in each case, are not recorded, it is quite impossible to determine on the proper remedy to be given; but we may remark on the first case, that arnica is very seldom used in phthisis. If the reader wishes proof of this, let him turn to that article in Jahr's Repertory, and he will find that arnica is not to be found among the *eighteen* medicines *most* useful in alleviating the sufferings of the consumptive. The next case is one of cerebral congestion, with great giddiness; this was probably a case to which arnica was adapted, for we find its administration was followed by good effects; but this good fortune was plainly owing to chance, for there is nothing in the case to point out to us, without trial, whether arnica, belladonna, or nux vomica, not to mention others, would prove specific; so that there was at least twice as much probability of the wrong medicine being chosen as the right, and, in the former case, the ill success which must have followed would have been laid to the blame of the system. We are at a loss to know why arnica was given in a case of hydropericarditis; we do not remember of a single case in which it was indicated; the presumption is, that arsenic, lachesis, or spigelia, were more appropriate to the case. As to the last case, we may observe, that it would perhaps be impossible to select any medicine out of the whole pharmacopœia less likely to prove beneficial in dysmenorrhœa than arnica. That this is not a simple assertion on our part, may be seen by once more turning to the Repertory of Jahr, when it will be found that, though no less than thirty substances are enumerated as occasionally remedial in this complaint, arnica is not there. We might proceed in this way through the remaining cases, but we think sufficient has been said to convince every one that these experiments had nothing of Homœopathy but the name. We may just refer, however, to two cases of diarrhœa, (cases 32 and 33,) which Andral, by departing from his usual practice of mentioning but a single symptom, has unwittingly given us the means of showing to have been wrongly treated. The diarrhœa of pulsatilla, though not unfrequently accompanied with colic, is, for the most part, more free from pain than that produced by other medicines; so that, when we meet with such a case as No. 32, unless the temperament be strongly indicative of pulsatilla, we naturally search among other remedies for the specific, and none is more frequently required than chamomilla. On the other hand, pulsatilla is likely to be useful in such cases as No. 33, for which chamomilla is certainly *not* suited; so that, in these two cases, the only ones in which there are any land-marks by which to guide our course, Andral chose the medicine least likely, on homœopathic principles, to effect a cure. It surprises us to find cases of intermittent fever among those experimented on, for these affections are, without exception, the most difficult of any to treat on homœopathic principles; requiring, in the first place, that the symptoms be detailed with extraordinary minuteness; and, in the next, that the physician have a most thorough acquaintance with the intimate character of the numerous medicines, (Böninghausen enumerates nearly sixty, which are required in their treatment.) Much judgment is also required to know at what period to administer the remedy.

We have now to state a circumstance for which our readers are scarcely prepared. It is seldom, whatever system we follow, that one medicine suffices for the cure of a chronic complaint, even when the experience of years has guided the choice, and it is rare indeed that *one* dose of the medicine brings about the desired result. To this obvious principle, however, M. Andral shut his eyes when experimenting homœopathically; for we gather from an attentive perusal of the article already referred to, what the author was doubtless ashamed to state in so many words: *That though three-fourths of the cases treated were such as required a long course of treatment to cure, none of them received more than one dose of the homœopathic remedy*, the administration of which was followed by some days ("quelques jours") of inaction, at the expiry of which, if not cured, the patient was handed over to Allopathy. It was expected, it would seem, that scarcely had the globule been swallowed, but the cure should be effected, if it lay in the power of Homœopathy to cure at all! Diseases of every kind, bronchitis, pleurisy, and consumption, chronic inflammation of the stomach, and hypertrophy of the heart,—diseases which had existed weeks, months, and perhaps years,—Homœopathy must cure them all by one dose each, or it is held to be a delusion! Were ever conditions like these imposed upon a system before? Notwithstanding all this, however, we learn that, of fifty-four cases thus treated, eight made permanent recoveries, and seven others were better *the day after getting the medicine.* We are told that time of itself brings about such results, ("le temps seul amène ce résultat;") but we would just suggest, that, in chronic diseases, and in many acute ones, time is just as likely to bring about progress as retrocession of the disease; and, to say the least, it is remarkable that the improvement coincided so closely with the taking of the medicine; at all events, it would have been but fair to follow up, by a repetition of the medicine, the good already begun: instead of this, these seven patients were allowed to relapse, and thus to swell the list of failures. These facts require no comment.

The professed object of such trials as these, is to obtain such a body of evidence as shall, on the acknowledged principles of medical statistics, suffice to establish the comparative efficacy of the old system and the new. Were it demonstrated by adequate statistics, that Homœopathy came short in its results of the dominant system, and that this inferiority depended not on any weakness incident to its recent birth and fettered growth, and which it might reasonably be expected to outgrow, but on some inherent and irremediable defect; we say, were this satisfactorily proved, we should feel bound at once to abandon it; but we are not sure that we should think the *utter inefficacy* of its infinitesimal doses to be thereby demonstrated. On the contrary, our respect for *Allopathy*, all defective as it is, would preserve us from such a conclusion. We would ask those who adduce the supposed inferiority of homœopathic practice as proving its absolute powerlessness, "Do you not perceive that, in so speaking, you are casting a slur on the system you practise? Do you not see that you are saying in other words, 'Every system that has *any* efficacy in it, must be equal or superior to ours; our system has so little power over disease, that to have *less* is to have *none?*" Happily for Allopathy, and for the mass of mankind who must long continue to be treated on its principles, the reasoning of such wholesale declaimers against Homœopathy is false, and therefore the degradation of the old system, which it implies, cannot be maintained. It would be just as reasonable to conclude that, because one body A, was proved to be hotter than another body B, *therefore* B contained *no* heat. The absolute powerlessness of a system of therapeutics, can only be proved by comparing it with the true zero of medicine, that is to say, the expectant method, and showing that the results are similar. This has not been done; till it be, the enemies of any new system dare not in conscience say it has no power.

But we are very far from anticipatiug *any* injury to Homœopathy from a statistical comparison of its results with those of the old system. On the contrary, we look forward with confidence to statistics, as one of the means destined to be most powerful in establishing the value of the system. Before, however, either favourable or adverse conclusions can be drawn from a body of cases, we must be assured that the system was fairly and intelligently applied, which we have shown was by no means the case in those before us; and it is therefore useless to proceed to consider the inferences deducible from them, for from false facts no ingenuity can obtain true deductions. But wo think it may not be amiss to consider for a little, whether, even supposing the facts to have been good, they were of such a nature as to be of service in a statistical inquiry.

The object of such trials being, as we have already observed, to institute a comparison between the merits of the two rival systems, it is obviously requisite that such diseases be chosen to operate upon, as admit of the display of the powers of medicine; for, where both systems are powerless to cure, no deduction favourable to either the one or the other can be drawn. It is therefore matter of surprise, that so intelligent a man as M. Andral (and a statistician withal) should have included in his trial so a large a proportion of intractable or absolutely incurable cases. Nothing would have been easier than to have avoided this, for M. Andral did not take indiscriminately all patients entering his wards during a certain period of time, (which, though on the whole the fairest mode of proceeding, inasmuch as it secures an unbiassed allotment of cases, would also be in some measure objectionable, as it would necessarily include some patients incurable by any system, and therefore make the results *quoad* these cases, indecisive of the question;) on the contrary, he *selected* his patients, as we infer from the following considerations. The experiments, of which we have a particular account, lasted 242 days, or 35 weeks; each experiment (or rather observation, for after the first day nothing was done) lasted "some days," say a week, or at most a fortnight; they were carried on continuously, and were thirty-five in number. Putting these things together, it is evident that there can have been but one, or at most two or three patients treated homœopathically at a time, so that M. Andral had ample opportunity for selecting, out of a ward of at least twenty beds, cases amenable to treatment, and therefore of use in determining the question at issue. Why did he not do so?

Further, had the mode of proceeding so far been unobjectionable, still we should have been unable to state if the results made for or against the new system, for we are as yet unprovided with any statistics parallel to these in Allopathy; to obtain such, it would be necessary to institute experiments on cases treated with single doses of the appropriate medicine. We might perhaps make some approach to the results by ascertaining what per centage of patients are cured in the first week of treatment.

Lastly, even had the cases been judiciously selected, we have Andral's own authority for stating that their number was far too small to make the conclusions trustworthy. One of his pupils, Gavarret, (Principles Généraux de Statisque Médicale, p. 108, note,) quotes Andral as saying, "With thirty or forty observations, one may determine the diagnosis and pathological anatomy of a disease, but it needs years of research to arrive at a satisfactory result in therapeutics." M. Andral has thus pronounced his own condemnation, which supersedes the necessity of ours.

INDEX.

THE PHILOSOPHY OF LIVING.

BY HERBERT MAYO, M.D.,

FORMERLY SENIOR SURGEON OF MIDDLESEX HOSPITAL, PROFESSOR OF ANATOMY, ETC.

"For though we Christians do continually aspire and pant after the Land of Promise, yet it will be a token of God's favour towards our journeyings through the World's Wilderness, to have our shoes and garments, (I mean those of our frail bodies,) little worn or impaired."—BACON.

Doctor, no physicking. We are, as I already told you, a machine made to live. We are organized for that purpose, and such is our nature. Do not counteract the living principle. Let it alone; leave it the liberty of defending itself. It will do better than your drugs.—EMPEROR NAPOLEON

There is no danger of our knowing too much of the true "Philosophy of Living," and though many other writers have published books upon the subject, there are none that combine so much of sound observation, good practical sense and true philosophy, as this one. The popularity of the work in England is shown by its having gone through three editions. It is the most thorough treatise on the various temperaments, food, drink, exercise, sleep, bathing, dress, &c., that we have ever met with; and along with sound directions for preserving physical health is a chapter on the Health of the Mind, which deserves especial attention.—*Bulletin.*

THE MATERNAL MANAGEMENT OF CHILDREN IN HEALTH AND DISEASE.

BY THOMAS BULL, M.D.,

Member of the Royal College of Physicians, &c.

FROM THE THIRD LONDON EDITION.

"After a careful perusal of this work, we are satisfied that the publishers have conferred a favour upon the mothers of the country by placing within their reach a book that cannot fail to be of great assistance to all who have the charge of young children."—*Medical Examiner.*

"Mothers will be especially benefitted by the study of this excellent book; we can devise no readier method of having it reach the fire-side, than for physicians to recommend it in their intercourse with families."—*Boston Med. and Surg. Jour.*

This is a work of great value, and should be in the hands of every intelligent mother. Without any affectation of medical learning, it is a truly scientific work, none the less so, from the plainness of its language and the perspicuity of its style to the uninitiated in medical terminology. It is of rare value both to the profession and to the public.

"We consider this the best work of the kind that has fallen under our observation, and recommend it to all heads of families, as containing information vitally important." —*Daily Despatch.*

THE SURGICAL AND MECHANICAL TREATMENT OF THE TEETH,

INCLUDING DENTAL MECHANICS.

WITH ILLUSTRATIONS.

BY JAMES ROBINSON,

Surgeon Dentist to the Metropolitan Hospital, &c. &c.

ARTHUR'S MANUAL OF DISEASES OF THE TEETH,

INCLUDING

A DESCRIPTION OF THEIR STRUCTURE AND MODES OF TREATMEMT, &c.

A SMALL POCKET VOLUME.

THE AMERICAN MEDICAL FORMULARY,

BASED UPON THE

UNITED STATES AND BRITISH PHARMACOPŒIAS,

Including also numerous Standard Formulæ, derived from American and European Authorities, together with the Medical Properties and Uses of Medicines; Poisons, their Antidotes, Tests, &c. Designed for the Medical and Pharmaceutical Student.

BY JOHN J. REESE, M. D.,

Lecturer on Materia Medica and Therapeutics in the Philadelphia Medical Institute; Fellow of the College of Physicians, &c., &c.

"In the preparation of the Formulary of Dr. Reese, which is one of the series of the 'Medical Practitioners' and Students' Library,' the alphabetical order has been pursued; and in it, with a very few unimportant exceptions, every article that has a place in the Pharmacopœias of the United States or Great Britain, is described, and its medical properties and uses, as received by standard authorities, are noticed, while in the appendix is a list of some of the more common and useful dietetic preparations; a brief description of poisons, with reference to their treatment, antidotes, and tests; a table of the analysis of the most celebrated natural mineral water of the United States and Europe; a table of the doses of the most important medicines, &c.; all of which, we hesitate not to say, add much to the interest and value of the work, and will prove very acceptable to the reader." —*New York Journal of Medicine.*

"It contains much that is really valuable, and must serve as a standard work of reference upon the subjects of which it treats. We can confidently recommend the work, and hope it will meet with that favour which it so richly merits." —*Boston Medical and Surgical Journal.*

"The author has manifested much care and research in the preparation of the volume before us, and has presented us with a work, in general, of great accuracy, which cannot fail to be useful for reference, both to the practitioner and student." —*Medical Examiner.*

"This work contains all the officinal preparations recognised by the best standard works of the day, and we recommend Reese's Formulary, as a highly useful work of its class, to the profession." —*New Orleans Medical and Surgical Journal.*

"This is a very convenient manual for the student of medicine and pharmacy, presenting, in a space as brief as possible, a complex list of the medicinal preparations now in use in England and the United States. The appendix contains a good selection of recipes of dietetic preparations; a chapter on poisons and their antidotes; a table of doses, weights and measures, &c.; comprising a large body of most valuable information. We recommend it to our readers." —*Journal and Library of Dental Science.*

MEIGS ON CHILDREN,

A NEW EDITION, MUCH ENLARGED AND IMPROVED.

A PRACTICAL TREATISE

ON

THE DISEASES OF CHILDREN.

By J. FORSYTH MEIGS, M. D.,

LECTURER ON PATHOLOGY, THE PRACTICE OF MEDICINE, AND FORMERLY LECTURER ON THE DISEASES OF CHILDREN IN THE PHILADELPHIA MEDICAL ASSOCIATION, FELLOW OF THE COLLEGE OF PHYSICIANS, ETC. ETC.

SECOND EDITION. IN ONE VOLUME OCTAVO.

Dr: Meigs' descriptions of diseases are clear and concise; his pathological views are, in the main, sound, and his practical directions plain, simple and judicious. His work is far from being a mere compilation from the best authorities, or a simple array of the various and often discordant views of the leading writers on the diseases of children. He has, with judgement, selected his materials, testing them, in most instances, by the result of his own experience, and endeavouring throughout, to present an exact exposition of the present state of our knowledge on the several forms of diseases of which he treats."—*Amer. Med. Jour., Oct.*, 1848.

"The author is a son of the eminent Professor of Obstetrics in Jefferson Medical College, and, like him, is distinguished for his ardent devotion to obstetrics, and to the study and treatment of the diseases of women and children. In the preparation of the work no pains has been spared to make it both methodical and accurate, and as complete as the limits of the series would allow.

"The reader will find it to contain, in a brief compass, the most approved views o modern authoritative writers, expressed in plain and appropriate language."—*Medica. Examiner.*

"One of its essential recommendations is, it is not necessary to ramble through a forest of propositions to find the thing sought; the definition, for example, synonymes, causes, nature of the disease, symptoms, diagnosis, prognosis and treatment, follow each other in an orderly manner, so that there is no confusion in the general arrangement, and therefore none likely to be engendered in the mind of the reader. For students, we cannot divest ourselves of the idea, that this work is precisely what they need."—*British Med. and Surg. Journal.*

"We have given the greater part of the work a careful perusal, and in our opinion, it is a production in every way creditable to the author. That he has prosecuted personal observation in a careful, philosophical manner, and turned his opportunities to the best account, the work bears evidence. His arrangement of topics, and the practical conclusions at which he arrives, appear to us to be sound and judicious. Moreover, the work embodies, in a small compass, the most valuable precepts of the most approved modern authorities, on the subjects of which it treats."—*Buffalo Med. Jour. for August.*

"The diseases are arranged (and very properly, as we think,) according to the systems which they affect; and the work is both methodical and accurate, and as complete as the limits of the series will allow. The author has freely availed himself o. the labours of others, with due acknowledgement, and especially of those of Rilliet and Barthèz, and has incorporated with the text not a little practical experience of his own. He has produced, we think, a very sensible, accurate, and useful volume, which we unhesitatingly recommend to all who may need a compendium of truly practical character, upon this interesting and important branch of Medical Science. Dr. Meigs, we think, deserves great credit and many thanks, for the good service he has done to humanity and to the profession, for the lucid, able, scientific and practical compilation he has made of what was best known upon the subject, not less than for the additions he has made from his own experience to the common stock."—"*The Annalist.*"

"The work is throughout systematic, well written, and highly creditable to the author; and may be read profitably by every practitioner and student in the country."—*N. Y. Jour. of Med., Sept.*, 1848.

MINOR SURGERY, BANDAGING,

THE APPLICATION OF DRESSINGS, ETC.

With 145 Illustrations.

BY JOHN HASTINGS, M.D.,

LATE LECTURER ON SURGICAL ANATOMY AND OPERATIVE SURGERY, FELLOW OF THE COLLEGE OF PHYSICIANS, ETC. ETC.

From Valentine Mott, M.D.

"I have received a copy of Hastings' Manual of Surgery, for which you will please accept my thanks. To the author offer my congratulations, for having furnished the American student a valuable and convenient book."

From Prof. S. D. Gross, Louisville, Ky.

"I have carefully examined Hastings' Manual of Surgery, and find it to contain an excellent outline of the existing state of the science of which it treats. It seems to me to be well adapted as a text-book, and I shall take great pleasure in recommending it, from time to time, to my pupils."

From Dr. Charles Bell Gibson, Richmond, Va.

"I look upon Dr. Hastings' work as an excellent one, and shall recommend it everywhere within my reach, and especially to our class."

From Prof. E. R. Peaslee, Hanover, N. H.

"I am happy to be able to say that I am much pleased with Dr. Hastings' work, as being adapted to the object it has in view; and shall take pleasure in recommending it to the pupils of the medical schools with which I am connected."

From Prof. John Frederick May, Washington, D. C.

"So far as I have examined the work, I find it to be an excellent compendium and manual for students; and I shall accordingly take much pleasure in speaking of it tavourably to my class."

From the New Orleans Medical Journal.

"This very neat volume on the practical part of Surgery, is an excellent guide-book for the medical student and the young practitioner. It is confessedly a handsome compilation, and is carefully and industriously prepared, and neatly printed. The illustrations are numerous and well executed; and we are pleased with the book, considered in all its parts."

"In it the student will find the principles of Surgery detailed in a simple and concise manner; and while there are, of course, many things omitted that will be found in larger treatises, he will find sufficient of really practical and valuable information on the subject of surgical diseases, minor and operative surgery, to render him competent to manage cases that ordinarily come into the hands of the general practitioner. The portion devoted to operative surgery is written with great clearness and simplicity; everything being made as plain as possible to the comprehension of the student. The wood-cuts with which it is illustrated are correct and accurate delineations, and add no little to its value. The typographical execution of the volume is of a very superior character, and is a credit to the publishing house from which it emanates."

"As a guide-book to the student and practitioner, in this department of medical science, it does not savour of prolixity, and yet it is sufficiently minute to present a practical and general view of the subjects embraced within its scope. That there are works which contain nearly, if not quite all that is presented in the one before us, we have no doubt; but that it is thoroughly adapted to the end for which it was designed, we feel confident all will admit who give it a careful perusal. It presents a careful and sufficiently digested selection, and a clear and exact account of the most important facts and principles already furnished by the ablest observers, both at home and abroad. By reference to the volume, we find that the following authors have been fully consulted and used: Sir Astley Cooper, Sir B. Brodie; Messrs. Miller, Druitt, Ferguson, Lawrence; Drs. Gibson, Pancoast, Carpenter, Dunglison, Prout, M. M. Velpeau, Malgaigne, Ricord, Sichel, Weller, Rayer, Guthrie, Hennen, and others—authorities sufficient, with the careful and attractive manner in which it is executed, to ensure for it that success which its intrinsic merit demands.

www.ingramcontent.com/pod-product-compliance
Lightning Source LLC
LaVergne TN
LVHW020247110826
845151LV00003B/1038

* 9 7 8 1 4 2 5 5 2 9 1 6 1 *